Mastering Swift 2

Dive into the latest release of the Swift programming language with this advanced Apple development book for creating exceptional iOS and OS X applications

Jon Hoffman

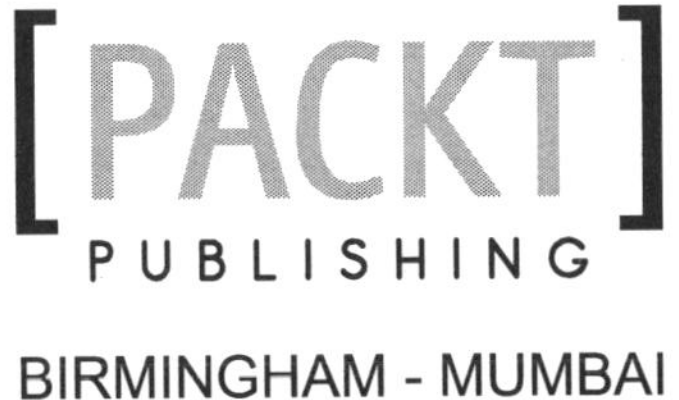

BIRMINGHAM - MUMBAI

Mastering Swift 2

First published: June 2015

Second edition: November 2015

Production reference: 1281015

Published by Packt Publishing Ltd.
Livery Place
35 Livery Street
Birmingham B3 2PB, UK.

ISBN 978-1-78588-603-4

www.packtpub.com

Cover Image by Jon Hoffman

Credits

Author
Jon Hoffman

Reviewer
Jannis Muething

Commissioning Editor
Wilson D'souza

Acquisition Editor
Tushar Gupta

Content Development Editor
Sumeet Sawant

Technical Editors
Jayesh Sonawane
Ankita Thakur

Copy Editor
Swati Priya

Project Coordinator
Shweta H. Birwatkar

Proofreader
Safis Editing

Indexer
Priya Sane

Production Coordinator
Shantanu N. Zagade

Cover Work
Shantanu N. Zagade

About the Author

Jon Hoffman has over 20 years of experience in the field of information technology. Over those 20 years, he has worked in the areas of system administration, network administration, network security, application development, and architecture. Currently, he works as a senior software engineer with Syn-Tech Systems.

He has developed extensively for the iOS platform since 2008. This includes several apps that he has published in the App Store and written for third parties, besides numerous enterprise applications.

In January of 2014, he authored his first book, *iOS and OS X Network Programming Cookbook, Packt Publishing*.

What really drives him is the challenges in the information technology field. There is nothing more exhilarating to him than overcoming a challenge. Some of his other interests are watching baseball (Go Sox) and basketball (Go Celtics). He also really enjoys taekwondo, where he and his eldest daughter, Kailey, earned their black belts together early in 2014. Kim (his wife) earned her black belt in December 2014 and his youngest daughter is currently working toward hers.

I would like to thank my wonderful wife, Kim. Without her support, encouragement, patience, and understanding, this book would have never been written. I would also like to thank my two wonderful daughters, Kailey and Kara, who have both been my inspiration and driving force since the day they were born. Thanks goes to the wonderful people at Packt Publishing who worked so hard to get this book published and made writing so enjoyable for me.

About the Reviewer

Jannis Muething works as a freelance iOS developer. Currently based in Dortmund, Germany, he is also studying computer science with a focus on medical applications. He has been developing for iOS devices since 2009. Since 2014, he is working for smartcircles mHealth AG, where he is the lead iOS developer. Prior to this, he had a job at Materna GmbH where he mainly did Java development. He can be found on the Web at `http://jannis.co` and on Twitter at `@j4nnis`.

www.PacktPub.com

Support files, eBooks, discount offers, and more

For support files and downloads related to your book, please visit www.PacktPub.com.

Did you know that Packt offers eBook versions of every book published, with PDF and ePub files available? You can upgrade to the eBook version at www.PacktPub.com and as a print book customer, you are entitled to a discount on the eBook copy. Get in touch with us at service@packtpub.com for more details.

At www.PacktPub.com, you can also read a collection of free technical articles, sign up for a range of free newsletters and receive exclusive discounts and offers on Packt books and eBooks.

https://www2.packtpub.com/books/subscription/packtlib

Do you need instant solutions to your IT questions? PacktLib is Packt's online digital book library. Here, you can search, access, and read Packt's entire library of books.

Why subscribe?

- Fully searchable across every book published by Packt
- Copy and paste, print, and bookmark content
- On demand and accessible via a web browser

Free access for Packt account holders

If you have an account with Packt at www.PacktPub.com, you can use this to access PacktLib today and view 9 entirely free books. Simply use your login credentials for immediate access.

Table of Contents

Preface

Swift is Apple's new programming language that was introduced at the Worldwide Developers Conference (WWDC) in 2014, alongside the integrated development environment Xcode 6 and iOS 8. Swift was arguably the most significant announcement at WWDC 2014, and very few people, including Apple insiders, were aware of the project's existence prior to it being announced.

At WWDC 2015, Apple made another big splash when they announced Xcode 7 and Swift 2, which is a major enhancement to the Swift language. During WWDC, Chris Lattner said that a lot of the enhancements were based on direct feedback that Apple received from the development community.

Swift can be thought of as Objective-C reimagined using modern concepts and safe programming patterns. In Apple's own words, Swift is like "Objective-C without the C". Chris, the creator of Swift, said that Swift took language ideas from Objective-C, Rust, Haskell, Ruby, Python, C#, CLU, and far too many others to list.

Apple has also stated that "Swift is a successor to the C and Objective-C languages". Therefore, it is imperative for iOS and OS X developers who want to keep their skills up to date to not only learn, but also master the Swift programming language.

The first five chapters of this book will introduce the reader to the Swift programming language. These chapters will give the reader a solid understanding of the Swift programming language. The remainder of the book will cover more advanced topics such as concurrency, network development, protocol extensions, and design patterns that will help the reader master this language.

This book is written in an example-based approach where each topic covered is backed by examples, which are written to reinforce the topic and show how to implement it within the reader's code.

Since Swift is constantly changing and evolving, I've started a blog at `http://masteringswift.blogspot.com/` to keep the readers up to date with what is new with Swift. The blog will also be used to enhance and expand on the material in the book.

What this book covers

Chapter 1, Taking the First Steps with Swift, will introduce you to the Swift programming language and discuss what inspired Apple to create Swift. We'll also go over the basic syntax of Swift and how to use Playgrounds to experiment and test Swift code.

Chapter 2, Learning about Variables, Constants, Strings, and Operators, will introduce you to variables and constants in Swift and when to use them. There will be brief overviews of the most common variable types with examples on how to use them. We'll conclude this chapter by showing examples of how to use the most common operators in the Swift language.

Chapter 3, Using Collections and Cocoa Data Types, will explain Swift's array, set, and dictionary collection types and show examples on how to use them. We'll also show how to use Cocoa and Foundation data types with Swift.

Chapter 4, Control Flow and Functions, will show you how to use Swift's control flow statements. These include looping, conditional, and control transfer statements. The second half of the chapter is all about functions and how to define and use them.

Chapter 5, Classes and Structures, is dedicated to Swift's classes and structures. We'll look at what makes them similar and what makes them different. We'll also look at access controls and object-oriented design. We'll close this chapter out by looking at memory management in Swift.

Chapter 6, Using Protocols and Protocol Extensions, will cover both protocols and protocol extensions in detail since protocols are very important to the Swift language, and having a solid understanding of them will help us write flexible and reusable code.

Chapter 7, Writing Safer Code with Availability and Error Handling, will cover the new approach to error handling, which Apple included in Swift 2, in depth as well as the new availability feature. Error handling is the process of responding to and recovering from error conditions

Chapter 8, Working with XML and JSON Data, will discuss what XML and JSON data are and their uses. We'll then see several examples of how to parse and build XML and JSON data using Apple's frameworks.

Chapter 9, Custom Subscripting, will discuss how we can use custom subscripts in our classes, structures, and enumerations. Subscripts in Swift can be used to access elements in a collection. We can also define custom subscripts for our classes, structures, and enumerations.

Chapter 10, Using Optional Types, will explain what optional types really are, what are the various ways to unwrap them, and optional chaining. For a developer who is just learning Swift, optional types can be one of the more confusing items to learn.

Chapter 11, Working with Generics, will explain how Swift implements generics. Generics allow us to write very flexible and reusable code that avoids duplication.

Chapter 12, Working with Closures, will teach us how to define and use closures in our code. Closures in Swift are similar to blocks in Objective-C except that they have a much cleaner and easier way of using syntax. We will conclude this chapter with a section on how to avoid strong reference cycles with closures.

Chapter 13, Using Mix and Match, will explain mix and match and demonstrate how we can include Swift code in our Objective-C projects and Objective-C code in our Swift projects. With all of the apps and frameworks written in Objective-C, it was important to allow Swift and Objective-C code to work together.

Chapter 14, Concurrency and Parallelism in Swift, will show how to use both Grand Central Dispatch and Operation Queues to add concurrency and parallelism to our applications. Understanding and knowing how to add concurrency and parallelism to our apps can significantly enhance the user experience.

Chapter 15, Swift Formatting and Style Guide, will define a style guide for the Swift language that can be used as a template for enterprise developers who need to create a style guide since most enterprises have style guides for the various languages that they develop in.

Chapter 16, Network Development with Swift, will explain the Apple API's to connect to remote servers and how best to use them. Network development can be both fun and challenging.

Chapter 17, Adopting Design Patterns in Swift, will show you how to implement some of the more common design patterns in Swift. A design pattern identifies a common software development problem and provides a strategy for dealing with it.

What you need for this book

To follow along with the examples in this book, you'll need to have an Apple computer with OS X 10.10 or higher installed. You'll also need to install Xcode Version 7.0 or higher with Swift Version 2 or higher.

Who this book is for

This book is intended for individuals looking for a book that will not only give them a solid introduction to the Swift programming language, but will also cover, in depth, the advanced topics such as ARC, design patterns, protocol extensions, and concurrency. This book is written for those developers who learn best by looking at, and working with, code because each concept covered in the book is backed by example code written to give the reader a good understanding of the current topic and demonstrate how to properly implement it.

Conventions

In this book, you will find a number of text styles that distinguish between different kinds of information. Here are some examples of these styles and an explanation of their meaning.

Code words in text, database table names, folder names, filenames, file extensions, pathnames, dummy URLs, user input, and Twitter handles are shown as follows: "If we had an OS X playground open, we would use an `NSColor` object to represent a color."

A block of code is set as follows:

```
var name = "Jon"
var language = "Swift"

var message1 = " Welcome to the wonderful world of "
var message2 = "\(name) Welcome to the wonderful world of \
(language)!"

print(name, message1, language, "!")
print(message2)
```

New terms and **important words** are shown in bold. Words that you see on the screen, for example, in menus or dialog boxes, appear in the text like this: "For most of the examples in this book, it is safe to assume that you can select either **iOS** or **OS X** unless it is otherwise noted."

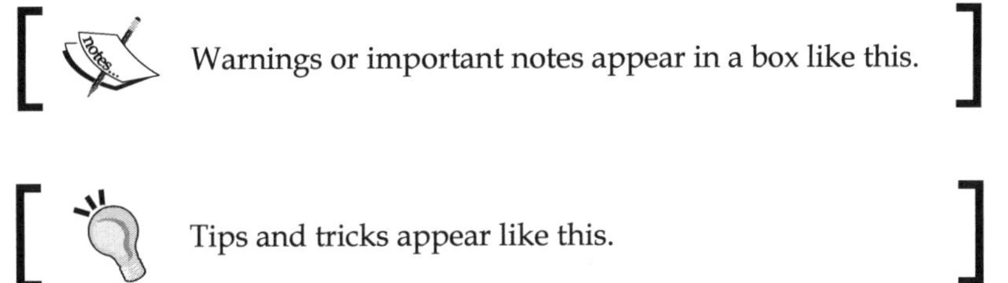

Warnings or important notes appear in a box like this.

Tips and tricks appear like this.

Reader feedback

Feedback from our readers is always welcome. Let us know what you think about this book—what you liked or disliked. Reader feedback is important for us as it helps us develop titles that you will really get the most out of.

To send us general feedback, simply e-mail `feedback@packtpub.com`, and mention the book's title in the subject of your message.

If there is a topic that you have expertise in and you are interested in either writing or contributing to a book, see our author guide at `www.packtpub.com/authors`.

Customer support

Now that you are the proud owner of a Packt book, we have a number of things to help you to get the most from your purchase.

Downloading the example code

You can download the example code files from your account at `http://www.packtpub.com` for all the Packt Publishing books you have purchased. If you purchased this book elsewhere, you can visit `http://www.packtpub.com/support` and register to have the files e-mailed directly to you.

Downloading the color images of this book

We also provide you with a PDF file that has color images of the screenshots/diagrams used in this book. The color images will help you better understand the changes in the output. You can download this file from: `https://www.packtpub.com/sites/default/files/downloads/6034OT_ColorImages.pdf`.

Errata

Although we have taken every care to ensure the accuracy of our content, mistakes do happen. If you find a mistake in one of our books—maybe a mistake in the text or the code—we would be grateful if you could report this to us. By doing so, you can save other readers from frustration and help us improve subsequent versions of this book. If you find any errata, please report them by visiting `http://www.packtpub.com/submit-errata`, selecting your book, clicking on the **Errata Submission Form** link, and entering the details of your errata. Once your errata are verified, your submission will be accepted and the errata will be uploaded to our website or added to any list of existing errata under the Errata section of that title.

To view the previously submitted errata, go to `https://www.packtpub.com/books/content/support` and enter the name of the book in the search field. The required information will appear under the **Errata** section.

Piracy

Piracy of copyrighted material on the Internet is an ongoing problem across all media. At Packt, we take the protection of our copyright and licenses very seriously. If you come across any illegal copies of our works in any form on the Internet, please provide us with the location address or website name immediately so that we can pursue a remedy.

Please contact us at `copyright@packtpub.com` with a link to the suspected pirated material.

We appreciate your help in protecting our authors and our ability to bring you valuable content.

Questions

If you have a problem with any aspect of this book, you can contact us at `questions@packtpub.com`, and we will do our best to address the problem.

1
Taking the First Steps with Swift

Ever since I was 12 years old and wrote my first program in the basic programming language, programming has been a passion for me. Even as programming became my career, it always remained more of a passion than a job, but over the past few years, that passion has waned. I was unsure why I was losing that passion. I attempted to recapture it with some of my side projects, but nothing really brought back the excitement that I used to have. Then, something wonderful happened! Apple announced Swift. Swift is such an exciting and progressive language that it has brought a lot of that passion back and made programming fun for me again.

In this chapter, you will learn:

- What Swift is
- Some of the features of Swift
- What Playgrounds are
- How to use Playgrounds
- What the basic syntaxes of the Swift language are

What is Swift?

Swift is Apple's new programming language that was introduced at the Worldwide Developers Conference (WWDC) in 2014 alongside the integrated development environment Xcode 6 and iOS 8. Swift was arguably the most significant announcement at WWDC 2014 and very few people, including Apple insiders, were aware of the project's existence prior to it being announced.

It was amazing, even by Apple's standards, that they were able to keep Swift a secret for as long as they could and that no one suspected they were going to announce a new development language. At WWDC 2015, Apple made another big splash when they announced Xcode 7 and Swift 2. Swift 2 is a major enhancement to the Swift language. During that conference, Chris Lattner said that a lot of the enhancements were based on direct feedback that Apple received from the development community.

Swift can be thought of as Objective-C reimagined using modern concepts and safe programming patterns. In Apple's own words, Swift is like Objective-C without the C. Chris Lattner, the creator of Swift, said Swift took language ideas from Objective-C, Rust, Haskell, Ruby, Python, C#, CLU, and far too many others to list. At WWDC 2014, Apple really stressed that Swift was safe by default. Swift was designed to eliminate many common programming errors, making applications more secure and less prone to bugs. Swift 2 added two additional core features to the language—availability and error handling—which are designed to make it even easier to write safe code.

The development of Swift started in 2010 by Chris. He implemented much of the basic language structure with only a few people being aware of its existence. It wasn't until late 2011 that other developers began to really contribute to Swift and in July of 2013, it became a major focus of the Apple Developer Tools group.

Chris started working at Apple in the summer of 2005. He has held several positions in the Developers Tools group, and is currently the director and architect of that group. On his home page (`http://www.nondot.org/sabre/`), he notes that Xcode's Playgrounds (read more on Playgrounds a little later in this chapter) became a personal passion of his because it makes programming more interactive and approachable. We will be using Playgrounds a lot in the book as a test and experimentation platform.

There are a lot of similarities between Swift and Objective-C. Swift adopts the readability of Objective-C's named parameters and dynamic object model. When we refer to Swift as having a dynamic object model, we are referring to the ability for types to change at runtime. This includes adding new (custom) types and changing/extending the existing types.

Swift also provides seamless access to the existing Cocoa and Cocoa Touch frameworks. This gives Objective-C developers a certain amount of familiarity when they begin to learn Swift because how these frameworks functioned with Objective-C is how they function with Swift.

While there are a lot of similarities between Swift and Objective-C, there are significant differences between them as well. Swift's syntax and formatting are a lot closer to Python than Objective-C, but Apple did keep the curly braces. I know Python people would disagree with me, and that is all right because we all have different opinions, but I like the curly braces. Swift actually makes the curly braces required for control statements, such as `if` and `while`, which eliminates bugs, such as the `goto fail`, in Apple's SSL library.

Swift was also built to be fast. At WWDC 2014, Apple showed a number of benchmarks, which proved that Swift significantly outperformed Objective-C. Swift uses the LLVM compiler, which is included with Xcode 7 to transform the Swift code into highly optimized native code that is tuned to get the most out of Apple's modern hardware.

If you are an iOS or OS X developer and you are still not convinced that learning Swift is a good idea, then maybe this one paragraph from Apple's Swift page (`https://developer.apple.com/swift/`) will help convince you:

> "*Swift is a successor to the C and Objective-C languages. It includes low-level primitives such as types, flow control, and operators. It also provides object-oriented features such as classes, protocols, and generics, giving Cocoa and Cocoa Touch developers the performance and power they demand.*"

The first line in that paragraph, which says that Swift is a successor to the C and Objective-C languages, is the most important line. This line and other Apple documentation tell us that Apple sees the Swift language as its application and systems programming language of the future. While Objective-C is not going away anytime soon, it sounds like it will be taking a backseat to Swift in the very near future.

Swift features

When Apple said that Swift is Objective-C without the C, they were really only telling us half of the story. Objective-C is a superset of C and provides object-oriented capabilities and a dynamic runtime to the C language. This meant that Apple needed to maintain compatibility with C, which limited the enhancements it could make to the Objective-C language. As an example, Apple could not change how the `switch` statement functioned and still maintains the C compatibility.

Since Swift did not need to maintain the same C compatibility as Objective-C, Apple was free to add any feature/enhancement to the language. This allowed Apple to include the best features from many of today's most popular and modern languages, such as Objective-C, Python, Java, Ruby, C#, Haskell, and many others.

The following chart shows a list of some of the most exciting enhancements that Swift includes:

Swift feature	Description
Type inference	Swift can automatically deduce the type of the variable or constant, based on the initial value.
Generics	Generics allow us to write code only once to perform identical tasks for different types of objects.
Collection mutability	Swift does not have separate objects for mutable or non-mutable containers. Instead, you define mutability by defining the container as a constant or variable.
Closure syntax	Closures are self-contained blocks of functionality that can be passed around and used in our code.
Optionals	Optionals define a variable that might not have a value.
Switch statement	The Switch statement has been drastically improved. This is one of my favorite improvements.
Multiple return types	Functions can have multiple return types using tuples.
Operator overloading	Classes can provide their own implementation of the existing operators.
enums with Associated values	In Swift, we can do a lot more than just defining a group of related values with enumerations.

There is one feature that I did not mention in the preceding chart because it is technically not a feature of Swift; it is a feature of Xcode and the compiler. This feature is **Mix and Match**, which allows us to create applications that contain both Objective-C and Swift files. It also allows us to systematically update the current Objective-C applications with Swift classes and use current Objective-C libraries/ frameworks in our Swift applications.

Mix and Match lets Objective-C and Swift files coexist in the same project. This allows us to begin using Swift without throwing away our existing Objective-C code base or projects.

Before we begin our journey into the wonderful world of Swift development, let's take a detour and visit a place that I have loved ever since I was a kid—the playground.

Playgrounds

When I was a kid, the best part of the school day was going to the playground. It really did not matter what we were playing; as long as we were on the playground, I knew it would be fun. When Apple introduced Playgrounds as part of Xcode 6, I was excited just by the name, but I wondered if Apple could make its Playground as fun as the playgrounds from my youth. While Apple's Playgrounds might not be as fun as playing kickball when I was 9 years old, it definitely brings a lot of fun back to experimenting and playing with code.

Getting started with Playgrounds

Playgrounds are interactive work environments that let us write code and see the results immediately. As changes are made to the code, the results also change in real time. This means that Playgrounds are a great way to learn and experiment with Swift.

Playgrounds also make it incredibly easy to try out the new APIs, prototype new algorithms, and demonstrate how code works. We will be using Playgrounds throughout this book to show how our sample code works. Therefore, before we really get into Swift development, let's spend some time learning about and getting comfortable with Playgrounds.

Do not worry if the Swift code does not make a lot of sense right now, as we go through the book, this code will begin to make sense. We are simply trying to get a feel of Playgrounds right now.

A Playground can have several sections, but the three that we will be using in this book are:

- **Coding Area**: This is where you enter your Swift code.
- **Results Sidebar**: This is where the results of your code are shown. Each time you type in a new line of code, the results are re-evaluated and the results' sidebar is updated with the new results.
- **Debug Area**: This area displays the output of the code, and it can be very useful for debugging.

The following screenshot shows how the sections are arranged in a Playground:

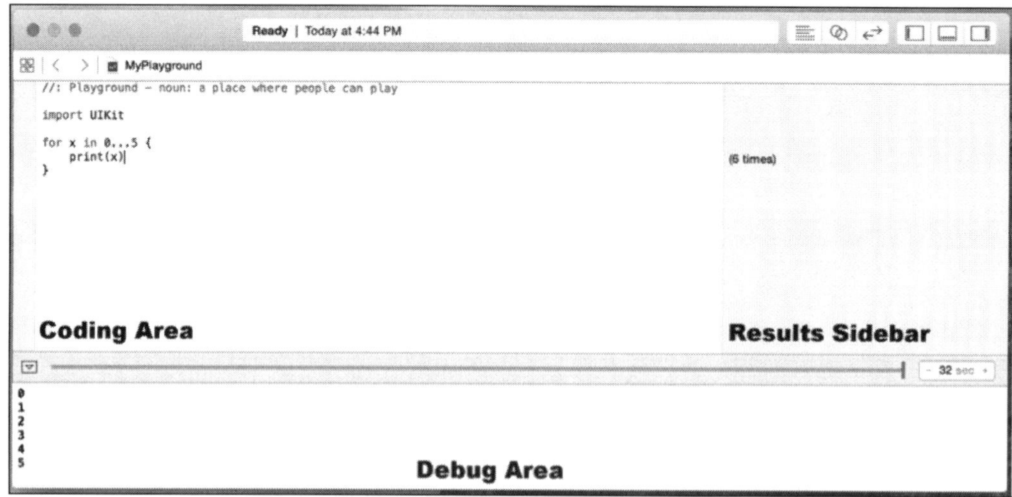

Let's start a new Playground. The first thing we need to do is to start Xcode. Once Xcode has started, we can select the **Get started with a playground** option, as shown in the following screenshot:

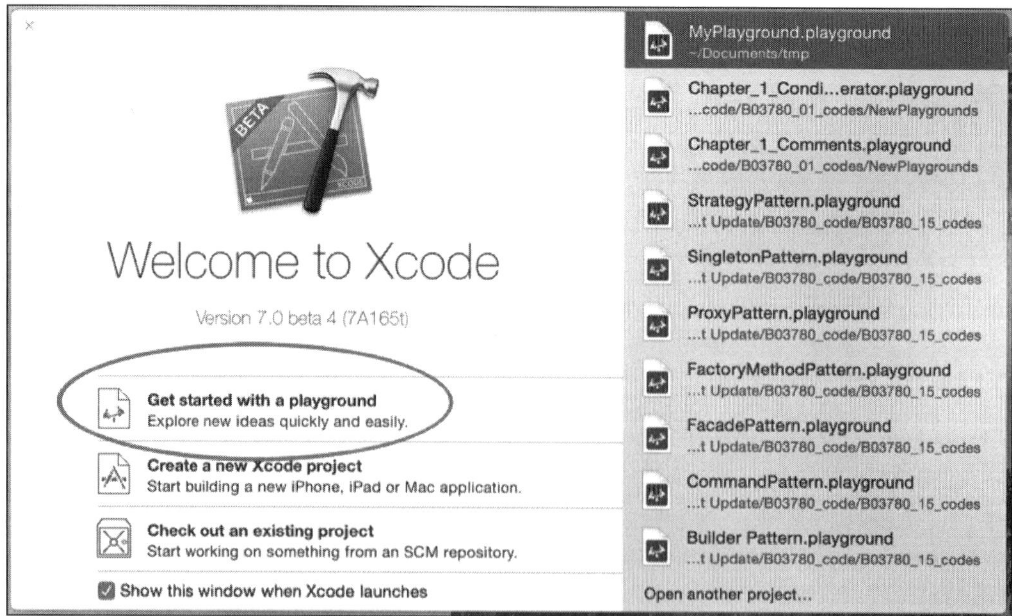

Alternatively, we can navigate to the Playground by going to **File** | **New** from the top menu bar, as shown in the following screenshot:

Next, we should see a screen similar to the following screenshot that lets us name our Playground and select whether the Playground is an **iOS** or **OS X** Playground.

For most of the examples in this book, it is safe to assume that you can select either **iOS** or **OS X** unless it is otherwise noted:

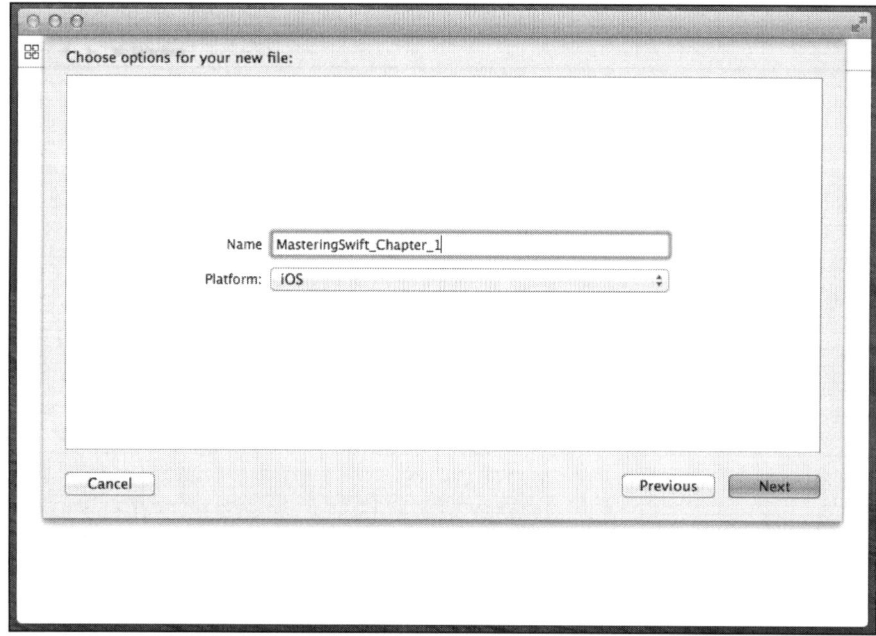

Finally, we are asked for the location to save our Playground. After we select the location, the Playground will open up and look similar to the following screenshot:

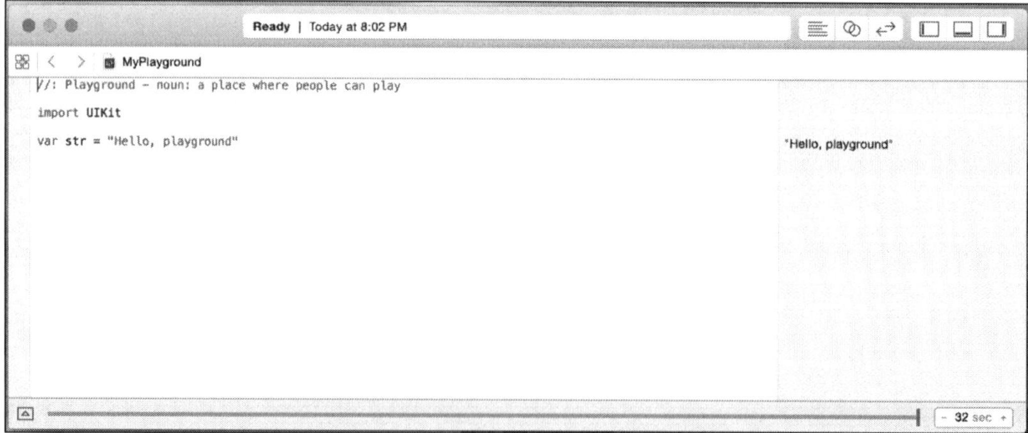

In the preceding screenshot, we can see that the coding area of the Playground looks similar to the coding area for an Xcode project. What is different here is the sidebar on the right-hand side. This sidebar is where the results of our code are shown. The code in the previous screenshot imports iOS' UIKit framework and sets a variable named `str` to the string, `Hello, playground`. You can see the content of the `str` string in the sidebar to the right of the code.

By default, a new Playground does not open the debug area. You can open it manually by pressing the *shift* + *command* + *Y* keys together. Later in the chapter, we will see why the debug area is so useful.

iOS and OS X Playgrounds

When you start a new iOS Playground, the Playground imports UIKit (Cocoa Touch). This gives us access to the UIKit framework that provides the core infrastructure for iOS applications. When we start a new OS X Playground, the Playground imports Cocoa. This gives us access to the OS X Cocoa framework.

What the last paragraph means is if we want to experiment with the specific features of either UIKit or Cocoa, we will need to open the correct Playground. As an example, if we have an iOS Playground open and we want to create an object that represents a color, we would use a `UIColor` object. If we had an OS X playground open, we would use an `NSColor` object to represent a color.

Showing images in a Playground

As you will see throughout this book, Playgrounds are great at showing the results of code as text in the results sidebar. However, they can also do a lot more than just text, such as images, graphs, and display views. Let's take a look at how we would show an image in a Playground. The first thing we need to do is to load the image into the resource directory of our Playground.

The following steps show how to load an image into the resource directory:

1. Let's begin by showing the project navigator sidebar. To do this, in the top menu bar, navigate to **View** | **Navigators** | **Show Project Navigator** or use the *command* + *1* keyboard shortcut. The project navigator looks similar to this:

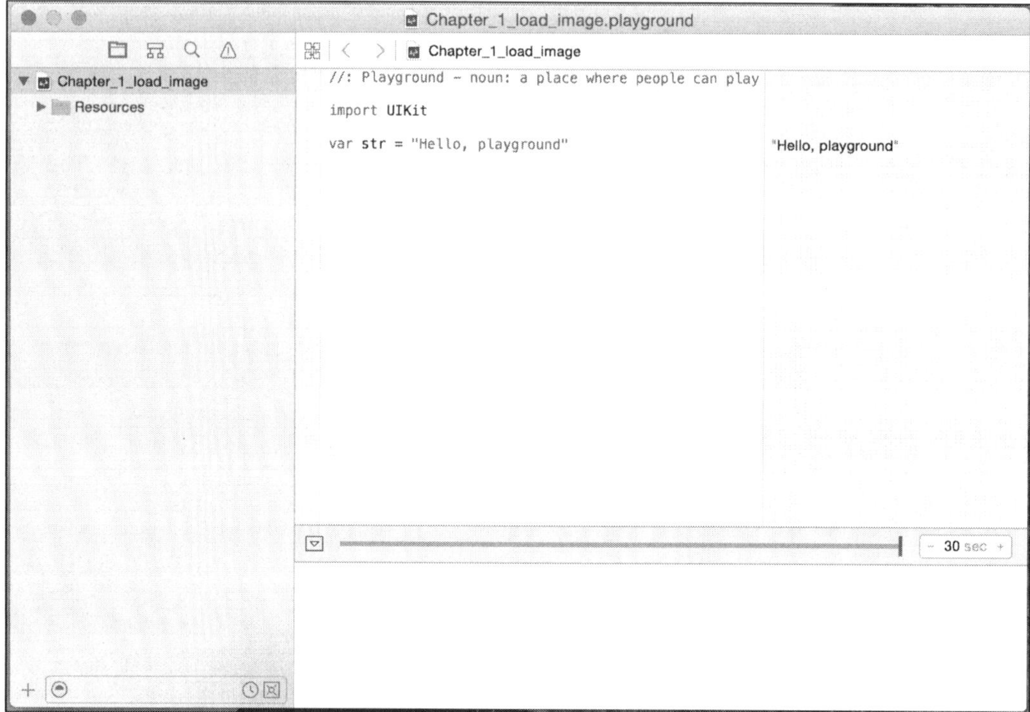

2. Once we have the Project Navigator open, we can drag the image into the `Resources` folder so that we can access it from our code. Once we drag the image file over it and drop it, it will appear in the `Resources` folder, as shown here:

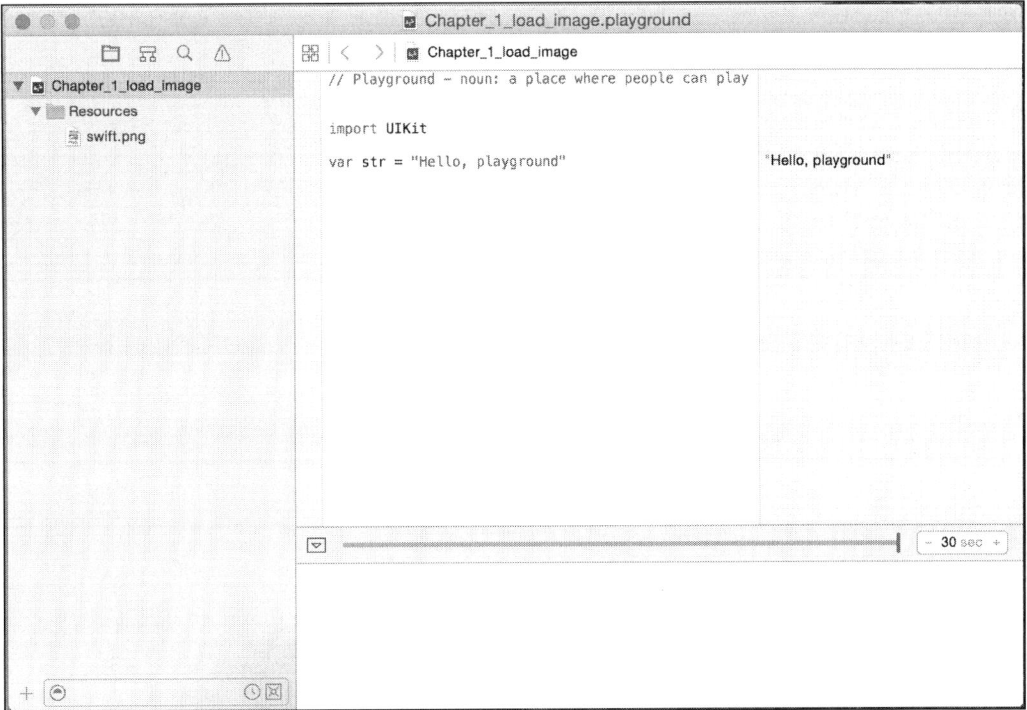

3. Now, we can access the image that is in our `Resources` folder within our code. The following screenshot shows how we would do this. The actual code that we use to access the image is not as important at this time as knowing how to access resources within a playground:

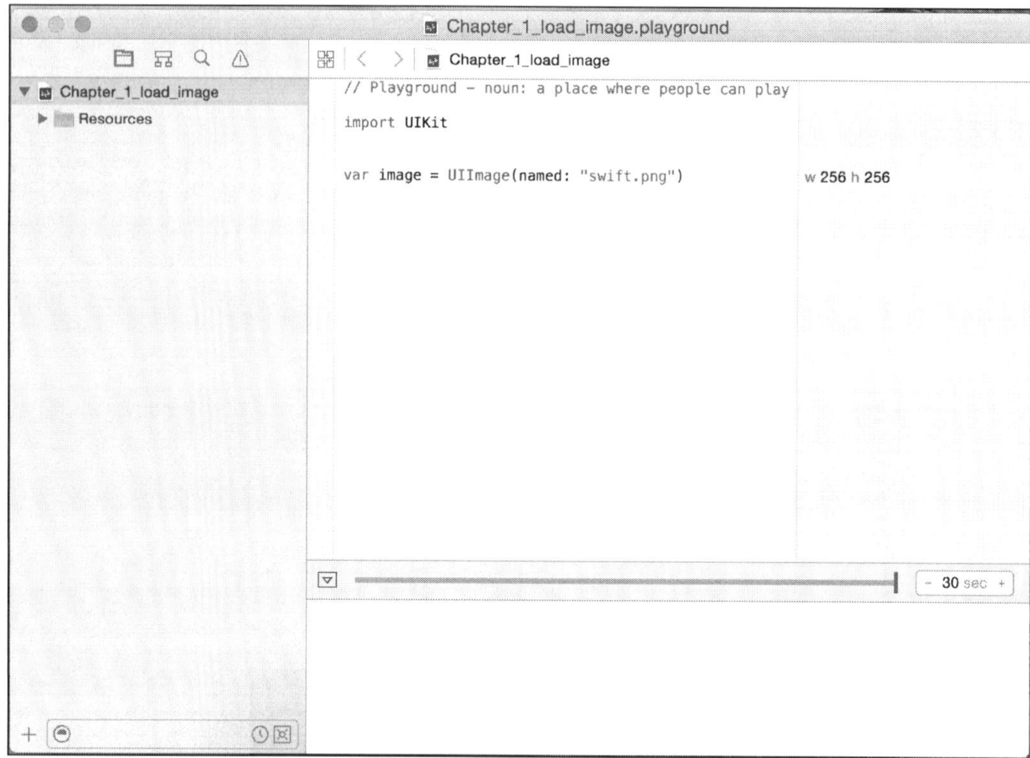

4. To view the image, we need to hover our cursor in the results sidebar over the section that shows the width and height of the image. In our example, the width and height section shows **w 256 h 256**. Once we hover the mouse pointer over the width and height, we should see two symbols, as shown in the following screenshot:

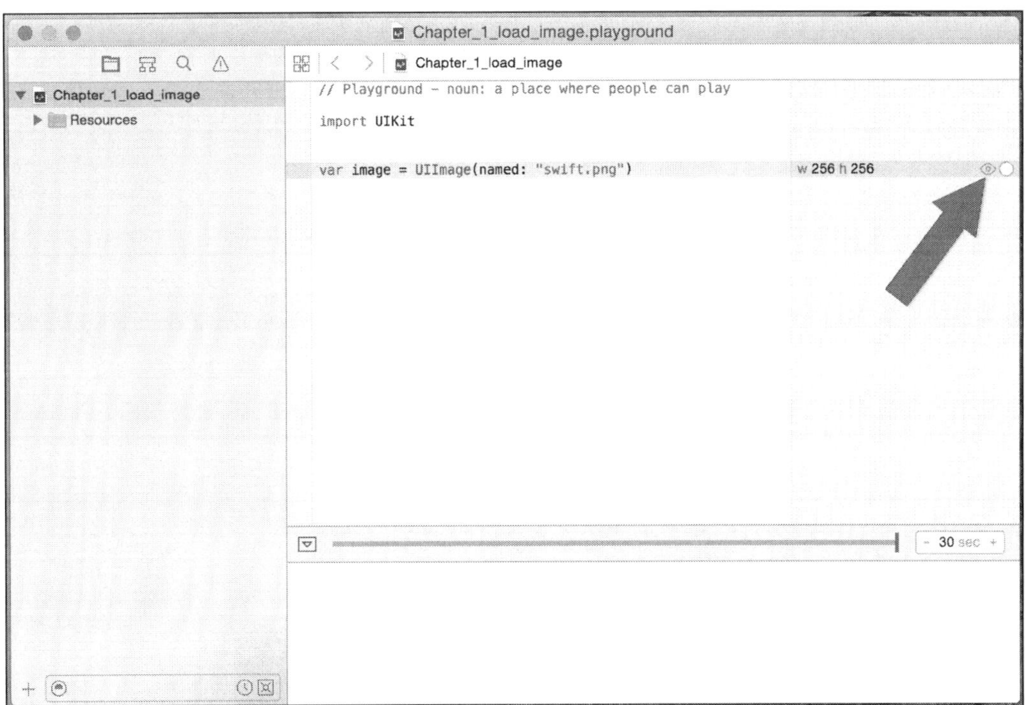

5. We can press either of the symbols to show the image. The one that is shaped like a circle with a plus sign in it will display the image within the playground's code section, while the one that looks like an eye will pop the image up outside the playground. The following screenshot shows what it shows if we press the circle with a plus sign in it:

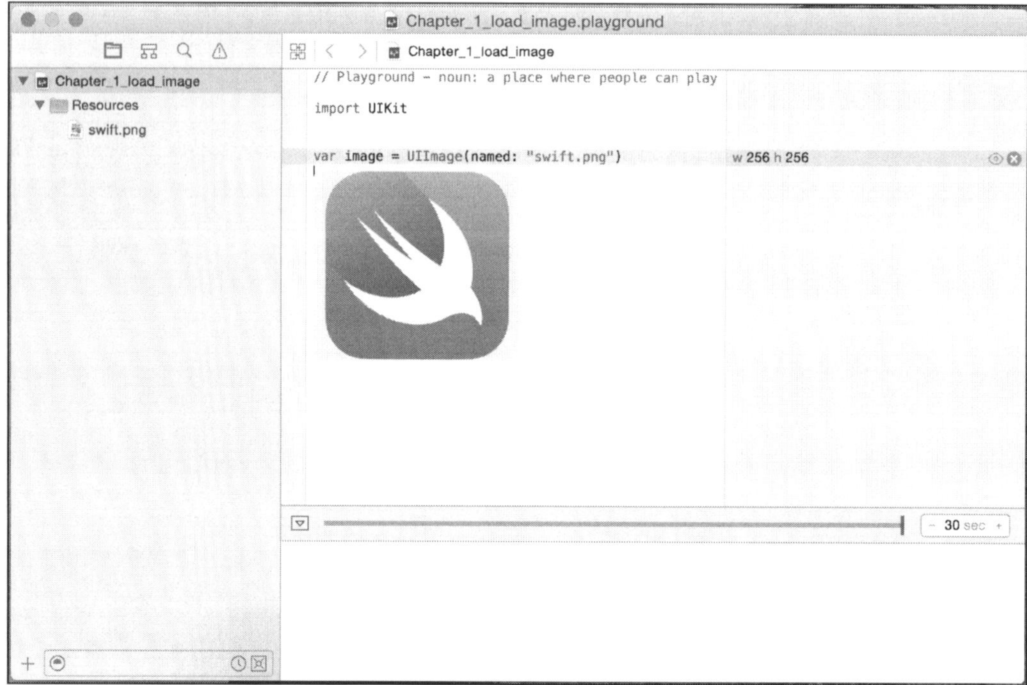

Having the ability to create and display graphs can be very useful when we want to see the progression of our code. Let's look at how we can create and display graphs in a playground.

Creating and displaying graphs in Playgrounds

We can also graph the value of numeric variables over time. This feature is really useful when we are prototyping new algorithms because it allows us to see the value of the variable throughout the course of the calculations.

To see how graphing works, take a look at the following Playground:

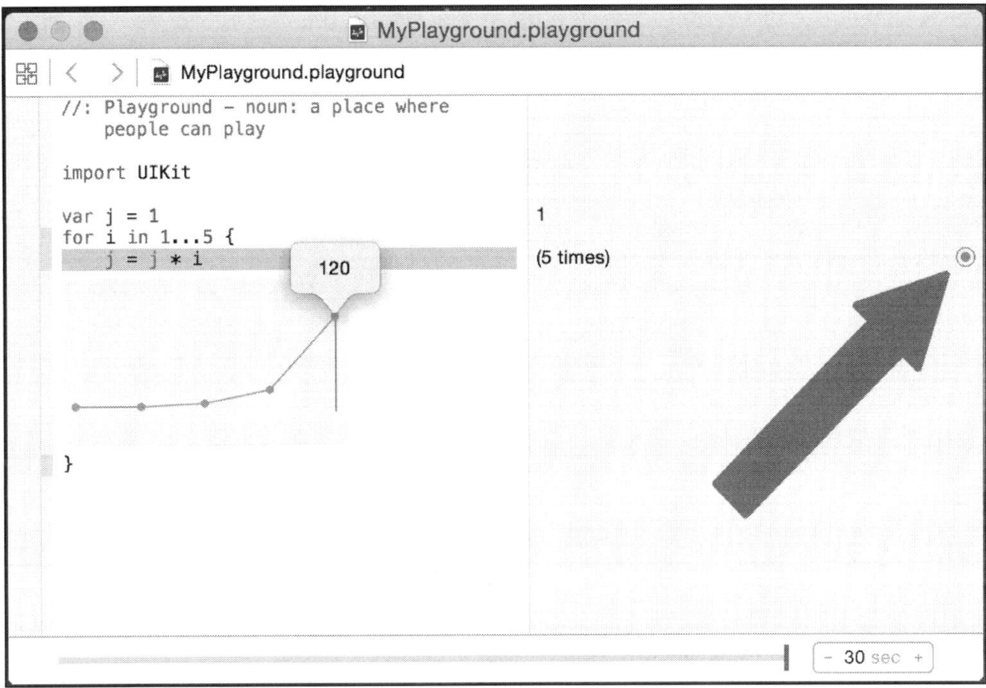

In this playground, we set the variable `j` to `1`. Next, we create a `for` loop that assigns numbers `1` through `5` to the variable `i`. At each step in the `for` loop, we set the value of the variable `j` to the current value of `j` multiplied by `i`. The graph shows the values of the variable `j` at each step of the `for` loop. We will be covering `for` loops in detail later in this book.

To bring up the graph, click on the symbol that is shaped like a circle with a dot in it. We can then move the timeline slider to see the values of variable `j` at each step of the `for` loop.

What Playgrounds are not

There is a lot more that we can do with Playgrounds, and we have only scratched the surface in our quick introduction here. As we proceed through the book, we will be using Playgrounds for almost all of the sample code and demonstrate other features of Playgrounds as they are used.

Before we leave this brief introduction, let's take a look at what Playgrounds are not so that we can understand when not to use Playgrounds:

- Playgrounds should not be used for performance testing: The performance you see from any code that is run in a Playground is not representative of how fast the code will run when it is in your projects
- Playgrounds do not support user interaction: Users cannot interact with code that is run in a Playground
- Playgrounds do not support on-device execution: You cannot run the code that is present in a Playground as an external application or on an external device

Swift language syntax

If you are an Objective-C developer, and you are not familiar with modern languages such as Python or Ruby, the code in the previous screenshots may have looked pretty strange. The Swift language syntax is a huge departure from Objective-C, which was based largely on Smalltalk and C.

The Swift language uses very modern concepts and syntax to create very concise and readable code. There was also a heavy emphasize on eliminating common programming mistakes. Before we get into the Swift language itself, let's take a look at some of the basic syntax of the Swift language.

Comments

Writing comments in Swift code is a little different from writing comments in Objective-C code. We still use the double slash `//` for single line comments and the `/*` and `*/` for multiline comments.

What has changed is how we document the parameters and the return value. To document any parameter, we use the `:parm:` field, and for the return value, we use the `:return:` field.

The following Playground shows examples of both single line and multiline comments to properly comment a function:

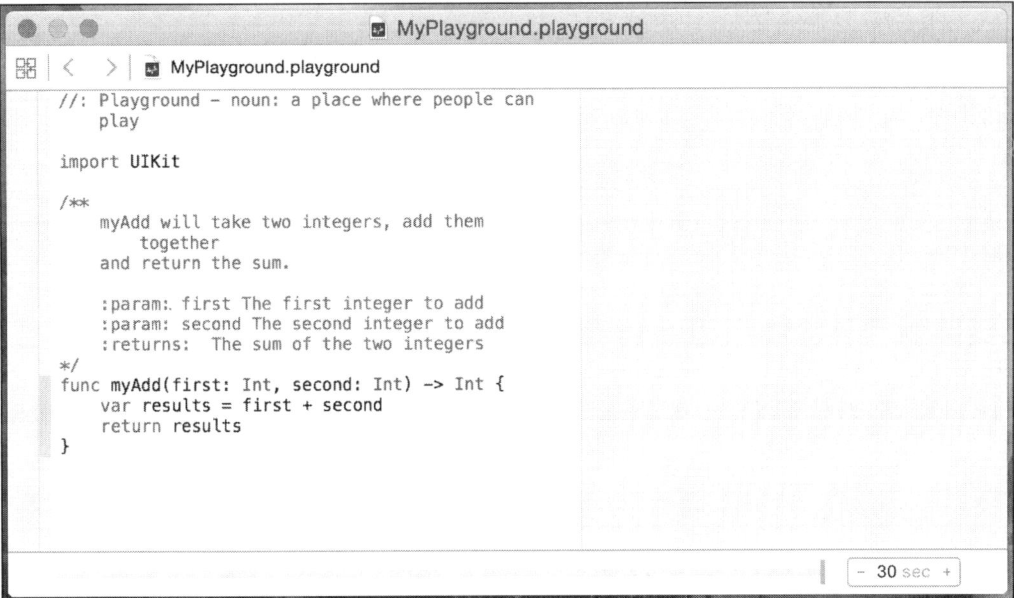

To write good comments, I would recommend using single line comments within a function to give quick one-line explanations of your code. We will then use the multiline comments outside of functions and classes to explain what the function and class does. The preceding Playground shows a good use of comments. By using proper documentation, as we did in the preceding screenshot, we can use the documentation feature within Xcode. If we hold down the *option* key and then click on the function name anywhere in our code, Xcode will display a popup with the description of the function.

This next screenshot shows what that popup would look similar to:

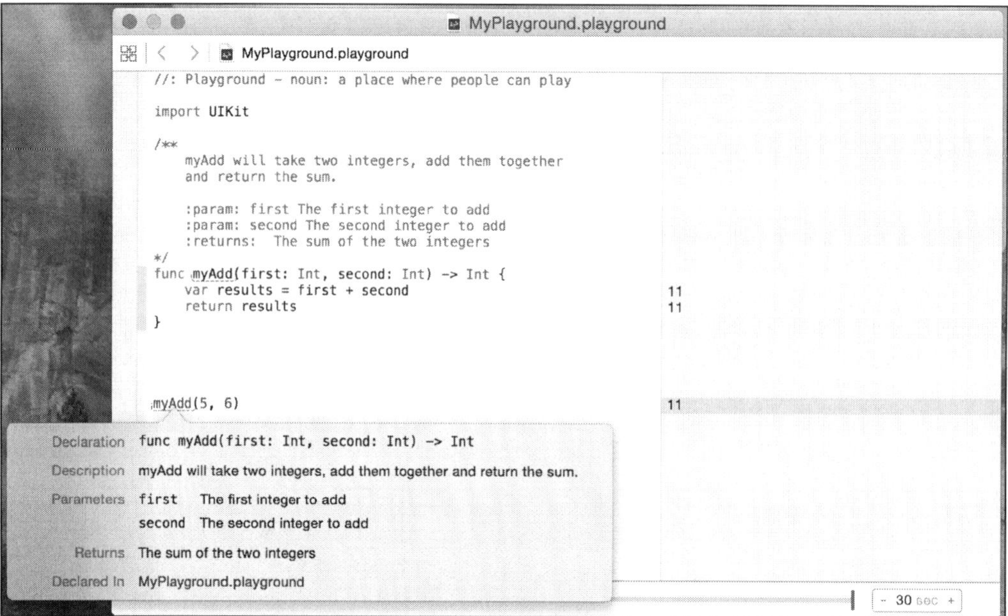

This screenshot shows the documentation feature of Xcode if we hold down the `option` key and then click on the `myAdd()` method. We can see that the documentation contains five fields. These fields are:

- **Declaration**: This is the function's declaration
- **Description**: This is the description of the function as it appears in the comments
- **Parameters**: The parameter descriptions are prefixed with the `:param:` tag in the comment section
- **Returns**: The return description is prefixed with the `:return:` tag in the comment section
- **Declared In**: This is the file that the function is declared in so that we can easily find it

Semicolons

You may have probably noticed, from the code samples so far, that we are not using semicolons at the end of lines. The semicolons are optional in Swift; therefore, both lines in the following Playground are valid in Swift. You can see the results of the code in the results sidebar, as shown in the following screenshot:

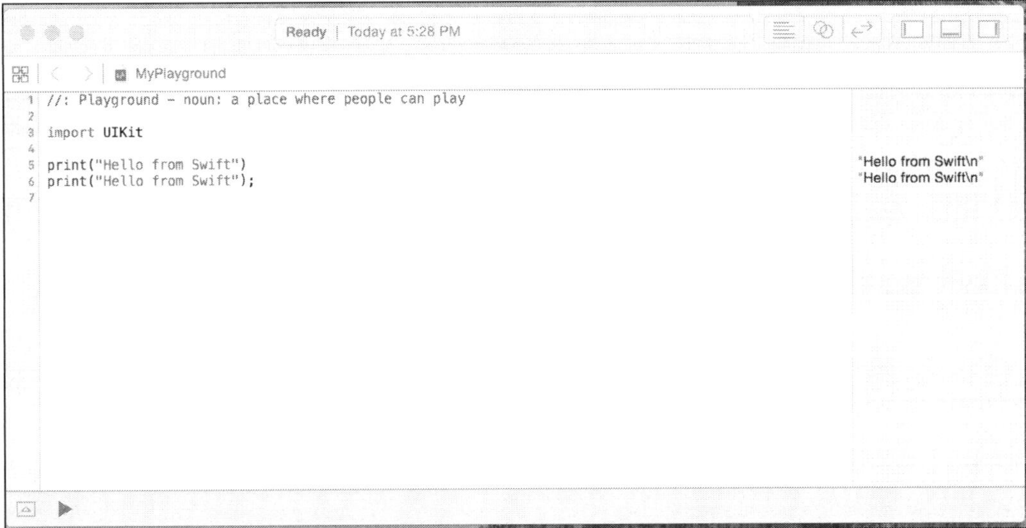

For style purposes, it is strongly recommended that you do not use semicolons in your Swift code. If you are really set on using semicolons in your code, then be consistent and use them on every line of code; however, Swift will not warn you if you forget them. I will stress again, that it is recommended that you do not use semicolons in Swift.

Parentheses

In Swift, parentheses around conditional statements are optional, for example, both `if` statements in the following Playground are valid. You can see the results of the code in the sidebar, as shown in the following screenshot:

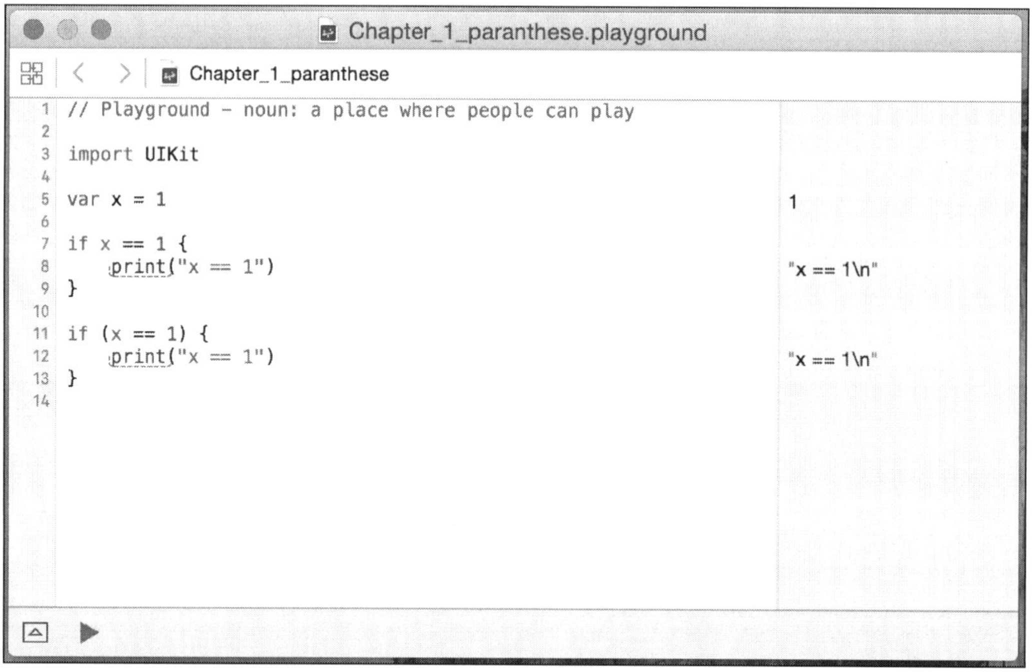

Chapter_1_paranthese.playground

Chapter_1_paranthese

```
// Playground - noun: a place where people can play

import UIKit

var x = 1

if x == 1 {
    print("x == 1")
}

if (x == 1) {
    print("x == 1")
}
```

1

"x == 1\n"

"x == 1\n"

For style purposes, it is recommended that you do not include the parentheses in your code unless you have multiple conditional statements on the same line. For readability purposes, it is good practice to put parentheses around the individual conditional statements that are on the same line.

See the following Playground for samples:

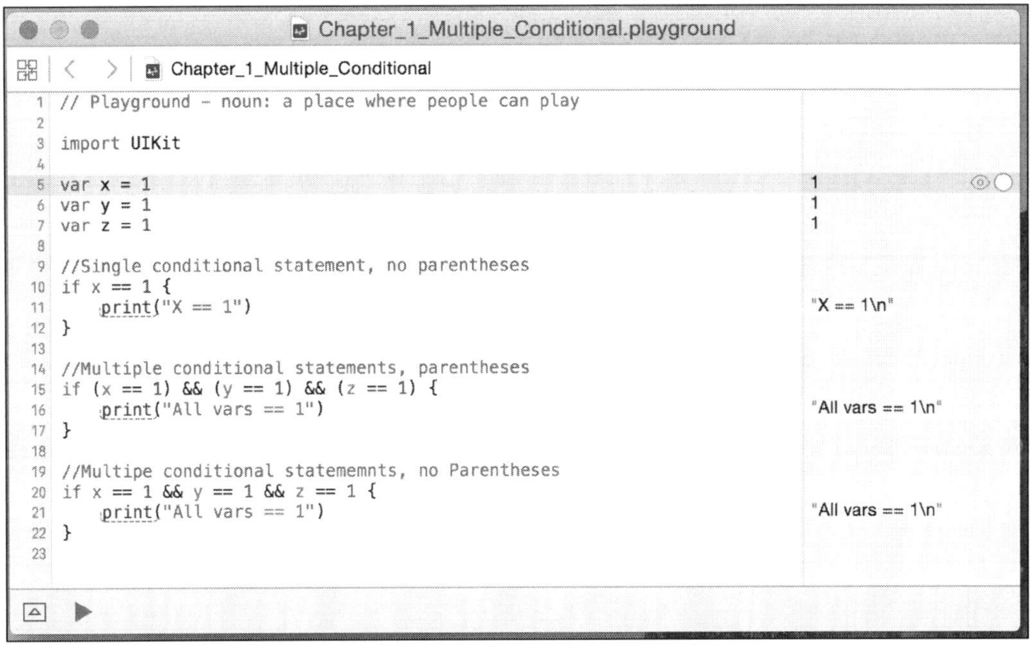

Chapter_1_Multiple_Conditional.playground

Chapter_1_Multiple_Conditional

```
// Playground - noun: a place where people can play

import UIKit

var x = 1
var y = 1
var z = 1

//Single conditional statement, no parentheses
if x == 1 {
    print("X == 1")
}

//Multiple conditional statements, parentheses
if (x == 1) && (y == 1) && (z == 1) {
    print("All vars == 1")
}

//Multipe conditional statememnts, no Parentheses
if x == 1 && y == 1 && z == 1 {
    print("All vars == 1")
}
```

```
1
1
1
"X == 1\n"
"All vars == 1\n"
"All vars == 1\n"
```

Curly braces

In Swift, unlike most other languages, the curly bracket is required after statements. This is one of the safety features that are built into Swift. Arguably, there have been numerous security bugs that may have been prevented if the developer would have used curly braces. A good example of this is Apple's `goto fail` bug. These bugs could also have been prevented by other means such as unit testing and code reviews, but requiring developers to use curly braces, in my opinion, is a good security standard.

The following Playground shows you what error you get if you forget to include the curly braces:

Chapter_1_curly_braces.playground

Chapter_1_curly_braces

```
// Playground - noun: a place where people can play

import UIKit

let x = 1

if x == 1 {
    print("x == 1")
}

if x == 1
    print("x == 1")
```

An assignment operator does not return a value

In most other languages, the following line of code is valid, but it probably is not what the developer meant to do:

```
if (x = 1) {}
```

Downloading the example code

You can download the example code files from your account at `http://www.packtpub.com` for all the Packt Publishing books you have purchased. If you purchased this book elsewhere, you can visit `http://www.packtpub.com/support` and register to have the files e-mailed directly to you.

In Swift, this statement is not valid. Using an assignment operator (=) in a conditional statement (`if` and `while`) will throw an error. This is another safety feature built into Swift. It prevents the developer from forgetting the second equals sign (=) in a comparison statement. This error is shown in the following Playground:

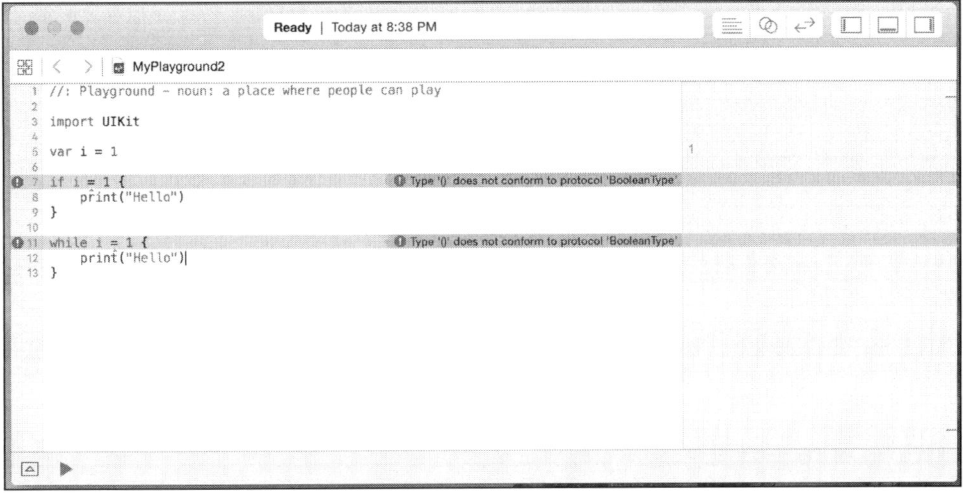

Spaces are optional in conditional and assignment statements

For both conditional (`if` and `while`) and assignment (=) statements, the white spaces are optional. Therefore, in the following Playground, both `The i block` and `The j block` of code are valid:

```
Chapter_1_white_space.playground
Chapter_1_white_space
// Playground - noun: a place where people can play

import UIKit

//The i block
var i=1                                   1
if i==1 {
    print("HI")                           "HI\n"
}

//The j block
var j = 1                                 1
if j == 1 {
    print("HI")                           "HI\n"
}
```

For style purposes, I would recommend adding the white spaces (such as `The j block` for readability purposes), but as long as you pick one style and be consistent, either style should be acceptable.

Hello World

All good computer books that are written to teach a computer language have a section that shows a user how to write a Hello World application. This book is no exception. In this section, we will show you how to write two different Hello World applications.

Our fist Hello World application will be the traditional Hello World application that simply prints Hello World to the console. Let's begin by creating a new Playground and naming it `Chapter_1_Hello_World`. The Playground can be either an iOS or an OS X Playground.

In Swift, to print a message to the console, we use the `print()` function. The `print()` function has been greatly enhanced in Swift 2. Prior to Swift 2, we had two separate print functions: `print()` and `println()`. Now both of these functions have been combined into the single `print()` function.

In the most basic form, to print out a single message, we would use the print function as shown in the following code:

```
print("Hello World")
```

Usually, when we use the `print()` function, we want to print more than just static text. We can include the value of variables and/or constants using a special sequence of characters, `\( )`, or by separating the values within the `print()` function with commas. The following code shows how to do this:

```
var name = "Jon"
var language = "Swift"

var message1 = " Welcome to the wonderful world of "
var message2 = "\(name) Welcome to the wonderful world of \
(language)!"

print(name, message1, language, "!")
print(message2)
```

We can also define two parameters in the print function that change how the message is displayed in the console. These parameters are the **separator** and **terminator** parameters. The separator parameter defines a string that is used to separate the values of the variables/constant in the `print()` function. By default, the `print()` function separates each variable/constant with a space. The terminator parameter defines what character is put at the end of the line. By default, the newline character is added at the end of the line.

The following code shows how we would create a comma-separated list that does not have a newline character at the end:

```
var name1 = "Jon"
var name2 = "Kim"
var name3 = "Kailey"
var name4 = "Kara"

print(name1, name2, name3, name4, separator:", ",
terminator:"")
```

There is one other parameter that we can add to our `print()` function. This is the **toStream** parameter. This parameter will let us redirect the output of the `print()` function. In the following example, we redirect the output to a variable named `line`:

```
var name1 = "Jon"
var name2 = "Kim"
var name3 = "Kailey"
var name4 = "Kara"

var line = ""

print(name1, name2, name3, name4, separator:", ",
terminator:"", toStream:&line)
```

The `print()` function use to simply be a useful tool for basic debugging, but now with the new enhanced `print()` function, we can use it for a lot more.

Summary

In this chapter, we showed you how to start and use Playgrounds to experiment with Swift programming. We also covered the basic Swift language syntax and discussed proper language styles. The chapter concluded with two Hello World examples.

In the next chapter, we will see how to use variables and constants in Swift. We will also look at the various data types and how to use operators in Swift.

2
Learning about Variables, Constants, Strings, and Operators

The first program I ever wrote was written in the BASIC programming language, and was the typical Hello World application. This application was pretty exciting at first, but the excitement of printing static text wore off pretty quickly. For my second application, I used BASIC's input command to prompt the user for a name and then printed out a custom hello message to the user with their name in it. At the age of 12, it was pretty cool to display Hello Han Solo. This application led me to create numerous Mad Lib style applications that prompted the user for various words and then put those words into a story that was displayed after the user had entered all the required words. These applications introduced me to, and taught me, the importance of variables. Every useful application I created since then has used variables.

In this chapter, we will cover the following topics:

- What variables and constants are
- The difference between explicit and inferred typing
- Explaining numeric, string, and Boolean types
- Defining what optional types are
- Explaining how enumerations work in Swift
- Explaining how Swift's operators work

Constants and variables

Constants and variables associate an identifier (such as `myName` or `currentTemperature`) with a value of a particular type (such as `String` or `Int`), where the identifier can be used to retrieve the value. The difference between a constant and a variable is that a variable can be updated or changed, while a constant cannot be changed once a value is assigned to it.

Constants are good for defining the values that you know will never change, such as the freezing temperature of water or the speed of light. Constants are also good for defining a value that we use many times throughout our application, such as a standard font size or maximum characters in a buffer. There will be numerous examples of constants throughout this book.

Variables tend to be more common in software development than constants, however. This is mainly because developers tend to prefer variables to constants. In Swift 2 and Xcode 7, we are warned if we declare a variable that is never changed. This should increase the use of constants. We can make useful applications without using constants (although it is a good practice to use them); however, it is almost impossible to create a useful application without variables.

The use of constants is encouraged in Swift. If we do not expect or want the value to change, we should declare it as a constant. This adds a very important safety constraint to our code that ensures that the value never changes.

You can use almost any character in the identifier of a variable or constant (even Unicode characters); however, there are a few rules that you must follow:

- An identifier must not contain any whitespace
- An identifier must not contain any mathematical symbols
- An identifier must not contain any arrows
- An identifier must not contain private use or invalid Unicode characters
- An identifier must not contain line- or box-drawing characters
- An identifier must not start with a number, but they can contain numbers
- If you use a Swift keyword as an identifier, surround it with back ticks

Keywords are words that are used by the Swift programming language. Some examples of keywords that you will see in this chapter are `var` and `let`. You should avoid using Swift keywords as identifiers to avoid confusion when reading your code.

Defining constants and variables

Constants and variables must be defined prior to using them. To define a constant, you use the keyword, `let`, and to define a variable, you use the keyword, `var`. The following are some examples of constants and variables:

```
// Constants
let freezingTemperatureOfWaterCelsius = 0
let speedOfLightKmSec = 300000

// Variables
var currentTemperature = 22
var currentSpeed = 55
```

We can declare multiple constants or variables in a single line by separating them with a comma. For example, we could shrink the preceding four lines of code down to two lines, as shown here:

```
// Constants
let freezingTempertureOfWaterCelsius = 0,
speedOfLightKmSec = 300000

// Variables
var currentTemperture = 22, currentSpeed = 55
```

We can change the value of a variable to another value of a compatible type; however, as we noted earlier, we cannot change the value of a constant. Let's look at the following Playground. Can you tell what is wrong with the code from the error message that is shown in the following screenshot:

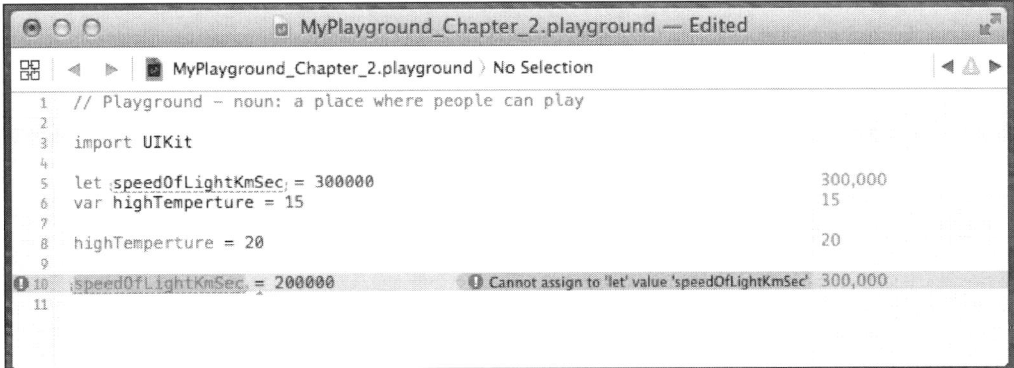

Did you figure out what was wrong with the code? Any physicist can tell you that we cannot change the speed of light, and in our code, the `speedOfLightKmSec` variable is a constant, so we cannot change it either. Therefore, when we try to change the `speedOfLightKmSec` constant, an error is reported. We are able to change the value of the `highTemperture` variable without an error because it is a variable. We mentioned the difference between variables and constants a couple of times because it is a very important concept to grasp, especially when we define mutable and immutable collection types later in *Chapter 3, Using Collections and Cocoa Data Types*.

Type safety

Swift is a type-safe language. In a type-safe language, we are required to be clear on the types of values we store in a variable. We will get an error if we attempt to assign a value to a variable that is of a wrong type. The following Playground shows what happens if we attempt to put a string value into a variable that expects integer values; note that we will go over the most popular types a little later in the chapter:

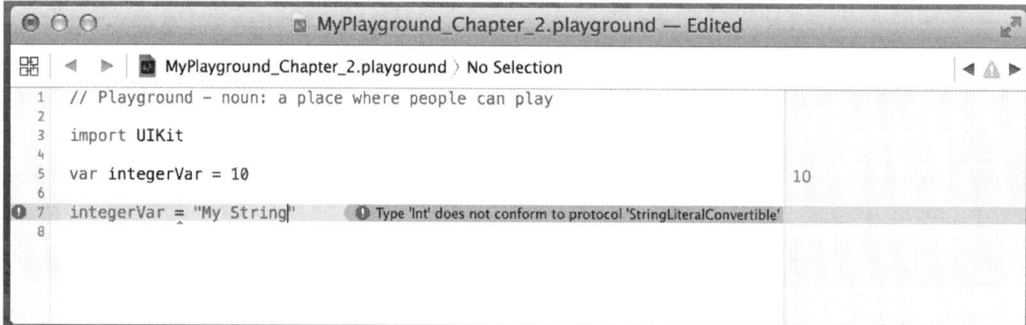

Swift performs a type check when it compiles code; therefore, it will flag any mismatched types with an error. The error message in this Playground explains pretty clearly that we are trying to insert a string literal into an integer variable.

So the question is, how does Swift know that `integerVar` is of the Int type? Swift uses type inference to figure out the appropriate type. Let's take a look at what type inference is.

Type inference

Type inference allows us to omit the variable type when we define it. The compiler will infer the type, based on the initial value. For example, in Objective-C, we would define an integer like this:

```
int myInt = 1
```

This tells the compiler that the `myInt` variable is of the Int type, and the initial value is the number `1`. In Swift, we would define the same integer like this:

```
var myInt = 1
```

Swift infers that the variable type is an integer because the initial value is an integer. Let's take a look at a couple of more examples:

```
var x = 3.14       // Double type
var y = "Hello"    // String type
var z = true       // Boolean type
```

In the preceding example, the compiler will correctly infer that variable `x` is Double, variable `y` is String, and variable `z` is Boolean, based on the initial values.

Explicit types

Type inference is a very nice feature in Swift and is one that you will probably get used to very quickly; however, there are times when we would like to explicitly define a variable's type. For example, in the preceding example, the variable, `x`, is inferred to be `Double`, but what if we wanted the variable type to be `Float`? We can explicitly define a variable type like this:

```
var x : Float = 3.14
```

Notice the `: Float`(colon and the word `Float`) after the variable identifier; this tells the compiler to define the variable to be of the `Float` type and gives it an initial value of `3.14`. When we define a variable in this manner, we need to make sure that the initial value is of the same type we are defining the variable to be. If we try to give a variable an initial value, that is, a different type than we are defining it as, we will receive an error.

We would also explicitly define the variable type if we were not setting an initial value. For example, the following line of code is invalid because the compiler does not know what type to set the variable, `x`, to:

```
var x
```

If we use this code in our application, we will receive a `Type annotation missing in pattern` error. If we are not setting an initial value for a variable, we are required to define the type like this:

```
var x: Int
```

Now that we have seen how to explicitly define a variable type, let's take a look at some of the most commonly used types.

Numeric types

Swift contains many of the standard numeric types that are suitable for storing various integer and floating-point values.

Integers

An integer is a whole number. Integers can be either signed (positive, negative, or zero) or unsigned (positive or zero). Swift provides several integer types of different sizes. The following chart shows the value ranges for the different integer types:

Type	Minimum	Maximum
Int8	-128	127
Int16	-32,768	32,767
Int32	-2,147,483,648	2,147,483,647
Int64	- 9,223,372,036,854,775,808	9,223,372,036,854,775,807
Int	- 9,223,372,036,854,775,808	9,223,372,036,854,775,807
UInt8	0	255
UInt16	0	65,535
UInt32	0	4,294,967,295
UInt64	0	18,446,744,073,709,551,615
UInt	0	18,446,744,073,709,551,615

Unless there is a specific reason to define the size of an integer, I would recommend using the standard `Int` or `UInt` type. This will save you from needing to convert between different types of integers.

In Swift, Int (as well as other numerical types) are actually named types, implemented in the Swift standard library using structures. This gives us a consistent mechanism for memory management for all the data types as well as properties that we can access. For the preceding chart, I retrieved the minimum and maximum values of each integer type using the `min` and `max` properties. Take a look at the following Playground to see how I retrieved the values:

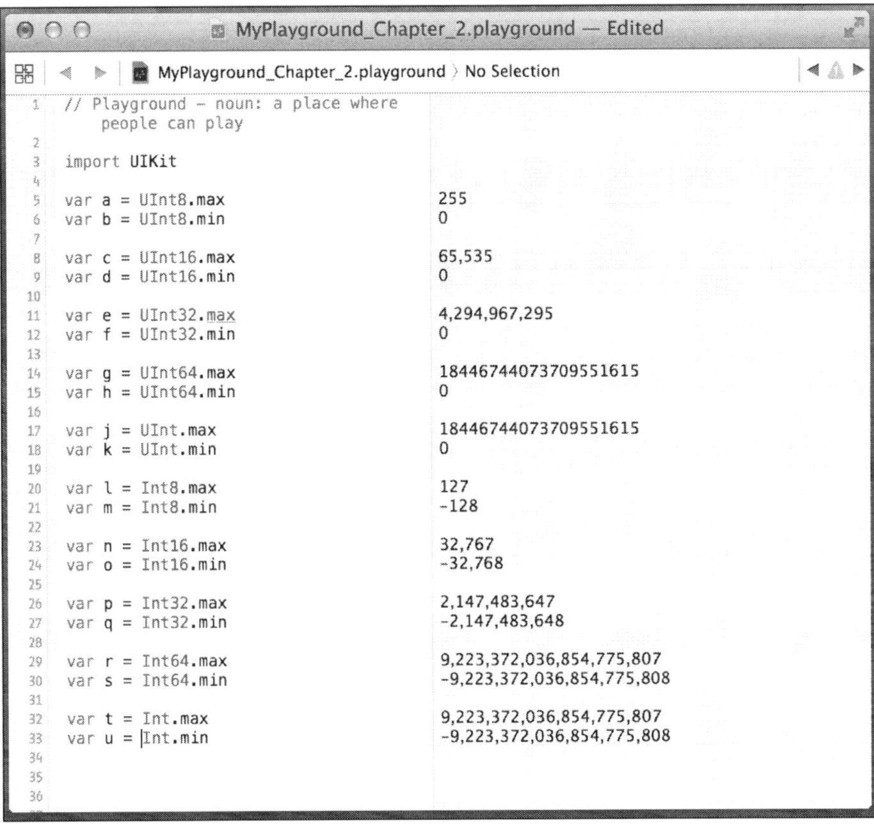

Integers can also be represented as binary, octal, and hexadecimal numbers. We just need to add a prefix to the number to tell the compiler which base the number should be in. The following chart shows the prefix for each numerical base:

Base	**Prefix**
Decimal	None
Binary	0b
Octal	0o
Hexadecimal	0x

The following Playground shows how the number, `95`, is represented in each of the numerical bases:

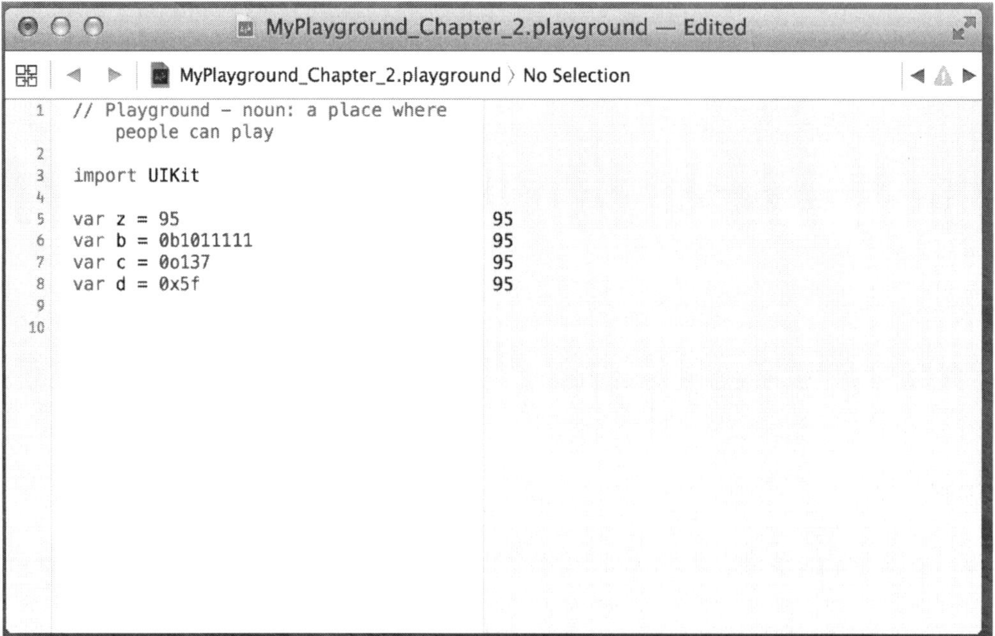

Swift also allows us to insert arbitrary underscores in our numeric literals. This can improve the readability of our code. As an example, if we were defining the speed of light, which is constant, we can define it like this:

```
let speedOfLightKmSec = 300_000
```

Swift will ignore these underscores; therefore, they do not affect the value of the numeric literals in any way.

Floating-point

A floating-point number is a number with a decimal component. There are two standard floating-point types in Swift Float and Double. Float represents a 32-bit floating-point number, while Double represents a 64-bit floating-point number. Swift also supports an extended floating-point type, that is, **Float80**. The Float80 type is an 80-bit floating-point number.

It is recommended that we use the Double type over the Float type unless there is a specific reason to use the latter. The Double type has a precision of at least 15 decimal digits, while the Float type can be as little as six decimal digits. Lets look at an example of how this can effect our application without us knowing it. The following screenshot shows the results if we add two decimal numbers together and put the results in both a Float type and Double type:

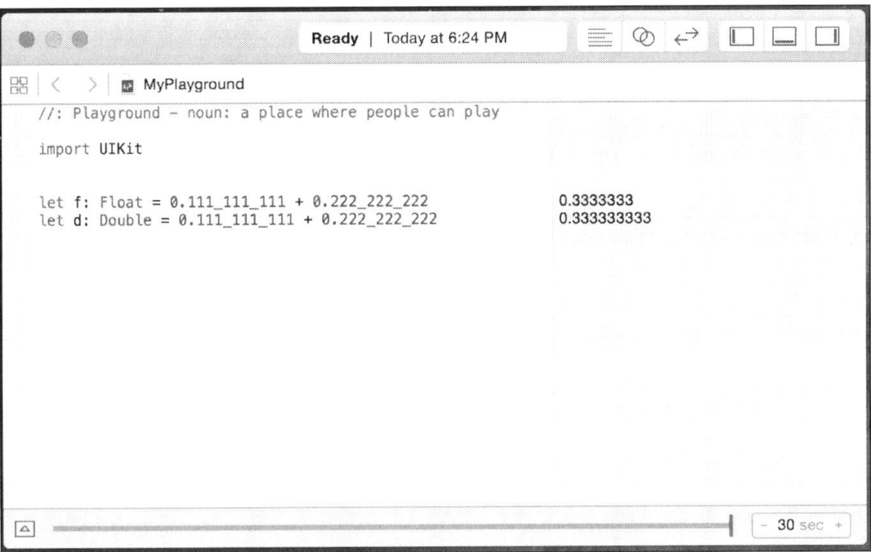

As we can see from the screenshots, the two decimal numbers that we are adding together contain nine digits post the decimal point; however, the results in the Float type only contains seven digits, while the results in the Double type contains the full nine digits.

The loss of precision can cause issues if we are working with currency or other numbers that need accurate calculations. The floating-point accuracy problem is not an issue confined to Swift; all the languages that implement the IEEE 754 floating-point standard have similar issues. The best practice is to use Double for floating-point numbers unless there is a specific reason not to.

What if we have two variables, one is an Int and the other is a Double? Do you think we can add them together as the following code depicts:

```
var a : Int = 3
var b : Double = 0.14
var c = a + b
```

If we put the preceding code into a Playground, we would receive the following error: `binary operator '+' cannot be applied to operands of type 'Int' and 'String'`

This error lets us know that we are trying to add two different types of numbers, which is not allowed. To add an Int and a Double together, we need to convert the Int value into a Double value. The following code shows how to convert an Int value into a Double value so that we can add them together:

```
var a : Int = 3
var b : Double = 0.14
var c = Double(a) + b
```

Notice how we use the `Double()` function to convert the Int value to a Double value. All the numeric types in Swift have a conversion convenience initializer, similar to the `Double()` function shown in the preceding code sample. For example, the following code shows how you can convert an `Int` variable to `Float` and `UInt16` variables:

```
var intVar = 32
var floatVar = Float(intVar)
var uint16Var = UInt16(intVar)
```

The Boolean type

Boolean values are often referred to as logical values because they can be either `true` or `false`. Swift has a built-in Boolean type called Bool that accepts one of the two built-in Boolean constants. These constants are `true` and `false`.

Boolean constants and variables can be defined like this:

```
let swiftIsCool = true
let swiftIsHard = false

var itIsWarm = false
var itIsRaining = true
```

Boolean values are especially useful when working with conditional statements, such as `if` and `while`. For example, what do you think this code would do:

```
let isSwiftCool = true
let isItRaining = false
if (isSwiftCool) {
    print("YEA, I cannot wait to learn it")
}
if (isItRaining) {
    print("Get a rain coat")
}
```

If you answered that this code would print out `YEA, I cannot wait to learn it`, then you would be correct. Since `isSwiftCool` is set to true, the `YEA, I cannot wait to learn it` message is printed out, but `isItRaining` is false; therefore, the `Get a rain coat` message is not.

You can also assign a Boolean value from a comparison operator like this:

```
var x = 2, y = 1
var z = x > y
```

In the preceding code, `z` is a Boolean variable containing a Boolean `true` value since `2` is greater than `1`.

The string type

A string is an ordered collection of characters, such as `Hello` or `Swift`. In Swift, the string type represents a string. We have seen several examples of strings already in this book, so the following code should look familiar. This code shows how to define two strings:

```
var stringOne = "Hello"
var stringTwo = " World"
```

Since a string is an ordered collection of characters, we can iterate through each character of a string. The following code shows how to do this:

```
varstringOne = "Hello"
for char in stringOne.characters {
    print(char)
}
```

The preceding code will display the results shown in the following screenshot:

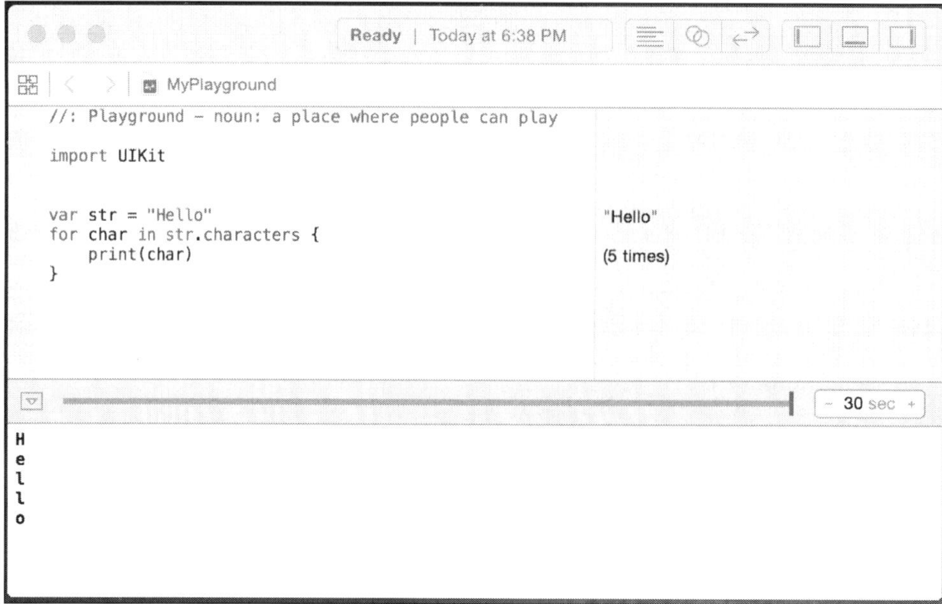

There are two ways to add one string to another string. We can concatenate them or include them inline. To concatenate two strings, we use the `+` or `+=` operator. The following code shows how to concatenate two strings. The first example appends `stringB` to the end of `stringA` and the results are put into a new `stringC` variable. The second example appends `stringB` directly to the end of `stringA` without creating a new string:

```
var stringC = stringA + stringB
stringA += stringB
```

To include a string inline, with another string, we use a special sequence of characters `\( )`. The following code shows how to include a string inline with another string:

```
var stringA = "Jon"
var stringB = "Hello \(stringA)"
```

In the previous example, `stringB` will contain the message, `Hello Jon`, because Swift will replace the `\(stringA)` sequence of characters with the value of `stringA`.

In Swift, we define the mutability of variables and collections by using the `var` and `let` keywords. If we define a string as a variable using `var`, the string is mutable; this means that we can change and edit the value of the string. If we define a string as a constant using `let`, the string is immutable, meaning that we cannot change or edit the value once it is set. The following code shows the difference between a mutable and an immutable string:

```
var x = "Hello"
let y = "HI"
var z = " World"

//This is valid, x is mutable
x += z

//This is invalid, y is not mutable.
y += z
```

Strings in Swift have three computed properties that can convert the case of the string. These properties are `capitalizedString`, `lowercaseString`, and `uppercaseString`. The following example demonstrates these properties:

```
var stringOne = "hElLo"
print("capitalizedString:  " + stringOne.capitalizedString)
print("lowercaseString:  " + stringOne.lowercaseString)
print("uppercaseString:  " + stringOne.uppercaseString)
```

If we run this code, the results will be as follows:

```
capitalizedString:  Hello
lowercaseString:  hello
uppercaseString:  HELLO
```

Swift provides four ways to compare a string; these are `string equality`, `prefix equality`, `suffix equality`, and `isEmpty`. The following example demonstrates these ways:

```
var stringOne = "Hello Swift"
var stringTwo = ""
stringOne.isEmpty  //false
stringTwo.isEmpty  //true
stringOne == "hello swift"  //false
stringOne == "Hello Swift"  //true
stringOne.hasPrefix("Hello")  //true
stringOne.hasSuffix("Hello")  //false
```

We can replace all the occurrences of a target string with another string. This is done with the `stringByReplacingOccurrencesOfString()` method. The following code demonstrates this:

```
var stringOne = "one,to,three,four"
print(stringOne.stringByReplacingOccurrencesOfString("to",
withString: "two"))
```

The preceding example will print `one,two,three,four` to the screen because we are replacing all the occurrences of `to` with `two`.

We can also retrieve substrings and individual characters from our strings. The following examples show various ways to do this:

```
var path = "/one/two/three/four"
//Create start and end indexes
var startIndex = path.startIndex.advancedBy(4)
var endIndex = path.startIndex.advancedBy(14)
path.substringWithRange(Range(start:startIndex, end:endIndex))   //
returns the String /two/three

path.substringToIndex(startIndex)  //returns the String /one
path.substringFromIndex(endIndex)  //returns the String /four
path.characters.last  //returns the last character in the String
which is r
path.characters.first  //returns the first character in the String
which is /
```

In the preceding example, we use the `substringWithRange()` function to retrieve the substring between a start and end index. The indexes are created with the `startIndex.advanceBy()` function. The `startIndex` property return the index of the first character in the string and then we use the `advancedBy()` method to advance the index to the desired number of positions.

The `substringToIndex()` function create a substring from the beginning of the string to the index. The `substringFromIndex()` function create a substring from the index to the end of the string. We then used the `last` property to get the last character of the string and the `first` property to get the first character.

We can retrieve the number of characters in a string by using the count property. The following example shows how you can use this function:

```
var path = "/one/two/three/four"
var length = path.characters.count
```

This completes our whirlwind tour of strings. I know we went through these properties and functions very quickly, but we will be using strings extensively throughout this book, so we will have a lot of time to get used to them.

Optional variables

All of the variables, which we have looked at so far, are considered to be non-optional variables. This means that the variables are required to have a non-nil value; however, there are times when we want or need our variables to contain `nil` values. This can occur if we return a `nil` from a function whose operation failed or if a value is not found.

In Swift, an optional variable is a variable that we are able to assign `nil` (no value) to. Optional variables and constants are defined using `?` (question mark). Let's look at the following Playground; it shows us how to define `Optional` and shows what happens if we assign a `nil` value to a `Non-Optional` variable:

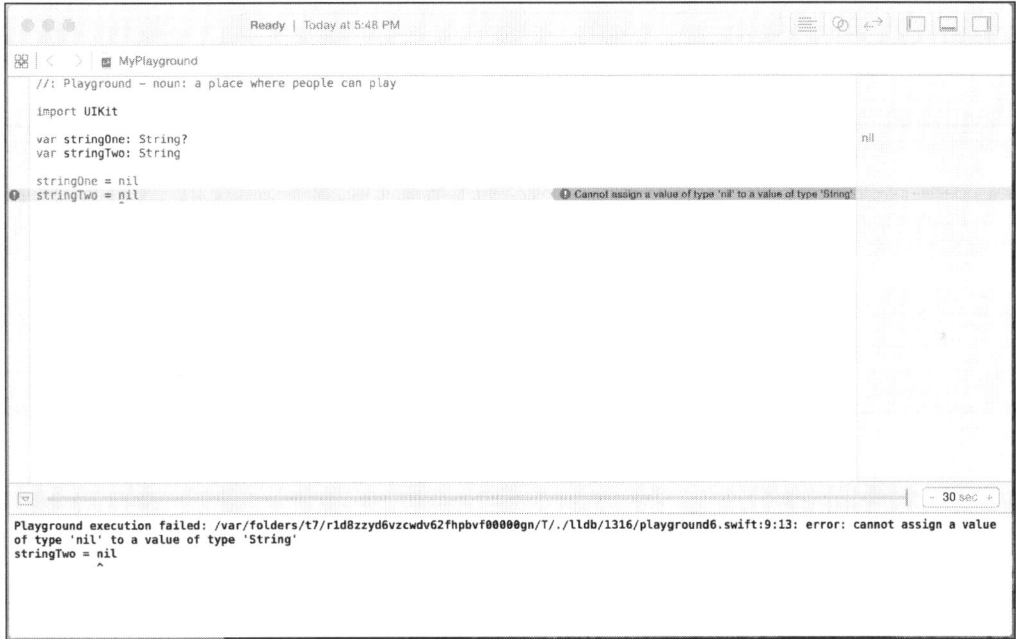

Notice the error we receive when we try to assign a `nil` value to the non-optional variable. This error message tells us that the `stringTwo` variable does not conform to the `NilLiteralConvertible` protocol. When we see this error, remember that it means that we are assigning a `nil` value to a variable or constant that is not defined as an optional type.

Optional variables were added to the Swift language as a safety feature. They provide a compile time check of our variables to verify that they contain a valid value. Unless our code specifically defines a variable as optional, we can assume that the variable contains a valid value, and we do not have to check for `nil` values. Since we are able to define a variable prior to initiating it, this could give us a `nil` value in a non-optional variable; however, the compiler checks for this. The following Playground shows the error that we receive if we attempt to use a non-optional variable prior to initiating it:

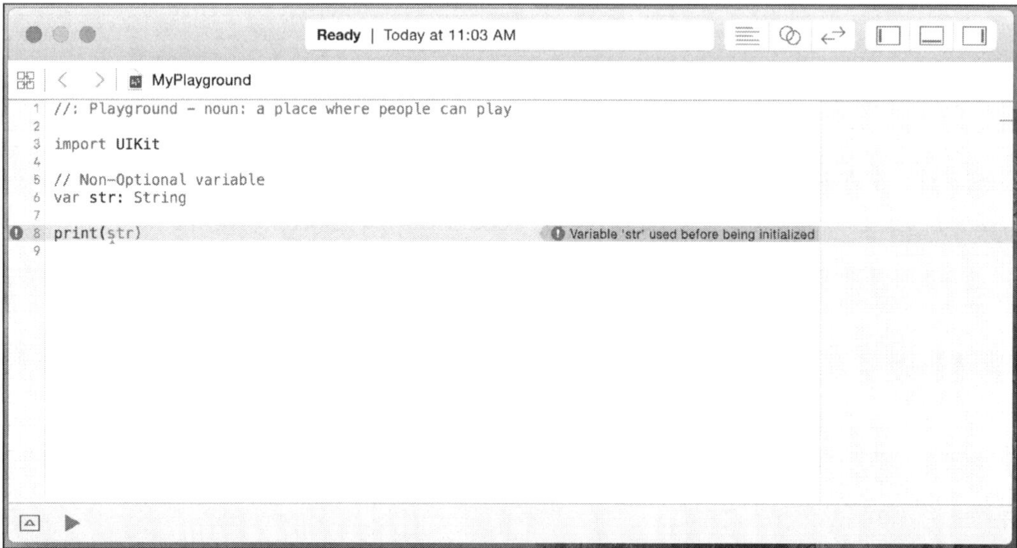

To verify that an optional variable or constant contains a valid (non-nil) value, our first thought may be to use the `!=` (not equals to) operator to verify that the variable is not equal to `nil`, but there are also other ways. These other ways are `Optional Binding` and `Optional Chaining`. Before we cover optional binding and optional chaining, let's see how to use the `!=` (not equals to) operator and what force unwrapping is.

To use force unwrapping, we must first make sure that the optional has a non-nil value and then we can use the explanation point to access that value. The following example shows how we can do this:

```
var name: String?
Name = "Jon"

if name != nil {
    var newString = "Hello " + name!
}
```

In this example, we create an optional variable named `name` and we assign it a value of `Jon`. We then use the `!=` operator to verify that the optional is not equal to `nil`. If it is not equal to `nil`, we are then able to use the explanation point to access its value. While this is a perfectly viable option, it is recommended that we use the optional binding method discussed next instead of force unwrapping.

We use optional binding to check whether an optional variable or constant has a non-nil value, and, if so, assign that value to a temporary variable. For optional binding, we use the `if-let` or `if-var` keywords together. If we use `if-let`, the temporary value is a constant and cannot be changed, while the `if-var` keywords puts the temporary value into a variable that allows us to change the value. The following code illustrates how optional binding is used:

```
if let temp = myOptional {
    print(temp)
    print("Can not use temp outside of the if bracket")
} else {
    print("myOptional was nil")
}
```

In the preceding example, we use the `if let` keywords to check whether the `myOptional` variable is `nil`. If it is not `nil`, we assign the value to the `temp` variable and execute the code between the brackets. If the `myOptional` variable is `nil`, we execute the code in the `else` bracket, which prints out the message, `myOptional was nil`. One thing to note is that the `temp` variable is scoped only for the conditional block and cannot be used outside of the conditional block.

It is perfectly acceptable with optional binding to assign the value to a variable of the same name. The following code illustrates this:

```
if let myOptional = myOptional {
    print(myOptional)
    print("Can not use temp outside of the if bracket")
} else {
    print("myOptional was nil")
}
```

To illustrate the scope of the temporary variable, let's take a look at the following code:

```
var myOptional: String?

myOptional = "Jon"
print("Outside: \(myOptional)")

if var myOptional = myOptional {
    myOptional = "test"
    print("Inside:  \(myOptional)")
}

print("Outside: \(myOptional)")
```

In this example, the first line that is printed to the console is `Inside: Optional( test)` because we are within the scope of the `if-var` statement where we assign the value of `test` to the `myOptional` variable. The second line that is printed to the console would be `Outside:  Optional(Jon)` because we are outside of the scope of the `if-var` statement where the `myOptional` variable is set to `Jon`.

We can also test multiple optional variables in one line. We do this by separating each optional check with a comma. The following example shows how to do this:

```
if let myOptional = myOptional, myOptional2 = myOptional2,
myOptional3 = myOptional3 {
  // only reach this if all three optionals
  // have non-nil values
}
```

Optional chaining allows us to call properties, methods, and subscripts on an optional that might be `nil`. If any of the chained values return `nil`, the return value will be `nil`. The following code gives an example of optional chaining using a fictitious `car` object. In this example, if either `car` or `tires` are `nil`, the variable `s` will be `nil`; otherwise, `s` will be equal to the `tireSize` property:

```
var s = car?.tires?.tireSize
```

The following Playground illustrates the three ways to verify whether the optionals contain a valid value prior to using them:

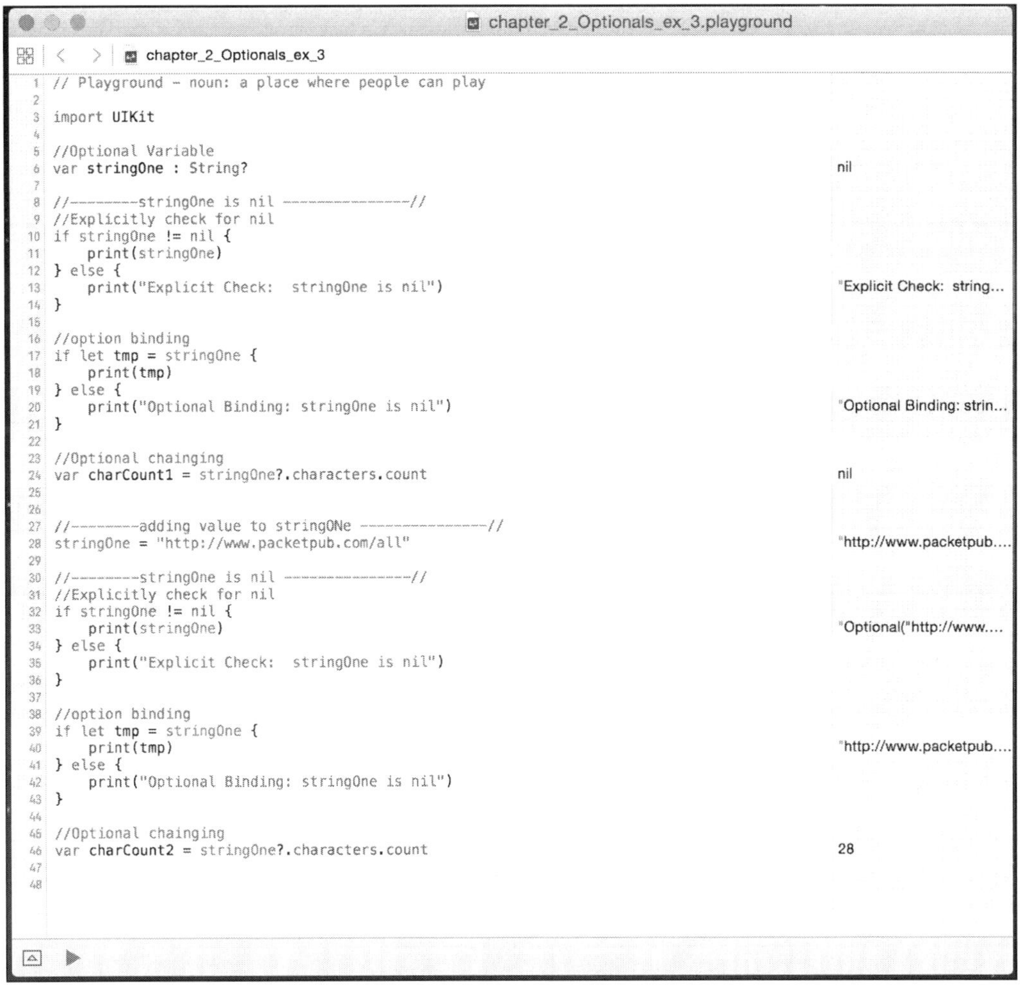

chapter_2_Optionals_ex_3.playground

```
// Playground - noun: a place where people can play

import UIKit

//Optional Variable
var stringOne : String?

//--------stringOne is nil --------------//
//Explicitly check for nil
if stringOne != nil {
    print(stringOne)
} else {
    print("Explicit Check:  stringOne is nil")
}

//option binding
if let tmp = stringOne {
    print(tmp)
} else {
    print("Optional Binding: stringOne is nil")
}

//Optional chainging
var charCount1 = stringOne?.characters.count


//--------adding value to stringONe --------------//
stringOne = "http://www.packetpub.com/all"

//--------stringOne is nil --------------//
//Explicitly check for nil
if stringOne != nil {
    print(stringOne)
} else {
    print("Explicit Check:  stringOne is nil")
}

//option binding
if let tmp = stringOne {
    print(tmp)
} else {
    print("Optional Binding: stringOne is nil")
}

//Optional chainging
var charCount2 = stringOne?.characters.count
```

In the preceding Playground, we begin by defining the optional string variable, `stringOne`. We then explicitly check for `nil` by using the `!=` operator. If `stringOne` is not equal to `nil`, we print the value of `stringOne` to the console. If `stringOne` is `nil`, we print the `Explicit Check: stringOne is nil` message to the console. As we can see in the results console, `Explicit Check: stringOne is nil` is printed to the console because we have not assigned a value to `stringOne` yet.

We then use optional binding to verify that `stringOne` is not `nil`. If `stringOne` is not `nil`, the value of `stringOne` is put into the `tmp` temporary variable, and we print the value of `tmp` to the console. If `stringOne` is `nil`, we print the `Optional Binding: stringOne is nil` message to the console. As we can see in the results console, `Optional Binding: stringOne is nil` is printed to the console because we have not assigned a value to `stringOne` yet.

We use optional chaining to assign the value of the `characters.count` property of the `stringOne` variable to the `charCount1` variable if `stringOne` is not `nil`. As we can see, the `charCount1` variable is `nil` because we have not assigned a value to `stringOne` yet.

We then assign a value of `http://www.packtpub.com/all` to the `stringOne` variable and rerun all the three tests again. This time `stringOne` has a non-nil value; therefore, the value of `charCount2` is printed to the console.

It would be tempting to say that I may need to set this variable to `nil`, so let me define it as optional, but that would be a mistake. The mindset for optionals should be to only use them if there is a specific reason for the variable to have `nil` value.

Enumerations

Enumerations (otherwise known as enums) are a special data type that enables us to group related types together and use them in a type safe manner. For those of us who are familiar with enums from other languages, such as C or Java, enums in Swift are not tied to integer values. We can define an enum with a type (string, character, integer, or floating-point) and then it's actual value (known as the raw value) will be the assigned value. Enums also support features that are traditionally supported only by classes such as computed properties and instance methods. We will discuss these advanced features in depth in *Chapter 5, Classes and Structures*. In this section, we will look at the traditional enum features.

We will define an enum that contains the list of `Planets` like this:

```
enum Planets {
    case Mercury
    case Venus
    case Earth
    case Mars
```

```
        case Jupiter
        case Saturn
        case Uranus
        case Neptune
    }
```

The values defined in an enum are considered to be the member values (or simply the members) of the enum. In most cases, you will see the member values defined like the preceding example because it is easy to read; however, there is a shorter version. This shorter version lets us define multiple members in a single line, separated by commas, as the following example shows:

```
enum Planets {
    case Mercury, Venus, Earth, Mars, Jupiter
    case Saturn, Uranus, Neptune
}
```

We can then use the `Planets` enum like this:

```
var planetWeLiveOn = Planets.Earth
var furthestPlanet = Planets.Neptune
```

The type for the `planetWeLiveOn` and `furthestPlanet` variables is inferred when we initialize the variable with one of the member values of `Planets`. Once the variable type is inferred, we can then assign a new value without the `Planets` prefix, as shown here:

```
planetWeLiveOn = .Mars
```

We can match an enum value using the traditional equals (==) operator or use a `switch` statement. The following example shows how to use the `equals` operator and the `switch` statement with an enum:

```
// Using the traditional == operator
if planetWeLiveOn == .Earth {
    print("Earth it is")
}
// Using the switch statement
switch planetWeLiveOn {
case .Mercury:
    print("We live on Mercury, it is very hot!")
case .Venus:
    print("We live on Venus, it is very hot!")
case .Earth:
```

```
    print("We live on Earth, just right")
case .Mars:
    print("We live on Mars, a little cold")
default:
    print("Where do we live?")
}
```

Enums can come prepopulated with raw values, which are required to be of the same type. This means that we can define our enum to contain string, character, integer, or floating-point values, but all of the members must be defined as the same type. The following example shows how to define an enum with string values:

```
enum Devices: String {
    case iPod = "iPod"
    case iPhone = "iPhone"
    case iPad = "iPad"
}
print("We are using an " + Devices.iPad.rawValue)
```

The preceding example creates an enum with three Apple devices. We then use the `rawValue` property to retrieve the raw value for the iPad member of the `Devices` enum. This example will print a message, saying `We are using an iPad`.

Let's create another `Planets` enum, but this time, assign numbers to the members, as follows:

```
enum Planets: Int  {
    case Mercury = 1
    case Venus
    case Earth
    case Mars
    case Jupiter
    case Saturn
    case Uranus
    case Neptune
}
print("Earth is planet number \(Planets.Earth.rawValue)")
```

The big difference between the two enum examples is that in the second example, we only assign a value to the first member (`Mercury`). If integers are used for the raw values of an enum, we do not have to assign a value to each member. If no value is present, the raw values will be auto-incremented.

In Swift, enums can also have associated values. Associate values allow us to store additional information along with member values. This additional information can vary each time we use the member. It can also be of any type, and the types can be different for each member. Let's take a look at how we might use associate types by defining a `Product` enum, which contains two types of products:

```
enum Product {
    case Book(Double, Int, Int)
    case Puzzle(Double, Int)
}
var masterSwift = Product.Book(49.99, 2015, 310)
var worldPuzzle = Product.Puzzle(9.99, 200)

switchmasterSwift {
case .Book(let price, let year, let pages):
    print("Mastering Swift was published in \(year) for the price
        of \(price) and has \(pages) pages")
case .Puzzle(let price, let pieces):
    print("Master Swift is a puzze with \(pieces) and sells for
    \(price)")
}

switchworldPuzzle {
case .Book(let price, let year, let pages):
    print("World Puzzle was published in \(year) for the price of
    \(price) and has \(pages) pages")
case .Puzzle(let price, let pieces):
    print("World Puzzle is a puzze with \(pieces) and sells for
    \(price)")
}
```

In the preceding example, we begin by defining a `Product` enum with two members—`Book` and `Puzzle`. The `Book` member has an associated value of `Double`, `Int`, `Int`, and the `Puzzle` member has an associated value of `Double, Int`. We then create two products `masterSwift` and `worldPuzzle`. We assign the `masterSwift` variable a value of `Product.Book` with the associated values of `49.99, 2015, 310`. We then assign the `worldPuzzle` variable a value of `Product.Puzzle` with the associated values of `9.99, 200`.

We can then check the `Products` enum using a `switch` statement, as we did in some of the preceding enum examples. We also extract the associated values within the `switch` statement. In the previous example, we extracted the associated values as constants with the `let` keyword, but you can also extract the associated values as variables with the `var` keyword.

If you put the previous code into a Playground, the following results will be displayed:

```
"Master Swift was published in 2015 for the price of 49.99
  and has 310 pages"
"World Puzzle is a puzzle with 200 and sells for 9.99"
```

Operators

An operator is a symbol or combination of symbols that we can use to check, change, or combine values. We have used operators in most of the examples so far in this book; however, we did not specifically call them operators. In this section, we will show how to use most of the basic operators that Swift supports.

Swift supports most standard C operators and also improves them to eliminate several common coding errors. For example, the assignment operator does not return a value to prevent it from being used when the equality operator (==) was meant to be used.

Let's look at the operators in Swift.

The assignment operator

The assignment operator initializes or updates a variable.

Prototype:

```
varA = varB
```

Example:

```
let x = 1
var y = "Hello"
a = b
```

Comparison operators

The comparison operator returns a Boolean `true` if the statement is true or a Boolean `false` if the statement is not true.

Prototypes:

```
Equality:  varA == varB
Not equal:  varA != varB
Greater than:  varA > varB
Less than:  varA < varB
Greater than or equal to:  varA >= varB
Less than or equal to:  varA <= varB
```

Example:

```
2 == 1 //false, 2 does not equal 1
2 != 1 //true, 2 does not equal 1
2 > 1  //true, 2 is greater than 1
2 < 1  //false, 2 is not less than 1
2 >= 1 //true, 2 is greater or equal to 1
2 <= 1 //false, 2 is not less or equal to 1
```

Arithmetic operators

The arithmetic operators perform the four basic mathematical operations.

Prototypes:

```
Addition:  varA + varB
Subtraction:  varA - varB
Multiplication:  varA * varB
Division:  varA / varB
```

Example:

```
var x = 4 + 2  //x will equal 6
var x = 4 - 2  //x will equal 2
var x = 4 * 2  //x will equal 8
var x = 4 / 2  //x will equal 2
var x = "Hello " + "world"  //x will equal "Hello World"
```

The remainder operator

The remainder operator calculates the remainder if the first operand is divided by the second operand.

Prototype:

```
varA % varB
```

Example:

```
var x = 10 % 3  //x will equal 1
var x = 10 % 2.6  //x will equal 2.2
```

Increment and decrement operators

The increment and decrement operators are shortcuts to increment or decrement a variable by `1`.

Prototypes:

```
++varA - Increments the value of varA and then returns the value
varA++ - Returns the values of varA and then increments varA
--varA - Decrements the value of varA and then returns the value
varA-- - Returns the value of varA and then decrements varA
```

Example:

```
var x = 5
var y = ++x  //Both x and y equals 6
var y = x++  //x equals 6 but y equals 5
var y = --x  //Both x and y equals 4
var y = x--  //x equals 4 but y equals 5
```

Compound assignment operators

The compound assignment operators combine an arithmetic operator with an assignment operator.

Prototypes:

```
varA += varB
varA -= varB
varA *= varB
varA /= varB
```

Example:

```
var x = 6
x += 2  //x is equal to 8
x -= 2  //x is equal to 4
x *= 2  //x is equal to 12
x /= 2  //x is equal to 3
```

The ternary conditional operator

The ternary conditional operator assigns a value to a variable, based on the evaluation of a comparison operator or Boolean value.

Prototype:

```
(boolValue ? valueA : valueB)
```

Example:

```
var x = 2
var y = 3
var z = (y > x ? "Y is greater" : "X is greater")  //z equals
  "Y is greater"
```

The logical NOT operator

The logical NOT operator inverts a Boolean value.

Prototype:

```
varA = !varB
```

Example:

```
var x = true
var y = !x  //y equals false
```

The logical AND operator

The logical AND operator returns `true` if both operands are true, otherwise it returns `false`.

Prototype:

```
varA && varB
```

Example:

```
var x = true
var y = false
var z = x && y  //z equals false
```

The logical OR operator

The logical OR operator returns `true` if either of the operands is true.

Prototype:

```
varA || varB
```

Example:

```
var x = true
var y = false
var z = x || y  //z equals true
```

For those who are familiar with C and languages that have a similar syntax to C, these operators should look pretty familiar. For those who aren't that familiar with the C operators, rest assured that you will use them enough and they will become second nature.

Summary

In this chapter, we covered a lot of different topics. These topics ranged from variables and constants to data types and operators. The items in this chapter will be the foundation of every application that you write; therefore, it is important to understand the concepts discussed here.

In the next chapter, we will look at how we can use the Swift collection types to store related data. These collection types are the dictionary and array types. We will also look at how we can use the Cocoa and Foundation data types in Swift.

3

Using Collections and Cocoa Data Types

Once I got past the basic Hello World beginner applications, I quickly began to realize the shortcomings of variables, especially with the Mad Libs style applications that I was starting to write. These applications requested that the user enter in numerous strings, and I was creating a separate variable for each input field that the user entered. Having all of these separate variables quickly became very cumbersome. I remember talking to a friend about this and he asked me why I was not using arrays. At that time, I was not familiar with arrays, so I asked him to show me what they were. Even though he had a TI-99/4A and I had a Commodore Vic-20, the concept of arrays was the same. Even today, the arrays found in modern development languages have the same basic concepts as the arrays I used on my Commodore Vic-20. While it is definitely possible to create a useful application without using collections, when used right, collections do make application development significantly easier.

In this chapter, we will cover the following topics:

- What an array is in Swift and how to use it
- What a dictionary is in Swift and how we can use it
- What a Set is in Swift and how we can use it
- What a tuple is in Swift and how we can use it
- How to use Cocoa data types in Swift
- How to use Foundation data types in Swift

Swift collection types

A collection is a group or store of data that has a shared significance. Swift provides three native collection types for storing data. These collection types are arrays, sets, and dictionaries. An array stores the data in an ordered list, sets are an unordered collection of unique data, and dictionaries are an unordered collection of key/value pairs. In an array, we access the data by the location (index) in the array; in a set, we tend to iterate over the set; and dictionaries are usually accessed using a unique key.

The data stored in a Swift collection is required to be of the same type. This means, as an example, that we are unable to store a string value and an array of integers. Since Swift does not allow us to mismatch data types in a collection, we can be certain of the data type when we retrieve data from a collection. This is another feature, which on the surface might seem like a shortcoming, but is actually a design feature that helps eliminate common programming mistakes. We will see how to work around this feature by using the `AnyObject` and `Any` aliases in this chapter.

Mutability

For those who are familiar with Objective-C, you will know that there are different classes for mutable and immutable collections. For example, to define a mutable array, we use the `NSMutableArray` class, and to define an immutable array, we use the `NSArray` class. Swift is a little different because it does not contain separate classes for mutable and immutable collections. Instead, we define whether a collection is constant (immutable) or a variable (mutable) by using the `let` and `var` keywords. This should seem familiar since, in Swift, we define constants with the `let` keyword and variables with the `var` keyword.

It is good practice to create immutable collections unless there is a specific need to change the objects within the collection. This allows the compiler to optimize the performance.

Let's begin our tour of collections by looking at the most common collection type—the array type.

Arrays

Arrays are a very common component of modern programming languages and can be found virtually in all the modern programming languages. In Swift, arrays are an ordered list of objects of the same type. This is different from the `NSArray` class in Objective-C, which can contain objects of different types.

When an array is created, we must declare the type of data to be stored in it by explicit type declaration or through type inference. Typically, we only explicitly declare the data type of an array when we are creating an empty array. If we initialize an array with data, we should let the compiler use type inference to infer the most appropriate data type for the array.

Each object in an array is called an element. Each of these elements is stored in a set order and can be accessed by its location (index) in the array.

Creating and initializing arrays

We can initialize an array with an array literal. An array literal is a set of values that we prepopulate the array with. The following example shows how to define an immutable array of integers using the `let` keyword:

```
let arrayOne = [1,2,3]
```

As we mentioned, if we need to create a mutable array, we will use the `var` keyword to define the array. The following example shows how to define a mutable array:

```
var arrayTwo = [4,5,6]
```

In the preceding two examples, the compiler inferred the type of values stored in the array by looking at the type of values stored in the array literal. If we needed to create an empty array, we will need to explicitly declare the type of values to store in the array. The following example shows how to declare an empty array that can be used to store integers:

```
var arrayThree = [Int]()
```

In the preceding examples, we created arrays with integer values, and the majority of the array examples in this chapter will also use integer values; however, we can create arrays in Swift with any type. The only rule is that once an array is defined as containing a particular type, all the elements in the array must be of that type. The following example shows how we would create arrays of various data types:

```
var arrayOne = [String]()
var arrayTwo = [Double]()
var arrayThree = [MyObject]()
```

Swift does provide special type aliases for working with nonspecific types. These aliases are `AnyObject` and `Any`. We can use these aliases to define arrays whose elements are of different types, like this:

```
var myArray: [AnyObject] = [1,"Two"]
```

We should use the `Any` and `AnyObject` aliases only when there is an explicit need for this behavior. It is always better to be specific about the types of data our collections contain.

We can also initialize an array to a certain size with all the elements of the array set to a predefined value. This can be very useful if we want to create an array and prepopulate it with the default values. The following example defines an array with seven elements, and each element contains the number `3`:

```
var arrayFour = [Int](count: 7, repeatedValue: 3)
```

While the most common array is a one-dimensional array, we can also create multidimensional arrays. A multidimensional array is really nothing more than an array of arrays. For example, a two-dimensional array is an array of arrays, while a three-dimensional array is an array of arrays of arrays. The following examples show the two ways to create a two-dimensional array in Swift:

```
var multiArrayOne = [[1,2],[3,4],[5,6]]
var multiArrayTwo = [[Int]]()
```

Accessing the array elements

We use the subscript syntax to retrieve values from an array. The subscript syntax for an array is where a number appears between two square brackets and that number specifies the location (index), within the array, of the element we wish to retrieve. The following example shows how to retrieve elements from an array using the subscript syntax:

```
let arrayOne = [1,2,3,4,5,6]
print(arrayOne[0])  //Displays '1'
print(arrayOne[3])  //Displays '4'
```

In the preceding code, we begin by creating an array of integers that contains six numbers. We then print out the value at index `0` and `3`.

If we want to retrieve an individual value within a multidimensional array, we will need to provide a subscript for each dimension. If we did not provide a subscript for each dimension, we will return an array rather than an individual value within the array. The following example shows how we can define a two-dimensional array and retrieve an individual value within the two dimensions:

```
var multiArray = [[1,2],[3,4],[5,6]]
var arr = multiArray[0] //arr contains the array [1,2]
var value = multiArray[0][1] //value contains 2
```

In the preceding code, we begin by defining a two-dimensional array. When we retrieve the value at index `0` of the first dimension (`multiArray[0]`), we retrieve the array, `[1,2]`. When we retrieve the value at index `0` of the first dimension and index `1` of the second dimension (`multiArray[0][1]`), we retrieve the integer, `2`.

We can retrieve the first and last elements of an array using the `first` and `last` properties. The `first` and `last` properties return an optional value since the values may be nil if the array is empty. The following example shows how to use the `first` and `last` properties to retrieve the first and last elements of both single-dimensional and multidimensional arrays:

```
let arrayOne = [1,2,3,4,5,6]
var first = arrayOne.first  //first contains 1
var last = arrayOne.last  //last contains 6

let multiArray = [[1,2],[3,4],[5,6]]
var arrFirst1 = multiArray[0].first //arrFirst1 contains 1
var arrFirst2 = multiArray.first //arrFirst2 contains[1,2]
var arrLast1 = multiArray[0].last //arrLast1 contains 2
var arrLast2 = multiArray.last  //arrLast2 contains [5,6]
```

Counting the elements of an array

At times, it is essential to know the number of elements in an array. To retrieve the number of elements, we would use the read-only `count` property. The following example shows how to use this property to retrieve the number of elements in both single-dimensional and multidimensional arrays:

```
let arrayOne = [1,2,3]
let multiArrayOne = [[3,4],[5,6],[7,8]]
print(arrayOne.count)  //Displays 3
print(multiArrayOne.count)  //Displays 3 for the three arrays
print(multiArrayOne[0].count)  //Displays 2 for the two elements
```

The value that is returned by the `count` property is the number of elements in the array and not the largest valid index of the array. For nonempty arrays, the largest valid index is the number of elements in the array minus one. This is because the first element of the array has an index number of zero. As an example, if an array has two elements, the valid indexes are `0` and `1`, while the count property would return `2`. The following code illustrates this:

```
let arrayOne = [0,1]
print(arrayOne[0])  //Displays 0
print(arrayOne[1])  //Displays 1
print(arrayOne.count) //Displays 2
```

If we attempt to retrieve an element from an array, using the subscript syntax, where the index is outside the range of the array, the application will throw an `Array index out of range` error. Therefore, if we are unsure of the size of an array, it is good practice to verify that the index is not outside the range of the array. The following examples illustrate this concept:

```
//This example will throw an array index out of range error
var arrayTwo = [1,2,3,4]
print(arrayTwo[6])

//This example will not throw an array index out of range error
var arrayOne = [1,2,3,4]
if (arrayOne.count> 6) {
    print(arrayOne[6])
}
```

In the preceding code, the first block of code would throw an `array index out of range` error exception because we are attempting to access the value from the array `arrayTwo` at index `6`; however, there are only four elements in the array. The second example would not throw the `array index out of range` error exception because we are checking whether the `arrayOne` array contains more than six elements, and if it does not, we do not attempt to access the value at index `6`.

Is the array empty?

To check whether an array is empty (does not contain any elements), we use the `isEmpty` property. This property will return `true` if the array is empty, or `false` if it has elements. The following example shows how to check whether an array is empty or not:

```
var arrayOne = [1,2]
var arrayTwo = [Int]()
arrayOne.isEmpty  //Returns false because the array is not empty
arrayTwo.isEmpty  //Returns true because the array is empty
```

Appending to an array

A static array is somewhat useful, but having the ability to add elements dynamically is what makes arrays really useful. To add an item to the end of an array, we can use the `append` method. The following example shows how to append an item to the end of an array:

```
var arrayOne = [1,2]
arrayOne.append(3)  //arrayOne will now contain 1, 2 and 3
```

Swift also allows us to use the addition assignment operator (+=) to append an array to another array. The following example shows how to use the addition assignment operator to append an array to the end of another array:

```
var arrayOne = [1,2]
arrayOne += [3,4]  //arrayOne will now contain 1, 2, 3 and 4
```

The way you append an element to the end of an array is really up to you. Personally, I prefer the assignment operator because, to me, it is a bit easier to read, but we will be using both in this book.

Inserting a value into an array

We can insert a value into an array by using the `insert` method. The `insert` method will move all the items, starting at the specified index up one spot, to make room for the new element and then inserts the value into the specified index. The following example shows how to use the insert method to insert a new value into an array:

```
var arrayOne = [1,2,3,4,5]
arrayOne.insert(10, atIndex: 3) //arrayOne now contains 1, 2,
  3, 10, 4 and 5
```

> You cannot insert a value that is outside the current range of the array. Attempting to do so will throw an `Index out of range exception`. For example, in the preceding code, if we attempt to insert a new integer at index 10, we will receive an `Index out of range exception error` because `arrayOne` only contains five elements. The exception to this is that we are able to insert an item directly after the last element; therefore, we can insert an item at index `6`. However, it is recommended that we use the `append` function to append an item to avoid errors.

Replacing elements in an array

We use the subscript syntax to replace elements in an array. Using the subscript, we pick the element of the array we wish to update and then use the assignment operator to assign a new value. The following example shows how we will replace a value in an array:

```
var arrayOne = [1,2,3]
arrayOne[1] = 10  //arrayOne now contains 1,10,3
```

You cannot update a value that is outside the current range of the array. Attempting to do so will throw the same `Index out of range` exception that was thrown when we tried to insert a value outside the range of the array.

Removing elements from an array

There are three methods that we can use to remove one or all the elements in an array. These methods are `removeLast()`, `removeAtIndex()`, and `removeAll()`. The following example shows how to use the three methods to remove elements from the array:

```
var arrayOne = [1,2,3,4,5]
arrayOne.removeLast()  //arrayOne now contains 1, 2, 3 and 4
arrayOne.removeAtIndex(2)  //arrayOne now contains 1, 2 and 4
arrayOne.removeAll()  //arrayOne is now empty
```

The `removeLast()` and `removeAtIndex()` methods will also return the value of the element that it is removing. Therefore, if we want to know the value of the item that was removed, we can rewrite the `removeAtIndex` and `removedLast` lines to capture the value, as shown in the following example:

```
var arrayOne = [1,2,3,4,5]
var removed1 = arrayOne.removeLast()  //removed1 contains the
value 5
var removed = arrayOne.removeAtIndex(2)  //removed contains the
value 3
```

Adding two arrays

To create a new array by adding two arrays together, we use the addition (+) operator. The following example shows how to use the addition (+) operator to create a new array that contains all the elements of two other arrays:

```
let arrayOne = [1,2]
let arrayTwo = [3,4]
var combine = arrayOne + arrayTwo //combine contains 1, 2, 3 and 4
```

In the preceding code, `arrayOne` and `arrayTwo` are left unchanged, while the combine array contains the elements from `arrayOne`, followed by the elements from `arrayTwo`.

Reversing an array

We can create a new array from the original array with the elements in reverse order using the `reverse()` method. The original array will remain unchanged by the `reverse` method. The following example shows how to use the `reverse()` method:

```
var arrayOne = [1,2,3]
var reverse = arrayOne.reverse() //reverse contains 3,2 and 1
```

In the preceding code, the elements of `arrayOne` are left unchanged, while the `reverse` array will contain all the elements from `arrayOne`, but in the reverse order.

Retrieving a subarray from an array

We can retrieve a `subarray` from an existing array by using the subscript syntax with a range. The following example shows how to retrieve a range of elements from an existing array:

```
let arrayOne = [1,2,3,4,5]
var subArray = arrayOne[2…4] //subArray contains 3, 4 and 5
```

The … operator (three periods) is known as a range operator. The range operator, in the preceding code, says I want all the elements, `2` to `4`, inclusively (included elements 2 and 4 as well as what is between them). There is another range operator, which is `..<`, the same as the … range operator, but it excludes the last element. The following example shows how to use the `.<` operator.

```
let arrayOne = [1,2,3,4,5]
var subArray = arrayOne[2..<4] //subArray contains 3 and 4
```

In the preceding example, the `subArray` will contain two elements `3` and `4`.

Making bulk changes to an array

We can use the subscript syntax with a range operator to change the values of multiple elements. The following example shows how to use the subscript syntax to change a range of elements.

```
var arrayOne = [1,2,3,4,5]
arrayOne[1…2] = [12,13]//arrayOne contains 1,12,13,4 and 5
```

In the preceding code, the elements at index `1` and `2` will be changed to number `12` and `13`. After this, when the code runs, `arrayOne` will contain `1`, `12`, `13`, `4`, and `5`.

The number of elements that you are changing in the range operator does not need to match the number of values that you are passing in. Swift makes the bulk changes—it first removes the elements defined by the range operator and then inserts the new values. The following example demonstrates this concept:

```
var arrayOne = [1,2,3,4,5]
arrayOne[1…3] = [12,13]
//arrayOne now contains 1, 12, 13 and 5 (four elements)
```

In the preceding code, `arrayOne` starts with five elements. We then say that we want to replace the range of elements `1` to `3` inclusively. This causes elements `1` to `3` (three elements) to be removed from the array. We then add two elements (`12` and `13`) to the array, starting at index `1`. After this is complete, `arrayOne` will contain these four elements: `1`, `12`, `13`, and `5`. Let's see what happens if we try to add more elements than we remove:

```
var arrayOne = [1,2,3,4,5]
arrayOne[1...3] = [12,13,14,15]
//arrayOne now contains 1, 12, 13, 14, 15 and 5 (six elements)
```

In the preceding code, `arrayOne` starts with five elements. We then say that we want to replace the range of elements `1` to `3` inclusively. This causes elements `1` to `3` (three elements) to be removed from the array. We then add four elements (`12`, `13`, `14`, and `15`) to the array, starting at index `1`. After this is complete, `arrayOne` will contain these six elements: `1`, `12`, `13`, `14`, `15`, and `5`.

Algorithms for arrays

Swift arrays have several methods that take a closure as the argument. These methods transform the array and the closures affect how the array is transformed. Closures are self-contained blocks of code that can be passed around, and are similar to blocks in Objective-C and lambdas in other languages. We will discuss closures in depth in *Chapter 12, Working with Closures*. For now, we just want to get familiar with how the algorithms work in Swift.

sortInPlace

The sortInPlace algorithm sorts the array in place. This means when the `sortInPlace()` method is used, the original array is replaced by the sorted one. The closure takes two arguments (represented by `$0` and `$1`), and it should return a Boolean value that indicates whether the first element should be placed before the second element. The following code shows how to use the sort algorithm:

```
var arrayOne = [9,3,6,2,8,5]
arrayOne.sortInPlace(){ $0 < $1 }
//arrayOne contains 2,3,5,6,8 and 9
```

The preceding code will sort the array in increasing order. We can tell this because our rule will return `true` if the first number (`$0`) is less than the second number (`$1`). Therefore, when the sort algorithm begins, it compares the first two numbers (`9` and `3`) and returns `true` if the first number (`9`) is less than the second number (`3`). In our case, the rule returns `false`, so the numbers are reversed. The algorithm continues sorting, in this manner, until all of the numbers are sorted.

The preceding example sorted the array in numerically increasing order; if we wanted to reverse the order, we would reverse the arguments in the closure. The following code shows how to reverse the sort order:

```
var arrayOne = [9,3,6,2,8,5]
arrayOne.sortInPlace(){ $1 < $0 }
//arrayOne contains 9,8,6,5,3 and 2
```

When we run this code, `arrayOne` will contain the elements `9`, `8`, `6`, `5`, `3`, and `2`.

sort

While the sortInPlace algorithm sorts the array in place (replaces the original array), the `sort` algorithm does not change the original array, it instead creates a new array with the sorted elements from the original array. The following example shows how to use the sorted algorithm:

```
var arrayOne = [9,3,6,2,8,5]
let sorted = arrayOne.sort(){ $0 < $1 }
//sorted contains 2,3,5,6,8 and 9
//arrayOne contains 9,3,6,2,8 and 5
```

When we run this code, `arrayOne` will contain the original unsorted array (`9`, `3`, `6`, `2`, `8`, and `5`) and the sorted array will contain the new sorted array (`2`, `3`, `5`, `6`, `8`, and `9`).

filter

The filter algorithm will return a new array by filtering the original array. This is one of the most powerful array algorithms and may end up to be the one we use the most. If we need to retrieve a subset of an array, based on a set of rules, I recommend using this algorithm rather than trying to write your own method to filter the array. The closure takes one argument and it should return a Boolean `true` if the element should be included in the new array, as shown in the following code:

```
var arrayOne = [1,2,3,4,5,6,7,8,9]
let filtered = arrayFiltered.filter{$0 > 3 && $0 < 7}
//filtered contains 4,5 and 6
```

In the preceding code, the rule that we are passing to the algorithm returns `true` if the number is greater than `3` or less than `7`; therefore, any number that is greater than `3` or less than `7` is included in the new filtered array.

Let's take a look at another example; this one shows how we can retrieve a subset of cities that contain the letter o in their name from an array of cities:

```
var city = ["Boston", "London", "Chicago", "Atlanta"]
let filtered = city.filter{$0.rangeOfString("o") != nil}
//filtered contains "Boston", "London" and "Chicago"
```

In the preceding code, we use the `rangeOfString()` method to return `true` if the string contains the letter o. If the method returns `true`, the string is included in the filtered array.

map

The map algorithm returns a new array that contains the results of applying the rules in the closure to each element of the array. The following example shows how to use the map algorithm to divide each number by `10`:

```
var arrayOne = [10, 20, 30, 40]
let applied = arrayOne.map{ $0 / 10}
//applied contains 1,2,3 and 4
```

In the preceding code, the new array contains the numbers `1`, `2`, `3`, and `4`, which is the result of dividing each element of the original array by `10`.

The new array created by the map algorithm is not required to contain the same element types as the original array; however, all the elements in the new array must be of the same type. In the following example, the original array contains integer values, but the new array created by the map algorithm contains string elements:

```
var arrayOne = [1, 2, 3, 4]
let applied = arrayOne.map{ "num:\($0)"}
//applied contains "num:1", "num:2", "num:3" and "num:4"
```

In the preceding code, we created an array of strings that appends the numbers from the original array to the `num:`string.

forEach

We can use `forEach` to iterate over a sequence. The following example shows how we would do this:

```
var arrayOne = [10, 20, 30, 40]
arrayOne.forEach{ print($0) }
```

This example will print the following results to the console:

```
10
20
30
40
```

While using the `forEach` method is very easy, it does have some limitations. The recommended way to iterate over an array is to use the `for-in` loop, which we will see in the next section.

Iterating over an array

We can iterate over all elements of an array, in order, with a `for-in` loop. We will discuss the `for-in` loop in greater detail in *Chapter 4, Control Flow and Functions*. The `for-in` loop will execute one or more statements for each element of the array. The following example shows how we would iterate over the elements of an array:

```
var arr = ["one", "two", "three"]
for item in arr {
    print(item)
}
```

In the preceding example, the `for-in` loop iterates over the `arr` array and executes the `print(item)` line for each element in the array. If we run this code, it will display the following results in the console:

```
one
two
three
```

There are times when we would like to iterate over an array, as we did in the preceding example, but we would also like to know the index as well as the value of the element. To do this, we can use the `enumerate` method, which returns a tuple (see the *Tuples* section later in this chapter) for each item in the array that contains both `index` and `value` of the element. The following example shows how to use the `enumerate` function:

```
var arr = ["one", "two", "three"]
for (index,value) in arr.arr.enumerate() {
    print"\(index) \(value)")
}
```

The preceding code will display the following results in the console:

```
0 one
1 two
2 three
```

Now that we have introduced arrays in Swift, let's take a look at what a dictionary is.

Dictionaries

While dictionaries are not as commonly used as arrays, they have an additional functionality that makes them incredibly powerful. A dictionary is a container that stores multiple key-value pairs, where all the keys are of the same type, and all the values are of the same type. The key is used as a unique identifier for the value. A dictionary does not guarantee the order in which the key-value pairs are stored since we look up the values by the key, rather than by the index of the value.

Dictionaries are good for storing items that map to unique identifiers, where the unique identifier should be used to retrieve the item. As an example, countries with their abbreviations are a good example of items that can be stored in a dictionary. In the following chart, we show countries with their abbreviations as key-value pairs:

Key	Value
US	United States
IN	India
UK	United Kingdom

Creating and initializing dictionaries

We can initialize a dictionary using a dictionary literal, similar to how we initialized an array with the array literal. The following example shows how to create a dictionary using the key-value pairs in the preceding chart:

```
let countries = ["US":"UnitedStates","IN":"India","UK":"United
  Kingdom"]
```

The preceding code creates an immutable dictionary that contains each of the key-value pairs in the preceding chart. Just like the array, to create a mutable dictionary, we will use the `var` keyword rather than `let`. The following example shows how to create a mutable dictionary containing the countries:

```
var countries = ["US":"UnitedStates","IN":"India","UK":"United
Kingdom"]
```

In the preceding two examples, we created a dictionary where the key and value were both strings. The compiler inferred that the key and value were strings because that was the type of values we put in. If we wanted to create an empty dictionary, we would need to tell the compiler what the key and value types are. The following examples create various dictionaries with different key-value types:

```
var dic1 = [String:String]()
var dic2 = [Int:String]()
var dic3 = [String:MyObject]()
```

> If we want to use a custom object as the key in a dictionary, we will need to make our custom object conform to the Hashable protocol from Swift's standard library. We will discuss protocol and classes in *Chapter 5, Classes and Structures*, but, for now, just understand that it is possible to use custom objects as a key in a dictionary.

Accessing dictionary values

We use the subscript syntax to retrieve the value for a particular key. If the dictionary does not contain the key we are looking for, the dictionary will return `nil`; therefore, the variable returned from this lookup is an optional variable. The following example shows how to retrieve a value from a dictionary using its key in the subscript syntax:

```
let countries = ["US":"United States", "IN":"India","UK":"United
Kingdom"]
var name = countries["US"]
```

In the preceding code, the variable name will contain the string, `United States`.

Counting key or values in a dictionary

We use the `count` property of the dictionary to get the number of key-value pairs in the dictionary. The following example shows how to use the `count` property to retrieve the number of key-value pairs in the dictionary:

```
let countries = ["US":"United States", "IN":"India","UK":"United
Kingdom"];
var cnt = countries.count  //cnt contains 3
```

In the preceding code, the `cnt` variable will contain the number `3` since there are three key-value pairs in the `countries` dictionary.

Is the dictionary empty?

To test whether the dictionary contains any key-value pairs at all, we can use the `isEmpty` property. The `isEmpty` property will return `false` if the dictionary contains one or more key-value pairs and `true` if it is empty. The following example shows how to use the `isEmpty` property to determine whether our dictionary contains any key-value pairs:

```
let countries = ["US":"United States", "IN":"India","UK":"United
  Kingdom"]
var empty = countries.isEmpty
```

In the preceding code, the `isEmpty` property is false as there are three key-value pairs in the countries dictionary.

Updating the value of a key

To update the value of a key in a dictionary, we can either use the subscript syntax or the `updateValue(value:, forKey:)` method. The `updateValue(value:, forKey:)` method has an additional feature that the subscript syntax doesn't—it returns the original value associated with the key prior to changing the value. The following example shows how to use both the subscript syntax and the `updateValue(value:, forKey:)` method to update the value of a key:

```
var countries = ["US":"United States", "IN":"India","UK":"United
Kingdom"]

countries["UK"] = "Great Britain"
//The value of UK is now set to "Great Britain"

var orig = countries.updateValue("Britain", forKey: "UK")
//The value of UK is now set to "Britain" and orig now
  contains "Great Britain"
```

In the preceding code, we use the subscript syntax to change the value associated with the key `UK` from `United Kingdom` to `Great Britain`. The original value of `United Kingdom` was not saved prior to replacing it, so we are unable to see what the original value is. We then used the `updateValue(value:, forKey:)` method to change the value associated with the key `UK` from `Great Britain to Britain`. With the `updateValue(value:, forKey:)` method, the original value of `Great Britain` is assigned to the `orig` variable, prior to changing the value in the dictionary.

Adding a key-value pair

To add a new key-value pair to a dictionary, we can use the subscript syntax or the same `updateValue(value:, forKey:)` method that we used to update the value of a key. If we use the `updateValue(value:, forKey:)` method and the key is not currently present in the dictionary, the `updateValue(value:, forKey:)` method will add a new key-value pair and return nil. The following example shows how to use the subscript syntax and also the `updateValue(value:, forKey:)` method to add a new key-value pair to a dictionary:

```
var countries = ["US":"United States", "IN":"India","UK":"United
  Kingdom"]

countries["FR"] = "France" //The value of "FR" is set to
  "France"

var orig = countries.updateValue("Germany", forKey: "DE")
//The value of "DE" is set to "Germany" and orig is nil
```

In the preceding code, the countries dictionary starts with three key-value pairs and we then add a fourth key-value pair (`FR/France`) to the dictionary using the subscript syntax. We then use the updateValue(`value:, forKey:`) method to add a fifth key-value pair (`DE/Germany`) to the dictionary. The `orig` variable is set to nil because the countries dictionary did not contain a value associated with the `DE` key.

Removing a key-value pair

There may be times when we need to remove values from a dictionary. We can do this with the subscript syntax, using the `removeValueForKey()` method or the `removeAll()` method. The `removeValueForKey()` method returns the value of the key prior to removing it. The `removeAll()` method removes all the elements from the dictionary. The following example shows how to use the subscript syntax, the `removeValueForKey()` method, and the `removeAll()` method to remove key-value pairs from a dictionary:

```
var countries = ["US":"United States",
  "IN":"India","UK":"United Kingdom"];

countries["IN"] = nil //The "IN" key/value pair is removed

var orig = countries.removeValueForKey("UK")
//The "UK" key value pair is removed and orig contains
  "United Kingdom"

countries.removeAll() //Removes all key/value pairs from the
  countries dictionary
```

In the preceding code, the `countries` dictionary starts off with three key-value pairs. We then set the value associated with the key `IN` to `nil`, which removes the key-value pair from the dictionary. We use the `removeValueForKey()` method to remove the key associated with the `UK` key. Prior to removing the value associated with the `UK` key, the `removeValueForKey()` method saves the value in the `orig` variable. Finally, we use the `removeAll()` method to remove all the remaining key-value pairs in the countries dictionary.

Now let's look at the Set type.

Set

The Set type is a generic collection that is similar to the array type. While the array type is an ordered collection that may contain duplicate items, the Set type is an unordered collection where each item must be unique.

Similar to the key in a dictionary, the type stored in an array must conform to the Hashable protocol. This means that the type must provide a way to compute a hash value for itself. All of Swift's basic types, such as String, Double, Int and Bool, conform to the Hashable protocol and can be used in a set by default.

Let's look at how we would use the Set type.

Initializing a set

There are a couple of ways in which we can initialize a set. Just like the array and dictionary types, Swift needs to know what type of data is going to be stored in it. This means that we must either tell Swift the type of data to store in the set or initialize it with some data so that it can infer the data type.

Just like the array and dictionary types, we use the var and let keywords to declare if the set is mutable or not:

```
//Initializes an empty Set of the String type
var mySet = Set<String>()

//Initializes a mutable set of the String type with initial values
var mySet = Set(["one", "two", "three"])

//Creates aimmutable set of the String type.
let mySet = Set(["one", "two", "three"])
```

Inserting items into a set

We use the `insert` method to insert an item into a set. If we attempt to insert an item that is already in the set, the item will be ignored and no error will be thrown. Here are some examples on how to insert items into a set:

```
var mySet = Set<String>()
mySet.insert("One")
mySet.insert("Two")
mySet.insert("Three")
```

The number of items in a set

We can use the `count` property to determine the number of items in a Swift Set. Here is an example on how to use the `count` method:

```
var mySet = Set<String>()
mySet.insert("One")
mySet.insert("Two")
mySet.insert("Three")
print("\(mySet.count) items")
```

When executed, this code will print the message `"Three items"` to the console because the set contains three items.

Checking whether a set contains an item

We can very easily check to see whether a Set contains an item by using the `contains()` method, as shown here:

```
var mySet = Set<String>()
mySet.insert("One")
mySet.insert("Two")
mySet.insert("Three")
var contain = mySet.contains("Two")
```

In the preceding example, the `contain` variable is set to True because the set does contain the string `"Two"`.

Iterating over a set

We can use the `for` statement to iterate over the items in a Set. The following example shows how we would iterate through the items in a set:

```
for item inmySet {
    print(item)
}
```

The preceding example would print out each item in the set to the console.

Removing items in a set

We can remove a single item or all the items in a set. To remove a single item, we would use the `remove()` method, and to remove all the items, the `removeAll()` method. The following example shows how to remove items from a set:

```
//The remove method will return and remove an item from a set
var item = mySet.remove("Two")

//The removeAll method will remove all items from a set
mySet.removeAll()
```

Set operations

Apple has provided four methods that we can use to construct a set from two other sets. These operations can either be performed in place, on one of the sets, or used to create a new set. These operations are:

- `union` and `unionInPlace`: These create a set with all the unique vales from both sets
- `subtract` and `subtractInPlace`: These create a set with values from the first set that are not in the second set
- `intersect` and `intersectInPlace`: These create a set with values that are common to both sets
- `exclusiveOr` and `exclusiveOrInPlace`: These create a new set with values that are in either set but not in both sets

Let's look at some examples and see the results we get from each of these operations. For all the set operations examples, we will be using the following two sets:

```
var mySet1 = Set(["One", "Two", "Three", "abc"])
var mySet2 = Set(["abc","def","ghi", "One"])
```

Now let's look at our examples. The first example that we will look at is using the union method. This method will take the unique values from both sets to make another set:

```
var newSetUnion = mySet1.union(mySet2)
```

The `newSetUnion` variable would contain the following values: `"One", "Two", "Three", "abc", "def", "ghi"`. Now let's look at the subtract method. This method will create a set with the values from the first set that are not in the second set:

```
var newSetSubtract = mySet1.subtract(mySet2)
```

In this example, the `newSetSubtract` variable would contain the values `"Two"` and `"Three"` because those are the only two values that are not also in the second set.

Now let's look at the intersect method. The intersect method creates a new set from the values that are common between the two sets:

```
var newSetIntersect = mySet1.intersect(mySet2)
```

In this example, the `newSetIntersect` variable will contain the values `"One"` and `"abc"` since they are the values that are common between the two sets.

Now let's look at the `exclusiveOr` method. This method will create a new set with the values that are in either set but not in both:

```
//newSetExclusiveOr = {"Two", "Three", "def", "ghi"}
var newSetExclusiveOr = mySet1.exclusiveOr(mySet2)
```

In this example, the `newSetExclusiveOr` variable will contain the values `"Two", "Three", "def"` and `"ghi"`.

These four operations (`union`, `subtract`, `intersect`, and `exclusiveor` methods) add additional functionality that is not present with arrays. Combined with the faster lookup speeds as compared to an array, the Set can be a very useful alternative when the order of the collection is not important and the objects in a collection must be unique.

Tuples

Tuples group multiple values into a single compound value. Unlike arrays and dictionaries, the values in a tuple do not have to be of the same type. The following example shows how to define a tuple:

```
var team = ("Boston", "Red Sox", 97, 65, 59.9)
```

In the preceding example, we created an unnamed tuple that contains two strings, two integers, and one double. We can decompose the values from this tuple into a set of variables, as shown in the following example:

```
var team = ("Boston", "Red Sox", 97, 65, 59.9)
var (city, name, wins, loses, percent) = team
```

In the preceding code, the `city` variable will contain `Boston`, the `name` variable will contain `Red Sox`, the `wins` variable will contain `97`, the `loses` variable will contain `65`, and, finally, the `percent` variable will contain `0.599`.

We could also retrieve the values from a tuple by specifying the location of the value. The following example shows how we would retrieve the values by their location:

```
var team = ("Boston", "Red Sox", 97, 65, 59.9)
var city = team.0
var name = team.1
var wins = team.2
var loses = team.3
var percent = team.4
```

To avoid this decomposing step, we can create a named tuple. A named tuple associates a name (key) with each element of the tuple. The following example shows how to create a named tuple:

```
var team = (city:"Boston", name:"Red Sox", wins:97, loses:65,
  percent:59.9)
```

To access the values from a named tuple, we use a dot syntax. In the preceding code, we will access the `city` element of the tuple like this: `team.city`. In the preceding code, the `team.city` element will contain `Boston`, the `team.name` element will contain `Red Sox`, the `team.wins` element will contain `97`, the `team.loses` element will contain `65`, and, finally, the `team.percent` element will contain `59.9`.

Tuples are incredible useful and can be used for all sorts of purposes. I have found that they are very useful for replacing classes and structs that are designed to simply store data and do not contain any methods. We will learn more about classes in *Chapter 5, Classes and Structures*.

Using Cocoa data types

So far, in this chapter, we have looked at several native Swift data types, such as the string, array, and dictionary types. While using these types is definitely preferred, as part of the Objective-C interoperability, Apple has provided convenient and effective ways to work with Cocoa data types from within our Swift applications.

Some of the Cocoa and Swift data types can be used interchangeably, while others are automatically converted between Cocoa and Swift data types. Those data types that can be used interchangeably or converted are called bridged data types.

Swift also provides an overlay for working with Foundation data types. This lets us work with Foundation data types in a way that feels more like native Swift types. If we need to use these Foundation data types, we need to add the following import statement to the top of the Swift file:

```
import Foundation
```

Let's take a look at how to work with some common Cocoa data types.

NSNumber

Swift will automatically bridge certain native numeric types, such as Int, UInt, Float, Bool, and Double to an `NSNumber` object. This allows us to pass these native numeric types to arguments that expect an `NSNumber` object. This automatic bridging only works one way because an `NSNumber` object can contain various numeric types; therefore, the Swift compiler will not know which numeric type to convert the `NSNumber` into. The following examples show how to go from a native Swift Int and Double to an `NSNumber`, and how to convert it back to the Swift Int and Double. Let's take a look at the following code:

```
var inum = 7     //Creates an Int
var dnum = 10.6 //Creates a Double
var insnum: NSNumber = inum  //Bridges the Int to a NSNumber
var dnsnum: NSNumber = dnum  //Bridges the Double to a NSNumber
var newint = Int(insnum)       //Creates an Int from a NSNumber
var newdouble = Double(dnsnum) //Creates a Double from a NSNumber
```

In the preceding code, Swift automatically converts the `inum` and `dnum` to `NSNumber` objects without any typecasting; however, when we try to convert the `NSNumber` objects back to `Int` or `Double` types of Swift, we need to typecast the `NSNumber` objects to tell Swift what type of numbers we are converting into.

NSString

Swift will automatically bridge its native `String` type to a `NSString` type; however, it will not automatically bridge an `NSString` object to the native String type. This allows us to pass the native string type to arguments that expect an `NSString` object. Therefore, when we use mix and match to integrate the Objective-C APIs with our Swift project, it automatically converts `String` types to the `NSString` objects when needed.

This automatic bridging allows us to call the `NSString` methods on our Swift strings. Swift automatically converts the string to an `NSString` object and calls the method. The following example shows how to convert our string value to a C string using the `cStringUsingEncoding()` method that comes from the `NSString` type:

```
var str = "Hello World from Swift"
str.cStringUsingEncoding(NSUTF8StringEncoding)
```

To convert an `NSString` object to a string type, we will use the `as` keyword. Since an `NSString` object can always be converted to a string type, we do not need to use the optional version of this typecasting operator (`as?`). The following example shows how to convert an `NSString` object to a string type:

```
func testFunc(test: String) {
    print(test)
}
var nsstr: NSString = "abc"
testFunc(nsstr as String)
```

In the next example, we convert an `NSString` object to a native Swift string type, and then call the `toInt()` method, from the Swift string type, to convert the string to an integer, as shown in the following code:

```
var nsstr: NSString = "1234"
var num = Int(nsstr as String)//num contains the number 1234
```

In the preceding code, the `num` variable will contain the number `1234` and not the string `1234`.

NSArray

Swift will automatically bridge between the `NSArray` class and the Swift native array type. Since the elements of an `NSArray` object are not required to be of the same type, when we bridge from an `NSArray` object to a Swift array, the elements of the Swift array are set to the `[AnyObject]` type. The `[AnyObject]` type is an object that is an instance of an Objective-C or Swift class or can be bridged to one.

The following example shows how we can create an `NSArray` object in Swift that contains both string and Int types and then creates a Swift array from that `NSArray` object:

```
var nsarr: NSArray = ["HI","There", 1,2]
var arr = nsarr as? [AnyObject]
```

In the preceding code, `nsarr: NSArray` contains four elements—`HI`, `There`, `1`, and `2`. In `nsarrNSArray`, two of the elements are string types and two are Int types. When we convert the nsarr: `NSArray` to a Swift array, the `arr` array becomes an array of `AnyObject` types.

If the `NSArray` contains a specific object type, once it is bridged to a Swift array, we can downcast the Swift array of `[AnyObject]` to a Swift array of the specific object types. The only catch to this downcasting is if any element of the array is not of the object type specified, the downcasting will fail and the new array will be set to nil. The following example shows how to downcast an array:

```
var nsarr: NSArray = ["HI","There"]
var arr = nsarr as [AnyObject]
var newarr = arr as? [String]
```

In the preceding example, `newarr` will be an array of strings that contains two elements. Now, let's change the original `NSArray` to include two integers as well as the two strings. The new code will now look similar to this:

```
var nsarr: NSArray = ["HI","There", 1, 2]
var arr = nsarr as [AnyObject]
var newarr = arr as? [String]
```

Since the original `NSArray` defines an array of both strings and integers, when we attempt to downcast the Swift array from an array of `[AnyObject]` to an array of string, the downcasting fails and the `newarr` variable is set to nil.

When we use the `as?` keyword to cast an `NSArray` object as an array type, it is recommended that we use optional binding since it is possible to receive a nil value. The following example illustrates how to do this cast with optional binding:

```
var nsarr: NSArray = ["HI","There", 1,2]
if let arr = nsarr as? [String] {
    // arr is a native Swift array type.
}
```

Now let's look at the `NSDictionary` object and how we can use it within our Swift code.

NSDictionary

We use the `as` and `as?` keywords to convert between an `NSDictionary` object and a Swift dictionary type. The following example shows how to do this:

```
var nsdic: NSDictionary = ["one":"HI", "two":"There"]
if let dic = nsdic as? [String: String] {
    var newDic = dicasNSDictionary
}
```

In the previous example, we create an `NSDictionary` object that contains two key-value pairs. All of the keys and values in this `NSDictionary` object are String types. In the second line, the `nsdic2as? [String: String]` converts the `NSDictionary` object to a dictionary type where both the keys and the values are String types. We then convert the dictionary type back to an `NSDictionaryobject` using the `as` keyword.

In the previous example, we used optional binding when we converted the `NSDictionary` object to a dictionary type because if any of the values in the `NSDictionary` object were not of the String type, the conversion would have failed. The following example illustrates this:

```
var nsdic2: NSDictionary = ["one":"HI", "two":2]
if let dic2 = nsdic2 as? [String:String] {
    // Would not reach this because
    // conversion failed
}
```

In this example, the conversion fails because one of the values is an integer type and not a String type. When we do the conversion from an `NSDictionary` object to a Swift dictionary we use the `as?` keyword because the conversion may fail, but when we convert from a Swift dictionary to an `NSDictionary` object, we use the `as` keyword because the conversion is always successful.

Now let's look at how we would use Foundation data types with Swift.

Foundation data types

When using Foundation data types, Swift provides an overlay that makes interacting with them feel like they are native Swift types. We use this overlay to interact with Foundation types, such as `CGSize` and `CGRect` for iOS applications (`NSSize` and `NSRect` for OS X applications). When developing iOS or OS X applications, we will interact with Foundation data types on a regular basis, so it is good to see this overlay in action.

Let's look at how to initialize some Foundation data types. The following example defines `NSRange`, `CGRect`, and `NSSize`:

```
var range = NSRange(location: 3, length: 5)
var rect = CGRect(x: 10, y: 10, width: 20, height: 20)
var size = NSSize(width: 20, height: 40)
```

The overlay also lets us access the properties and functions in a way that feels like native Swift types. The following example shows us how to access the properties and functions:

```
var rect = CGRect(x: 10, y: 10, width: 20, height: 20)
rect.origin.x = 20
//Changes the X value from 10 to 20

var rectMaxY = rect.maxY
//rectMaxY contains 30 (value of y + value of height)

var validRect = rect.isEmpty
//validRect contains false because rect is valid.
```

In the preceding code, we initialize a `CGRect` type. We then change the property of `x` from `10` to `20`, retrieve the value of the `maxY` property, and check the `isEmpty` property to see whether we have a valid `CGRect` type.

We just barely scratched the surface of the interoperability between Swift and Objective-C. We will discuss this interoperability in depth in *Chapter 13, Using Mix and Match,* later in this book.

Summary

In this chapter, we covered Swift collections, tuples, Foundation, and Cocoa data types. Having a good understanding of the native collection types of Swift is essential to architect and develop applications in Swift since all but the very basic applications use collections to store data in memory.

At the time of writing this book, Swift is exclusively used for developing applications in an Apple (iOS or OS X) environment, so it is essential to understand how Swift interacts with Cocoa and Foundation types. While we briefly covered this subject in this chapter, we will look at this interaction more in depth in *Chapter 13, Using Mix and Match,* later in this book.

4
Control Flow and Functions

While I was learning BASIC programming on my Vic-20, every month I would read several of the early computer magazines such as *Byte Magazine*. I remember one particular review that I read; it was for a game called *Zork*. While *Zork* was not a game that was available for my Vic-20, the concept of the game fascinated me because I was really into Sci-Fi and fantasy. I remember thinking how cool it would be to write a game like that, so I decided to figure out how to do it. One of the biggest concepts that I had to grasp at that time was controlling the flow of the application depending on the user's actions.

In this chapter, we will cover the following topics:

- What are conditional statements and how to use them
- What are loops and how to use them
- What are control transfer statements and how to use them
- How to create and use functions in Swift

What we have learned so far

Up to this point, we have been laying the foundation for writing applications with Swift. While it is possible to write a very basic application with what we have learned so far, it would be really difficult to write a useful application using only what we covered in the first three chapters.

Starting with this chapter, we will begin to move away from the foundations of the Swift language, and begin to learn the building blocks of application development with Swift. In this chapter, we will go over control flow and functions. To become a master of the Swift programming language, it is important that you fully understand and comprehend the concepts discussed in this chapter and in *Chapter 5, Classes and Structures*.

Before we cover control flow and functions, let's take a look at how curly brackets and parentheses are used in Swift.

Curly brackets

In Swift, unlike other C-like languages, curly brackets are required for conditional statements and loops. In other C-like languages, if there is only one statement to execute for a conditional statement or a loop, the curly brackets around that line are optional. This has lead to numerous errors and bugs, such as Apple's `goto fail` bug; therefore, when Apple was designing Swift, they decided to use curly brackets, even when there is only one line of code to execute. Let's look at some code that illustrates this. This first example is not valid in Swift because it is missing the curly brackets; however, it will be valid in most other languages:

```
if (x > y)
  x=0
```

In Swift, you are required to have the curly brackets, as illustrated in the following example:

```
if (x > y) {
  x=0
}
```

Parentheses

Unlike other C-like languages, the parentheses around conditional expressions in Swift are optional. In the preceding example, we put parentheses around the conditional expression, but they are not required. The following example would be valid in Swift, but not valid in most C-like languages:

```
if x > y {
  x=0
}
```

Control flow

Control flow, also known as flow of control, refers to the order in which statements, instructions, or functions are executed within an application. Swift supports all of the familiar control flow statements that are in C-like languages. These include loops (including `for` and `while`), conditional statements (including `if` and `switch`) and the transfer of the control statements (including `break` and `continue`). In addition to the standard C control flow statements, Swift has also added additional statements, such as the `for-in` loop, and enhanced some of the existing statements, such as the `switch` statement.

Let's begin by looking at conditional statements in Swift.

Conditional statements

A conditional statement will check a condition and execute a block of code only if the condition is true. Swift provides both the `if` and `if-else` conditional statements. Let's take a look at how to use these conditional statements to execute blocks of code if a specified condition is true.

The if statement

The `if` statement will check the conditional statement and if it is true, it will execute the block of code. The `if` statement takes the following format:

```
if condition {
   block of code
}
```

Now, let's look at how to use the `if` statement:

```
let teamOneScore = 7
let teamTwoScore = 6
if teamOneScore > teamTwoScore {
    print("Team One Won")
}
```

In the preceding example, we begin by setting the `teamOneScore` and `teamTwoScore` constants. We then use the `if` statement to check whether the value of `teamOneScore` is greater than the value of `teamTwoScore`. If the value is greater, we print `Team One Won` to the console. If we run this code, we will indeed see that `Team One Won` is printed to the console, but if the value of `teamTwoScore` was greater than the value of `teamOneScore`, nothing would be printed to the console. That would not be the best way to write an application because we would want the user to know which team actually won. The `if-else` statement can help us with this problem.

Conditional code execution with the if-else statement

The `if-else` statement will check the conditional statement and if it is true, it will execute a block of code. If the conditional statement is not true, it will execute a separate block of code. The `if-else` statement follows this format:

```
if condition {
    block of code if true
} else {
    block of code if not true
}
```

Let's modify the preceding example to use the `if-else` statement to tell the user which team won:

```
var teamOneScore = 7
var teamTwoScore = 6
if teamOneScore > teamTwoScore {
    print("Team One Won")
} else {
    print("Team Two Won")
}
```

This new version will print out `Team One Won`, if the value of `teamOneScore` is greater than the value of `teamTwoScore`; otherwise, it will print out the message, `Team Two Won`. What do you think the code will do if the value of `teamOneScore` was equal to the value of `teamTwoScore`? In the real world, we will have a tie, but in the preceding code, we will print out `Team Two Won`; this would not be fair to team one. In cases like this, we can use multiple `else if` statements and a plain `else` statement, as shown in the following example:

```
var teamOneScore = 7
var teamTwoScore = 6
if teamOneScore > teamTwoScore {
    print("Team One Won")
} else if teamTwoScore > teamOneScore {
    print("Team Two Won")
} else {
    print("We have a tie")
}
```

In the preceding code, if the value of `teamOneScore` is greater than the value of `teamTwoScore`, we print `Team One Won` to the console. We then have another `if` statement that checks to see whether the value of `teamTwoScore` is greater than the value of `teamOneScore`, but this `if` statement follows an `else` statement, which means the `if` statement is checked only if the previous conditional statement is false. Finally, if both the `if` statements were false, then we assume that the values are equal and print `We have a tie` to the console.

A conditional statement checks the condition once, and if the condition is met, it executes the block of code. What if we wanted to continuously execute the block of code until a condition is met? For this, we would use one of the looping statements that are in Swift. Let's take a look at looping statements in Swift.

The for loops

The for loop variants are probably the most widely used looping statements. Swift offers the standard C-based for loop and also an extra `for-in` loop. The standard C-based `for` loop executes a block of code until a condition is met, usually by incrementing or decrementing a counter. The `for-in` statement will execute a block of code for each item in a range, collection, or sequence. We usually use one of the for loop variants when we need to iterate over a collection, or have a set number of times we want to execute a block of code.

Using the for loop variant

Let's begin by looking at the standard C-based `for` loop and how we would use it. The format for the `for` statement looks similar to this:

```
for initialization; condition; update-rule {
   block of code
}
```

As shown in the preceding format, the `for` loop has three sections:

- `Initialization`: This is where we initialize any variables needed; this can contain multiple initializations, separated by commas, if needed
- `Condition`: This is the condition to check; when the condition is false, the loop will exit
- `Update-rule`: This is what needs to be updated at the end of each loop

It is important to understand the order in which the sections are called. When the execution of the code encounters a `for` loop, the initialization section of the `for` loop is called to initialize the variables. Next, the condition section is executed to verify whether the block of code should be executed, and, if so, it will execute the block of code. Finally, the update-rule is called to perform any updates before looping back and starting over.

The following example shows how to use the `for` loop to go through a range of numbers:

```
for var index = 1; index <= 4; index++ {
    print(index)
}
```

In the preceding example, the `index` variable is initialized to the number `1`. At the beginning of each loop, we check whether the `index` variable is equal to or less than number `4`. If the `index` variable is equal to or less than number `4`, the inner block of code is executed, and this prints the value of the `index` variable to the console. Finally, we increment the `index` variable before looping back and starting over. Once the index variable is greater than `4`, the `for` loop exits. If we run the preceding example, the numbers `1` through `4` will indeed be printed to the console.

One of the most common uses of a `for` loop is to iterate through a collection and perform a block of code for each item in that collection. Let's look at how to loop through an array, followed by an example of how to loop through a dictionary:

```
var countries = ["USA","UK", "IN"]
for var index = 0; index < countries.count; index++ {
    print(countries[index])
}
```

In the preceding example, we begin by initializing the `countries` array with the abbreviations of three countries. In the `for` loop, we initialize the `index` variable to `0` (the first index of the array), and in the condition statement of the `for` loop, we check whether the index variable is less than the number of elements in the `countries` array. Each time we loop, we retrieve and print the value from the `countries` array at the index specified by the `index` variable.

One of the biggest mistakes that new programmers make when they use a `for` loop to iterate through an array is to use the less than or equal to (<=) operator rather than the less than (<) operator. Using a less than or equal to (<=) operator would cause one too many iterations through the loop and generate an `Index out of Bounds` exception when the code is run. In the preceding example, a less than or equal to operator will generate a count from 0 to 3 inclusively because there are three elements in the array; however, the elements in the array have indexes from 0 to 2 (0, 1, and 2). So, when we try to retrieve the value at index `3`, the `Index out of Bounds` exception will be thrown. It is recommended to use a `for-in` loop to iterate through an array rather than a standard `for` loop. We will look at the `for-in` loop a little later in this chapter.

Let's look at how we would iterate through a dictionary with a standard C-based `for` loop:

```
var dic = ["USA": "United States", "UK": "United Kingdom",
  "IN":"India"]

var keys  = Array(dic.keys)
for var index = 0; index < keys.count; index++ {
  print(dic[keys[index]])
}
```

In the preceding example, we begin by creating a dictionary object that contains country names as the values with their abbreviations as the keys. We then use the `keys` property of the dictionary to get an array of keys. In the `for` loop, we initialize the `index` variable to `0`, verify whether the `index` variable is less than the number of elements in the countries array, and increment the `index` variable at the end of each loop. Each time we loop, we print the country's name to the console.

Now, let's look at how to use the `for-in` statement and how it can help prevent common mistakes that occur when we use the standard `for` statement.

Using the for-in loop variant

In the standard `for` loop, we provide an index and then loop until a condition is met. While this approach is very good, when we want to loop through a range of numbers, it can cause bugs, as mentioned earlier, if our conditional statements are not correct. The `for-in` loop is designed to prevent these types of exceptions.

The `for-in` loop iterates over a collection of items or a range of numbers and executes a block of code for each item in the collection or range. The format for the `for-in` statement looks similar to this:

```
for variable in Collection/Range {
  block of code
}
```

As we can see in the preceding code, the `for-in` loop has two sections:

- `Variable`: This variable will change each time the `for-in` loop executes and hold the current item from the collection or range
- `Collection/Range`: This is the collection or range to iterate through

Let's take a look at how to use the `for-in` loop to iterate through a range of numbers:

```
for index in 1...5 {
    print(index)
}
```

In the preceding example, we iterate over a range of numbers from `1` to `5` and print each of the numbers to the console. This particular `for-in` statement uses the closed range operator (...) to give the `for-in` loop a range to go through. Swift also provides a second range operation called the half-open range operator (`..<`). The half-open range operator iterates through the range of numbers, but does not include the last number. Let's look at how to use the half-range operator:

```
for index in 1..<5 {
  print(index)
}
```

In the closed range operator example (...), we will see the numbers `1` though `5` printed to the console. In the half-range operator example, the last number (`5`) will be excluded; therefore, we will see the numbers `1` though `4` printed to the console.

Now, let's look at how to iterate over an array with the `for-in` loop:

```
var countries = ["USA","UK", "IN"]
for item in countries {
    print(item)
}
```

In the preceding example, we iterate through the `countries` array and print each element of the `counties` array to the console. As we can see, iterating through an array with the `for-in` loop is safer, cleaner, and a lot easier than using the standard C-based `for` loop. Using the `for-in` loop prevents us from making common mistakes, such as using the `<=` (less than or equal too) operator rather than the `<` (less than) operator in our conditional statement.

Let's look at how to iterate over a dictionary with the `for-in` loop:

```
var dic = ["USA": "United States", "UK": "United Kingdom",
  "IN":"India"]
```

```
for (abbr, name) in dic {
  print("\(abbr) --  \(name)")
}
```

In the preceding example, we used the `for-in` loop to iterate through each key-value pair of a dictionary. In this example, each item in the dictionary is returned as a (key,value) tuple. We can decompose (key,value) tuple members as named constants within the body of the `for-in` loop. One thing to note is that since a dictionary does not guarantee the order that items are stored in, the order that they are iterated over may not be the same as the order they were inserted in.

Now, let's look at another type of loop, the `while` loop.

The while loop

The `while` loop executes a block of code until a condition is met. Swift provides two forms of `while` loops; these are the `while` and `repeat-while` loops. In Swift 2.0, Apple replaced the `do-while` loop with the `repeat-while` loop. The `repeat-while` loop functions exactly as what the `do-while` loop did. Apple now uses the `do` statement for error handling.

We use the `while` loops when the number of iterations to perform is not known and is usually dependent on some business logic. A `while` loop is used when you want to run a loop zero or more times, while a `repeat-while` loop is used when you want to run the loop one or more times.

Using the while loop

The `while` loop starts by evaluating a conditional statement and then repeatedly executes a block of code if the conditional statement is true. The format for the `while` statement is as follows:

```
while condition {
  block of code
}
```

Let's look at how to use a `while` loop. In the following example, the `while` loop will continue to loop if a randomly-generated number is less than `4`. In this example, we are using the `arc4random()` function to generate a random number between `0` and `4`:

```
var ran = 0
while ran < 4 {
    ran = Int(arc4random() % 5)
}
```

In the preceding example, we begin by initializing the `ran` variable to `0`. The `while` loop then checks the `ran` variable, and if its value is less than `4`, a new random number, between `0` and `4`, is generated. The `while` loop will continue to loop while the randomly-generated number is less than `4`. Once the randomly-generated number is equal to or greater than `4`, the `while` loop will exit.

In the preceding example, the `while` loop checks the conditional statement prior to generating a new random number. What if we did not want to check the conditional statement prior to generating a random number? We could generate a random number when we first initialize the `ran` variable, but that would mean we would need to duplicate the code that generates the random numbers, and duplicating code is never an ideal solution. It would be preferable to use the `repeat-while` loop for such instances.

Using the repeat-while loop

The difference between the `while` and `repeat-while` loops is that the `while` loops check the conditional statement prior to executing the block of code the first time; therefore, all the variables in the conditional statements need to be initialized prior to executing the `while` loop. The `repeat-while` loop will run through the loop block prior to checking the `conditional` statement for the first time; this means that we can initialize the variables in the conditional block of code. Use of the `repeat-while` loop is preferred when the conditional statement is dependent on the code in the loop block. The `repeat-while` loop takes the following format:

```
repeat {
   block of code
} while condition
```

Let's take a look at this specific example by creating a `repeat-while` loop where we initialize the variable we are checking, in the conditional `while` statement, within the loop block:

```
var ran: Int
repeat {
    ran = Int(arc4random() % 5)
} while ran < 4
```

In the preceding example, we define the `ran` variable as an `Int`, but we do not initialize it until we enter the loop block and generate a random number. If we try to do this with the `while` loop (leaving the `ran` variable uninitialized), we will receive a `Variable used before being initialized` exception.

The switch statement

The `switch` statement takes a value and then compares it to the several possible matches, and executes the appropriate block of code based on the first successful match. The `switch` statement is an alternative to using the `if-else` statement when there could be several possible matches. The `switch` statement takes the following format:

```
switch value {
  case match1 :
    block of code
  case match2 :
    block of code
  ...... as many cases as needed
  default :
    block of code
}
```

Unlike the `switch` statements in most other languages, in Swift, it does not fall through to the next `case` statement; therefore, we do not need to use a `break` statement to prevent the fall through. This is another safety feature that is built into Swift since one of the most common programming mistakes, with the `switch` statement, made by beginner programmers is to forget the `break` statement at the end of the `case` statement. Let's look at how to use the `switch` statement:

```
var speed = 300000000
switch speed {
case 300000000:
    print("Speed of light")
case 340:
    print("Speed of sound")
default:
    print("Unknown speed")
}
```

In the preceding example, the `switch` statement takes the value of the `speed` variable and compares it to the two `case` statements, and if the value of speed matches either case, it will print out what the speed is. If the `switch` statement does not find a match, it will print out the `Unknown speed` message.

Every `switch` statement must have a match for all the possible values. This means that unless we are matching against an enum, each `switch` statement must have a `default` case. Let's look at a case where we do not have a `default` case:

```
var num = 5
switch num {
case 1 :
```

```
        print("number is one")
    case 2 :
        print("Number is two")
    case 3 :
        print("Number is three")
    }
```

If we put the preceding code into a Playground and attempt to compile the code, we will receive a `switch must be exhaustive, consider adding a default clause` error. This is a compile time error; therefore, we will not be notified until we attempt to compile the code.

It is possible to include multiple items in a single case. To set multiple items within a single case, we would need to separate the items with a comma. Let's look at how we would use the `switch` statement to tell us if a character was a vowel or a consonant:

```
var char : Character = "e"
switch char {
case "a", "e", "i", "o", "u":
    print("letter is a vowel")
case "b", "c", "d", "f", "g", "h", "j", "k", "l", "m",
"n", "p", "q", "r", "s", "t", "v", "w", "x", "y", "z":
    print("letter is a consonant")
default:
    print("unknown letter")
}
```

We can see in the preceding example that each case has its multiple items. Commas separate these items and the `switch` statement will attempt to match the `char` variable to each item listed in the `case` statement.

It is also possible to check the value of a `switch` statement to see whether it is included in a range. To do this, we would use a range operator in the `case` statement, as shown in the following example:

```
var grade = 93
switch grade {
case 90...100:
    print("Grade is an A")
case 80...89:
    print("Grade is a B")
case 70...79:
    print("Grade is an C")
case 60...69:
    print("Grade is a D")
```

```
    case 0...59:
        print("Grade is a F")
    default:
        print("Unknown Grade")
    }
```

In the preceding example, the `switch` statement takes the `grade` variable and compares it with the `grade` ranges in each `case` statement, and prints out the appropriate grade.

In Swift, any `case` statement can contain an optional guard condition that can provide an additional condition to validate. The guard condition is defined with the `where` keyword. Let's say, in our preceding example, we had students who were receiving special assistance in the class and we wanted to define a grade of `D` for them in the range of `55` to `69`. The following example shows how to do this:

```
var studentId = 4
var grade = 57
switch grade {
case 90...100:
    print("Grade is an A")
case 80...89:
    print("Grade is a B")
case 70...79:
    print("Grade is an C")
case 55...69 where studentId == 4:
    print("Grade is a D for student 4")
case 60...69:
    print("Grade is a D")
case 0...59:
    print("Grade is a F")
default:
    print("Unknown Grade")
}
```

One thing to keep in mind with the guard expression is that Swift will attempt to match the value starting with the first case statement and working its way down checking each case statement in order. This means that if we put the `case` statement with the guard expression after the Grade F `case` statement, then the `case` statement with the guard expression would never be reached. The following example illustrates this:

```
var studentId = 4
var grade = 57
switch grade {
case 90...100:
```

```
    print("Grade is an A")
case 80...89:
    print("Grade is a B")
case 70...79:
    print("Grade is an C")
case 60...69:
    print("Grade is a D")
case 0...59:
    print("Grade is a F")
//The following case statement would never be reached because the
//grades would always match one of the previous two
case 55...69 where studentId == 4:
    print("Grade is a D for student 4")
default:
    print("Unknown Grade")
}
```

A good rule of thumb is that if you are using guard expressions, always put the `case` statements with the guard condition before any similar `case` statements without guard expressions.

`Switch` statements are also extremely useful for evaluating enumerations. Since an enumeration has a finite number of values, if we provide a `case` statement for all the values in the enumeration, we do not need to provide a default case. The following example shows how we can use a `switch` statement to evaluate an enumeration:

```
 Product {
    case Book(String, Double, Int)
    case Puzzle(String, Double)
}

var order = Product.Book("Mastering Swift 2", 49.99, 2015)

switch order {
case .Book(let name, let price, let year):
    print("You ordered the book \(name) for \(price)")
case .Puzzle(let name, let price):
    print("You ordered the Puzzle \(name) for \(price)")
}
```

In this example, we begin by defining an enumeration named `Product` with two values each with the associated values. We then create an `order` variable of the product type and use the `switch` statement to evaluate it. Notice that we did not put a default case at the end of the `switch` statement. If we add additional values to the product enumeration at a later time, we would need to either put a default case at the end of the `switch` statement or add additional `case` statements to handle the additional values.

Using case and where statements with conditional statements

As we saw in the last section, the `case` and `where` statements within a `switch` statement can be very powerful. Starting with Swift 2, we are able to use these statements with other conditional statements such as the `if`, `for`, and `while` statements. Using the `case` and `where` statements within our conditional statements can make our code much smaller and easier to read. Let's look at some examples starting off with using the `where` statement to filter the results in a `for-in` loop.

Filtering with the where statement

In this section, we will see how we can use the `where` statement to filter the results of a `for-in` loop. For the example, we will take an array of integers and print out only the even numbers; however, before we look at how we would filter the results with the `where` statement, let's look at how we would do this without the `where` statement:

```
for number in 1…30 {
    if number % 2 == 0 {
        print(number)
    }
}
```

In this example, we use a `for-in` loop to cycle through the numbers `1` to `30`. Within the `for-in` loop, we use an `if` conditional statement to filter out the odd numbers. In this simple example, the code is fairly easy to read, but let's see how we can use the `where` statement to use less lines of code and make it easier to read:

```
for number in 1...30 where number % 2 == 0 {
    print(number)
}
```

We still have the same `for-in` loop as the previous example; however, now we put the `where` statement at the end, which, in this particular example, we only loop through the even numbers. Using the `where` statement shortens our example by two lines and also makes it easier to read because the filter statement is on the same line as the `for-in` loop rather than being embedded in the loop itself.

Now let's look at how we could filter with the `for-case` statement.

Filtering with the for-case statement

In this next example, we will use the `for-case` statement to filter through an array of tuples and print out only the results that match our criteria. The `for-case` example is very similar to using the `where` statement that we saw earlier where it is designed to eliminate the need for an `if` statement within a loop to filter the results. In this example, we will use the `for-case` statement to filter through a list of World Series winners and print out the year(s) a particular team won the World Series:

```
var worldSeriesWinners = [
    ("Red Sox", 2004),
    ("White Sox", 2005),
    ("Cardinals", 2006),
    ("Red Sox", 2007),
    ("Phillies", 2008),
    ("Yankees", 2009),
    ("Giants", 2010),
    ("Cardinals", 2011),
    ("Giants", 2012),
    ("Red Sox", 2013),
    ("Giants", 2014)
]

for case let ("Red Sox", year) in worldSeriesWinners {
    print(year)
}
```

In this example, we create an array of tuples named `worldSeriesWinners`, where each tuple in the array contains the name of the team and the year that they won the World Series. We then use the `for-case` statement to filter through the array and only print out the years that the Red Sox won the World Series. The filtering is done within the `case` statement where the `("Red Sox", year)` says that we want all the results that have the String, `"Red Sox"`, in the first item of the tuple and the value of the second item into the `year` constant. The `for` loop then loops through the results of the `case` statement, and we print out the value of the `year` constant.

The `for-case` statement also makes it very easy to filter out the nil values in an array of optionals. Let's take a look at an example of this:

```
let myNumbers: [Int?] = [1, 2, nil, 4, 5, nil, 6]

for case let .Some(num) in myNumbers {
    print(num)
}
```

In this example, we create an array of optionals named `myNumbers` that may contain an integer value or may contain nil. As we will see in *Chapter 10, Using Optional Types*, an optional is defined as an enum internally, as shown in the following code:

```
enum Optional<T> {
     case None,
     case Some(T)
}
```

If an optional is set to nil, it will have a value of `None`, but if it is not nil, then it will have a value of `Some` with an associate type of the actual value. In our example, when we filter for `.Some(num)`, we are looking for any optional that has the value of `.Some (non-nil value)`. As shorthand for `.Some()`, we could use the `?` (question mark) symbol, as we will see in the following example.

We can also combine `for-case` with a `where` statement to do additional filtering, as shown in the following example:

```
let myNumbers: [Int?] = [1, 2, nil, 4, 5, nil, 6]

for case let num? in myNumbers where num > 3 {
    print(num)
}
```

This example is the same as the previous example except that we added the additional filtering with the `where` statement. In the previous example, we looped through all of the non-nil values, but in this example, we loop through the non-nil values that are greater than 3. Let's see how we do this same filtering without the `case` or `where` statements:

```
for num in myNumbers {
    if let num = num {
        if num > 3 {
            print(num)
        }
    }
}
```

As we can see, using the `for-case` and `where` statements can greatly reduce the number of lines needed. It also makes our code much easier to read because all of the filtering statements are on the same line.

Let's look at one more filtering example. This time, we will look at the `if-case` statement.

Using the if-case statement

Using the `if-case` statement is very similar to using the `switch` statement. The majority of time the `switch` statement is preferred, but there are instances where the `if-case` statement is better. One of these times is when we are only looking for one or two possible matches, and we do not want to handle all of the possible matches. Let's look at an example of this:

```
enum Identifier {
    case Name(String)
    case Number(Int)
    case NoIdentifier
}

var playerIdentifier = Identifier.Number(42)

if case let .Number(num) = playerIdentifier {
    print("Player's number is \(num)")
}
```

In this example, we create an enumeration named `Identifier` that contains three possible values: `Name`, `Number`, and `NoIdentifier`. We create an instance of the `Identifier` enumeration named `playerIdentifier` with a value of `Number` and an associated value of `42`. We then use the `if-case` statement to see if the `playerIdentifier` has a value of `Number`, and if so, we print a message to the console.

Just like the `for-case` statement, we are able to do additional filtering with the `where` statement. The following example uses the same `Identifier` enumeration as we used in the previous example:

```
var playerIdentifier = Identifier.Number(42)

if case let .Number(num) = playerIdentifier where num == 2 {
    print("Player is either Xander Bogarts or Derek Jeter")
}
```

In this example, we still use the `if-case` statement to see if the `playerIdentifier` has a value of `Number`, but we added the `where` statement to see if the associate value is equal to `42`, and if so, we identify the player as either `Xander Bogarts or Derek Jeter`.

As we saw in our examples, using the `case` and `where` statements with our conditional statements can reduce the number of lines needed to do certain types of filtering. It can also make our code easier to read. Now let's take a look at control transfer statements.

Control transfer statements

Control transfer statements are used to transfer control to another part of the code. Swift offers five control transfer statements; these are `continue`, `break`, `fallthrough`, `guard`, `throws`, and `return`. We will look at the `return` statement in the *Functions* section later in this chapter and will discuss the `throws` statement in *Chapter 7, Writing Safer Code with Availability and Error Handling*.

The continue statement

The `continue` statement tells a loop to stop executing the code block and go to the next iteration of the loop. The following example shows how to use a `continue` statement to print out only the odd numbers in a range:

```
for i in 1...10 {
    if i % 2 == 0 {
        continue
    }
    print("\(i) is odd")
}
```

In the preceding example, we loop through a range of `1` through `10`. For each iteration of the `for-in` loop, we use the remainder (`%`) operator to see whether the number is odd or even. If the number is even, the `continue` statement tells the loop to immediately go to the next iteration of the loop. If the number is odd, we print out the number is odd and then move ahead. The output of the preceding code is as follows:

```
1 is odd
3 is odd
5 is odd
7 is odd
9 is odd
```

Now, let's look at the `break` statement.

The break statement

The `break` statement immediately ends the execution of a code block within the control flow. The following example shows how to break out of a `for` loop when we encounter the first even number:

```
for i in 1...10 {
    if i % 2 == 0 {
        break
    }
    print("\(i) is odd")
}
```

In the preceding example, we loop through the range of `1` through `10`. For each iteration of the `for` loop, we use the remainder (`%`) operator to see whether the number is odd or even. If the number is even, we use the `break` statement to immediately exit the loop. If the number is odd, we print out that the number is odd and then go to the next iteration of the loop. The preceding code has the following output:

```
1 is odd
```

The fallthrough statement

In Swift, the `switch` statements do not fall through like other languages; however, we can use the `fallthrough` statement to force them to fall through. The `fallthrough` statement can be very dangerous because once a match is found, the next case defaults to true and that code block is executed. The following example illustrates this:

```
var name = "Jon"
var sport = "Baseball"
switch sport {
case "Baseball":
    print("\(name) plays Baseball")
    fallthrough
case "Basketball":
    print("\(name) plays Basketball")
    fallthrough
default:
    print("Unknown sport")
}
```

In the preceding example, since the first case, `Baseball`, matches the code and the remaining code blocks also execute, the output looks similar to this:

```
Jon plays Baseball
Jon plays Basketball
Unknown sport
```

The guard statement

In Swift and most modern languages, our conditional statements tend to focus on testing if a condition is true. As an example, the following code tests to see whether the variable x is greater than 10, and if so, we preform some function; otherwise, we handle the error condition:

```
var x = 9
if x > 10 {
  // Functional code here
} else {
   // Do error condition
}
```

This type of code leads us to having our functional code embedded within our checks and with the error conditions tucked away at the end of our functions, but what if that is not what we really want. Sometimes, it may be nice to take care of our error conditions at the beginning of the function. I know, in our simple example, we could easily check if x is less than or equal to 10, and if so, we perform the error condition, but not all the conditional statements are that easy to rewrite, especially the items such as optional binding.

With Swift 2, Apple introduced the new `guard` statement. The `guard` statement focuses on performing a function if a condition is false; this allows us to trap errors and perform the error conditions early in our functions. We could rewrite our previous example using the `guard` statement like this:

```
var x = 9
guard x > 10 else {
  // Do error condition
  return
}
// Functional code here
```

In this new example, we check to see whether the variable x is greater than 10, and if not, we perform our error condition. If the variable x is greater than 10, our code continues. We notice that we have a `return` statement embedded within the error condition code. The code within the `guard` statement must contain a transfer of control statement; this is what prevents the rest of the code from executing. If we forget the transfer of `control` statement, Swift will show a compile time error.

Let's look at some more examples of the `guard` statement. The following example shows how we would use the `guard` statement to verify that an optional contains a valid value:

```
func guardFunction(str: String?) {
    guard let goodStr = str else {
        print("Input was nil")
        return
    }
    print("Input was \(goodStr)")
}
```

In this example, we create a function named `guardFunction()` that accepts an optional that contains a string or nil value. We then use the `guard` statement with optional binding to verify that the string optional does not contain a nil. If it does contain nil, then that code within the `guard` statement is executed and the `return` statement is used to exit the function. The really nice thing about using the guard statement with optional binding is the new variable is in scope for the rest of the function rather than just within the scope of the optional binding statement.

Now that we have seen how the control flow statements work in Swift, let's give an introduction to functions and classes in Swift.

Functions

In Swift, a function is a self-contained block of code that performs a specific task. Functions are generally used to logically break our code into reusable named blocks. We use the function's name to call the function.

When we define a function, we can also optionally define one or more parameters (also known as arguments). Parameters are named values that are passed into the function by the code that calls it. These parameters are generally used within the function to perform the task of the function. We can also define default values for the parameters to simplify how the function is called.

Every Swift function has a type associated with it. This type is referred to as the return type and it defines the type of data returned from the function to the code that called it. If a value is not returned from a function, the return type is `Void`.

Let's look at how to define functions in Swift.

Using a single parameter function

The syntax used to define a function in Swift is very flexible. This flexibility makes it easy for us to define simple C style functions or more complex Objective-C style functions, with local and external parameter names. Let's look at some examples of how to define functions. The following example accepts one parameter and does not return any value back to the code that called it (return type—`void`):

```
func sayHello(name: String) -> Void {
let retString = "Hello " + name
   print( retString)
}
```

In the preceding example, we defined a function named `sayHello` that accepts one variable that is named `name`. Inside the function, we print out a `Hello` greeting to the name of the person. Once the code within the function gets executed, the function exits and the control is returned back to the code that called it. Rather than printing out the greeting, if we want to return the greeting back to the code that called it, we can add a return type, as follows:

```
func sayHello2(name: String) ->String {
    let retString = "Hello " + name
    return retString
}
```

The `->` string defines that the return type associated with the function is a string. This means that the function must return a `string` variable back to the code that calls it. Inside the function, we build a `string` constant with the greeting message and then use the `return` keyword to return the `string` constant.

Calling a Swift function is very similar to how we call functions or methods in other languages such as C or Java. The following example shows how to call the `sayHello()` function that prints the greeting message to the screen from within the function:

```
sayHello("Jon")
```

Now, let's look at how to call the `sayHello2()` function that returns a value back to the code that called it:

```
var message = sayHello2("Jon")
print(message)
```

In the preceding example, we call the `sayHello2()` function and put the value returned in the `message` variable. If a function defines a return type, such as the `sayHello2()` function does, it must return a value of that type to the code that called it. Therefore, every possible conditional path within the function must end by returning a value of the specified type. This does not mean that the code that called the function has to retrieve the returned value. As an example, both lines in the following examples are valid:

```
sayHello2("Jon")
var message = sayHello2("Jon")
```

If you do not specify a variable for the return value to go into, the value is dropped.

Using a multiparameter function

We are not limited to just one parameter with our functions, we can also define multiple parameters. To create a multiparameter function, we list the parameters in the parentheses and separate the parameter definitions with commas. Let's look at how to define multiple parameters in a function:

```
func sayHello(name: String, greeting: String) {
    print("\(greeting) \(name)")
}
```

In the preceding example, the function accepts two arguments: `name` and `greeting`. We then print a `greeting` to the console using both the parameters.

Calling a multiparameter function is a little different from calling a single parameter function. When calling a multiparameter function, we separate the parameters with commas. We also need to include the parameter name for all the parameters except for the first one. The following example shows how to call a multiparameter function:

```
sayHello("Jon", greeting:"Bonjour")
```

We do not need to supply an argument for each parameter of the function if we define default values. Let's look at how to configure default values for our parameters.

Defining a parameter's default values

We can define default values for parameters by using the equal to operator (=) within the function definition when we declare the variables. The following example shows how to declare a function with parameter default values:

```
func sayHello(name: String, greeting: String = "Bonjour") {
    print("\(greeting) \(name)")
}
```

In the function declaration, we define one parameter without a default value (`name: String`) and one parameter with a default value (`greeting: String = "Bonjour"`). When a parameter has a default value declared, we are able to call the function with or without setting a value for that parameter. The following example shows how to call the `sayHello()` function without setting the `greeting` parameter, and also how to call it with setting the `greeting` parameter:

```
sayHello("Jon")
sayHello("Jon", greeting: "Hello")
```

In the `sayHello("Jon")` line, the `sayHello()` function will print out the message `Bonjour Jon` since it uses the default value for the `greeting` parameter. In the `sayHello("Jon", greeting: "Hello")` line, the `sayHello()` function will print out the message `Hello Jon` since we override the default value for the `greeting` parameter.

We can declare multiple parameters with default values and override only the ones we want by using the parameter names. The following example shows how we would do this by overriding one of the default values when we call it:

```
func sayHello4(name: String, name2: String = "Kim", greeting: String =
"Bonjour") {
    println("\(greeting) \(name) and \(name2)")
}

sayHello("Jon", greeting: "Hello")
```

In the preceding example, we declare one parameter without a default value (`name: String`) and two parameters with default values (`name2: String = "Kim", greeting: String = "Bonjour"`). We then call the function leaving the `name2` parameter with its default value, but override the default value of the `greeting` parameter.

The preceding example would print out the message, `Hello Jon and Kim`.

Returning multiple values from a function

There are a couple of ways to return multiple values from a Swift function. One of the most common ways is to put the values into a collection type (array or dictionary) and return the collection. The following example shows how to return a collection type from a Swift function:

```
func getNames() -> [String] {
    var retArray = ["Jon", "Kim", "Kailey", "Kara"]
    return retArray
}

var names = getNames()
```

In the preceding example, we declare the `getNames()` function with no parameters and a return type of `[String]`. The return type of `[String]` specifies the return type to be an array of string types.

One of the drawbacks of returning a collection type is that the values of the collection must be of the same type, or we must declare our collection type to be of the `AnyObject` type. In the preceding example, our array could only return string types. If we needed to return numbers with our strings, we could return an array of `AnyObjects` and then use typecasting to specify the object type. However, this would not be a very good design for our application since it would be very prone to errors. A better way to return values of different types would be to use a tuple type.

When we return a tuple from a function, it is recommended that we use a named tuple to allow us to use the dot syntax to access the returned values. The following example shows how to return a named tuple from a function and access the values from the named tuple that is returned:

```
func getTeam() -> (team:String, wins:Int, percent:Double) {
    let retTuple = ("Red Sox", 99, 0.611)
 return retTuple
}

var t = getTeam()
print("\(t.team) had \(t.wins) wins")
```

In the preceding example, we define the `getTeam()` function that returns a named tuple that contains three values—`String`, `Int`, and `Double`. Within the function, we create the tuple that we are going to return. Notice that we do not need to define the tuple that we are going to return as a named tuple as long as the value types within the tuple match the value types in the function definition. We can then call the function, as we would any other function, and use the dot syntax to access the values of the tuple that is returned. In the preceding example, the code would print out the following line:

```
Red Sox had 99 wins
```

Returning optional values

In the previous sections, we returned non-nil values from our function; however, that is not always what we need our code to do. What happens if we need to return a nil value from a function? The following code would throw an `expression does not conform to type 'NilLiteralConvertible'` exception:

```
func getName() ->String {
    return nil
}
```

The reason this code throws an exception is we define the return type as a `string` value; however, we are attempting to return `nil`. If there is a reason to return `nil`, we need to define the return type as an optional type to let the code calling it know that the value may be `nil`. To define the return type as an optional type, we use the question mark(`?`) the same way that we did when we defined a variable as an optional type. The following example shows how to define an optional return type:

```
func getName() ->String? {
    return nil
}
```

The preceding code would not throw an exception.

We can also set a tuple as an optional type or any value within a tuple as an optional type. The following example shows how we would return a tuple as an optional type:

```
func getTeam2(id: Int) -> (team:String, wins:Int, percent:Double)? {
    if id == 1 {
        return ("Red Sox", 99, 0.611)
    }
    return nil
}
```

In the following example, we could return a tuple as defined within our function definition or a `nil`; either option is valid. If we needed an individual value within our tuple to be `nil`, we would need to add an optional type within our tuple. The following example shows how to return a `nil` within our tuple:

```
func getTeam() -> (team:String, wins:Int, percent:Double?) {
    let retTuple: (String, Int, Double?) = ("Red Sox", 99, nil)
    return retTuple
}
```

In the preceding example, we can set the `percent` value to either a `Double` value or `nil`.

Adding external parameter names

In the preceding examples in this section, the parameters were defined similar to how we would define the parameters in C code, where we define the parameter names and value types. When we call the function, we also call the function similar to how we would call functions in C code, where we use the function name and specify the values we are passing to the function within parenthesis. In Swift, we are not limited to this syntax; we can also use external parameter names.

External parameter names are used when we call a function to indicate the purpose of each parameter. If we want to use external parameter names with our functions, we would need to define an external parameter name for each parameter in addition to its local parameter name. The external parameter name is added before the local parameter name in the function definition. The external and local parameter names are separated by a space.

Let's look at how to use external parameter names. But before we do so, let's review how we have previously defined functions. In the next two examples, we will define a function without external parameter names and then we will redefine that function with external parameter names:

```
func winPercentage(team: String, wins: Int, loses: Int) -> Double
{
    return Double(wins) / Double(wins + loses)
}
```

In the preceding example, we define the `winPercentage()` function that accepts three parameters. These parameters are `team`, `wins`, and `loses`. The `team` parameter is a `String` type and the `wins` and `loses` parameters are `Int` types. The following line of code shows how to call the `winPercentage()` function:

```
var per = winPercentage("Red Sox", wins: 99, loses: 63)
```

Now, let's define the same function with external parameter names:

```
func winPercentage(BaseballTeam team: String, withWins wins: Int,
  andLoses losses: Int) -> Double {
  return Double(wins) / Double(wins + losses)
}
```

In the preceding example, we redefine the `winPercentage` function with external parameter names. In this redefinition, we have the same three parameters: `team`, `wins`, and `losses`. The difference is how we define the parameters. When using external parameters, we define each parameter with both an external parameter name and a local parameter name separated by a space. In the preceding example, the first parameter has an external parameter name of `BaseballTeam`, an internal parameter name of `team`, and a type of `String`.

When we call a function with external parameter names, we need to include the external parameter names in the function call. The following code shows how to call the function in the preceding example:

```
var per = winPercentage(BaseballTeam:"Red Sox", withWins:99,
  andLoses:63)
```

While using external parameter names requires more typing, it does make your code easier to read. In the preceding example, it is easy to see that the function is looking for the name of a baseball team, the second parameter is the number of wins, and the last parameter is the number of losses.

Using variadic parameters

A variadic parameter is one that accepts zero or more values of a specified type. Within the functions definition, we define a variadic parameter by appending three periods(...) to the parameter's type name. The values of a variadic parameter are made available to the function as an array of the specified type. The following example shows how we would use a variadic parameter with a function:

```
func sayHello(greeting: String, names: String...) {
  for name in names {
    print("\(greeting) \(name)")
  }
}
```

In the preceding example, the `sayHello()` function takes two parameters. The first parameter is a String type, which is the greeting to use. The second parameter is a variadic parameter of the String type, which are the names to send the greeting to. Within the function, a variadic parameter is an array that contains the type specified; therefore, in our example, the `names` parameter is an array of `String` values. In this example, we use a `for-in` loop to access the values within the `names` parameter.

The following line of code shows how to call the `sayHello()` function with a variadic parameter:

```
sayHello("Hello", names: "Jon", "Kim")
```

The preceding line of code will print two greetings: `Hello Jon` and `Hello Kim`.

Parameters as variables

Parameters are constants by default, which means they cannot be changed within the function. Let's look at the following example:

```
func sayHello(greeting: String, name: String, count: Int) {
  while count > 0 {
    print("\(greeting) \(name)")
    count--
  }
}
```

If we try to run this example, we will get an exception because we will have attempted to change the value of the `count` parameter with the decrement operator (`--`). If we need to change the value of a parameter within our function, we need to specify that the parameter is a variable by using the `var` keyword in the function definition.

The following example shows how to declare the `count` parameter as a variable (rather than a constant) so that we can change the value within the function:

```
func sayHello(greeting: String, name: String, var count: Int) {
  while (count > 0) {
    println("\(greeting) \(name)")
    count--
  }
}
```

You can see how we added the `var` keyword prior to the `count` parameter name in the preceding example. This specifies whether the parameter is a variable and not a constant; therefore, we can change the value of the `count` parameter in the function.

Using inout parameters

Variable parameters, as we just described, can only change the value of the parameter within the function; therefore, any changes are lost after the function ends. If we want the changes to a parameter to persist once the function ends, we need to define the parameter as an `inout` parameter. Any changes made to an `inout` parameter are passed back to the variable that was used in the function call.

Two items to keep in mind when we use `inout` parameters are that these parameters cannot have default values and they cannot be a variadic parameter.

Let's look at how to use the `inout` parameters to swap the values of two variables:

```
func swap(inout first: String, inout second: String) {
  let tmp = first
  first = second
  second = tmp
}
```

This function will accept two parameters and swap the values of the variables that are used in the function call. When we make the function call, we put an ampersand (`&`) in front of the variable name indicating that the function can modify its value. The following example shows how to call the reverse function:

```
var one = "One"
var two = "Two"
swap(&one,&two)
print("one: \(one) two: \(two)")
```

In the preceding example, we set variable `one` to the value `One` and variable `two` to the value `Two`. We then call the reverse function with the `one` and `two` variables. Once the swap function returns, the variable named `one` will contain the value `Two`, while the variable named `two` will contain the value `One`.

Nesting functions

All the functions that we have shown so far are examples of global functions. Global functions are the ones that are defined at a global scope within the class or file that they are in. Swift also allows us to nest one function within another. Nested functions can only be called within the enclosed function; however, the enclosed function can return a nested function that allows it to be used outside the scope of the enclosed function. We will cover returning a function in *Chapter 12, Working with Closures*, later in this book.

Let's look at how to nest functions by creating a simple sort function that will take an array of integers and sort it:

```
func sort(inout numbers: [Int]) {
  //This is the nested function
  func reverse(inout first: Int, inout second: Int) {
    let tmp = first
    first = second
    second = tmp
  }
  //Nested function ends.

    var count = numbers.count

    while count > 0 {
      for var i = 1; i < count; i++ {
        if numbers[i] < numbers[i-1] {
          reverse(&numbers[i], second: &numbers[i-1])
        }
      }
    count--
    }
}
```

In the preceding code, we begin by creating a global function named `sort` that accepts an `inout` parameter, that is, an array of `Int`s. Within the `sort` function, the first thing we do is define the nested function that is named `reverse`. A function needs to be defined in the code prior to calling it, so it is good practice to put all the nested functions at the start of the global function so that we know they are defined prior to calling them. The `reverse` function simply swaps the two values that are passed in.

Within the body of the `sort` function, we implement the logic for the simple sort. Within that logic, we compare two numbers in the array, and if the numbers need to be reversed, we call the nested `reverse` function to swap the two numbers. This example shows how we can effectively use a nested function to organize our code to make it easy to maintain and read. Let's look at how to call the global sort function:

```
var nums: [Int] = [6,2,5,3,1]

sort(&nums)

for value in nums {
    print("--\(value)")
}
```

The preceding code creates an array of five integers and then passes the array to the `sort` function. When the `sort` function returns the `nums` array, it contains a sorted array.

Nested functions, when used properly, can be very useful. However, it is really easy to overuse them. Before creating a nested function, you might want to ask yourself why you want to use a nested function and what problem are you solving by using a nested function.

Putting it all together

To reinforce what we learned in this chapter, let's look at one more example. For this example, we will create a function that will test to see if a string value contains a valid IPv4 address or not. An IPv4 address is the address assigned to a computer that uses the Internet Protocol to communicate. An IP address consists of four numeric values, ranging from 0-255, separated by a dot (period). An example of a valid IP address is 10.0.1.250:

```
func isValidIP(ipAddr: String?) -> Bool {

    guard let ipAddr = ipAddr else {
        return false
    }

let octets = ipAddr.characters.split { $0 == "."}.map{String($0)}

    guard octets.count == 4 else {
        return false
```

```
        }

        func validOctet(octet: String) -> Bool {
            guard let num = Int(String(octet))
                where num >= 0 && num < 256 else {
                    return false
            }
            return true
        }

        for octet in octets {
            guard validOctet(octet) else {
                return false
            }
        }

        return true

    }
```

Since the parameter for the `isValidIp()` function is an optional type, the first thing we do is verify that the `ipAddr` parameter is not nil. To do this, we used a `guard` statement with optional binding and if the optional binding fails, we return a Boolean `false` value because nil is not a valid IP address.

If the `ipAddr` parameter contains a non-nil value, we then split the string into an array of strings, at the dots. Since an IP address is suppose to contain four numbers separated by a dot, we use the `guard` statement to check whether the array contains four elements. If it does not, we return `false` because we know that the `ipAddr` parameter did not contain a valid IP address.

Next, we create a nested function named `validOctet()` that has one String parameter named `octet`. This nested function will verify that the `octet` parameter contains a numeric value between 0 and 255, and if so, it will return a Boolean `true` value, otherwise, it will return a `false` Boolean value.

Finally, we loop through a values in the array that we created by splitting the original `ipAddr` parameter at the dots and pass the values to the `validOctet()` nested function. If all the four values get verified by the `validOctet()` function, we have a valid IP address and we return a Boolean `true` value; however, if any of the values fail the `validOctet()` function, we return a Boolean `false` value.

Summary

In this chapter, we covered control flow and functions in Swift. It is essential to understand the concepts in this chapter before going on. Every application that we write, beyond the simple Hello World applications, will rely very heavily on the control flow statements and functions.

The control flow statements are used to make decisions within our application, and the functions will be used to group our code into the sections that are reusable and organized.

5
Classes and Structures

The first programming language that I learned was BASIC. It was a good language to begin programming with, but once I traded in my Commodore Vic-20 for a PCjr (yes, I had a PCjr and I really enjoyed it), I realized that there were other, more advanced languages out there, and spent a lot of time learning Pascal and C. It wasn't until I started college that I heard the term "object-oriented language". At that time, object-oriented languages were so new that there were no real courses on them, but I was able to experiment a little with C++. After I graduated, I left object-oriented programming behind, and it really wasn't until several years later, when I started to experiment with C++ again, that I really discovered the power and flexibility of object-oriented programming.

In this chapter, we will cover the following topics:

- Creating and using classes and structures
- Adding properties and property observers to classes and structures
- Adding methods to classes and structures
- Adding initializers to classes and structures
- Using access controls
- Creating a class hierarchy
- Extending a class
- Understanding memory management and ARC

What are classes and structures?

In Swift, classes and structures are very similar. If we really want to master Swift, it is very important to understand what makes classes and structures so similar and also what sets them apart because they are the building blocks of your applications. Apple describes classes and structures as:

> *"Classes and structures are general-purpose, flexible constructs that become the building blocks of your program's code. You define properties and methods to add functionality to your classes and structures by using the already familiar syntax of constants, variables, and functions."*

Let's begin by taking a quick look at some of the similarities between classes and structures.

Similarities between classes and structures

In Swift, classes and structures are more similar than they are in other languages, such as Objective-C. The following is a list of some of the features that classes and structures share:

- Properties: These are used to store information in our classes and structures
- Methods: These provide functionality for our classes and structures
- Initializers: These are used when initializing instances of our classes and structures
- Subscripts: These provide access to values using the subscript syntax
- Extensions: These help in extending both classes and structures

Now let's take a quick look at some of the differences between classes and structures.

Differences between classes and structures

While classes and structures are very similar, there are also several very important differences. The following is a list of some of the differences between classes and structures in Swift:

- Type: A structure is a value type while a class is a reference type
- Inheritance: A structure cannot inherit from other types while a class can
- Deinitializers: Structures cannot have custom deinitializers while a class can
- Multiple references: We can have more than one reference to a class instance; however, with structures, we cannot

Throughout this chapter, we will be emphasizing the differences between classes and structures to help us understand when to use each. Before we really dive into classes and structures, let's take a look at the difference between value types (structures) and reference types (classes). In order to understand when to use classes and structures and how to properly use them, it is important to understand the difference between value and reference types.

Value versus reference types

Structures such as enums and tuples are value types. This means when we pass instances of a structure within our application, we pass a copy of the structure and not the original structure. Classes are reference types, which means when we pass an instance of a class within our application, we pass a reference to the original instance. It is very important to understand the difference between value and reference types. We will give a very high-level view here, and will provide additional details in the *Memory management* section at the end of this chapter.

When we pass structures within our application, we are passing copies of the structures and not the original structures. Since a function gets its own copy of the structure, it can change it as needed, without affecting the original instance of the structure.

When we pass an instance of a class within our application, we are passing a reference to the original instance of the class. Since we pass an instance of a class to a function, the function is getting a reference to the original instance; therefore, any changes made within the function will remain once the function exits.

To illustrate the difference between value and reference types, let's look at a real-world object—a book. If we had a friend that wanted to read *Mastering Swift*, we could either buy them their own copy or share ours.

If we bought our friend their own copy of the book, then any notes they made within the book would remain in their copy of the book and would not be reflected in our copy. This is how pass by value works with structures and variables. Any changes that are made to the structure or variable within the function are not reflected in the original instance of the structure or variable.

If we share our copy of the book, then any notes they made within the book would stay in the book when they returned it to us. This is how pass by reference works. Any changes that are made to the instance of the class remains when the function exits.

To read more about value versus reference types, see the *Memory management* section at the end of this chapter.

Creating a class or structure

We use the same syntax to define classes and structures. The only difference is we define a class using the `class` keyword, and a structure by using the `struct` keyword. Let's look at the syntax used to create both classes and structures:

```
class MyClass {
  // MyClass definition
}

struct MyStruct {
  // MyStruct definition
}
```

In the preceding code, we define a new class named `MyClass` and a new structure named `MyStruct`. This effectively creates two new Swift types named `MyClass` and `MyStruct`. When we name a new type, we want to use the standard naming convention set by Swift where the name is in camel case, with the first letter being uppercase. Any method or property defined within the class or structure should also be named using camel case with the first letter being lowercase.

Empty classes and structures are not that useful, so let's look at how we can add properties to our classes and structures.

Properties

Properties associate values with a class or a structure. There are two types of properties, which are as follows:

- Stored properties: They store variable or constant values as part of an instance of a class or structure. Stored properties can also have property observers that can monitor the property for changes and respond with custom actions when the value of the property changes.
- Computed properties: They do not store a value themselves, but retrieve and possibly set other properties. The value returned by a computed property can also be calculated when it is requested.

Stored properties

A stored property is a variable or constant that is stored as part of an instance of a class or structure. We can provide a default value for stored properties. These are defined with the `var` keyword. Let's look at how we would use stored properties in classes and structures. In the following code, we will create a structure named `MyStruct` and a class named `MyClass`. The structure and the class both contain two stored properties, `c` and `v`. The stored property `c` is a constant because it is defined with the `let` keyword, and `v` is a variable because it is defined with the `var` keyword. Let's take a look at the following code:

```
struct MyStruct {
  let c = 5
  var v = ""
}

class MyClass {
  let c = 5
  var v = ""
}
```

As we can see from the example, the syntax to define a stored property is the same for both classes and properties. Let's look at how we would create an instance of both the structure and class. The following code creates an instance of the `MyStruct` structure named `myStruct` and an instance of the `MyClass` class named `myClass`:

```
var myStruct = MyStruct()
var myClass = MyClass()
```

One of the differences between a structure and a class is that, by default, a structure creates an initializer that lets us populate the stored properties when we create an instance of the structure. Therefore, we could also create an instance of the `MyStruct` like this:

```
var myStruct = MyStruct(v: "Hello")
```

In the preceding example, the initializer is used to set the variable `v`, and the `c` constant will contain the number 5 that is set in the `struct` itself. If, for example, we did not give the constant an initial value, as shown in the following example, the default initializer would be used to also set the constant as well:

```
struct MyStruct {
  let c: Int
  var v = ""
}
```

The following example shows how the initializer for this new `struct` would work:

```
var myStruct = MyStruct(c: 10, v: "Hello")
```

This allows us to define a constant where we set the value when we initialize the class or struct at runtime rather than hardcoding the value of the constant in our code.

The order in which the parameters appear in the initializer is the order that we defined them in. In the previous example, we defined the c constant first; therefore, it is the first parameter in the initializer. We defined the v parameter second; therefore it is the second parameter in the initializer.

To set or read a stored property, we use the standard dot syntax. Let's look at how we would set and read stored properties in Swift:

```
var x = myClass.c
myClass.v = "Howdy"
```

Before we move on to computed properties, let's create a structure and class that will represent an employee. We will be using and expanding these throughout this chapter to show how classes and structures are similar and how they differ:

```
struct EmployeeStruct {
  var firstName = ""
  var lastName = ""
  var salaryYear = 0.0
}

public class EmployeeClass {
  var firstName = ""
  var lastName = ""
  var salaryYear = 0.0
}
```

The employee structure is named `EmployeeStruct` and the employee class is named `EmployeeClass`. Both the class and structure have three stored properties: `firstName`, `lastName`, and `salaryYear`.

Within our structure or class, we can now access these properties by using the name of the property or the `self` keyword. Every instance of a structure or class has a property named `self`. This property refers to the instance itself; therefore, we can use it to access the properties within the instance. The following examples show how we can access the properties with the `self` keyword within the instance of the structure or class:

```
self.firstName = "Jon"
self.lastName = "Hoffman"
```

Computed properties

Computed properties are properties that do not have backend variables that are used to store the values associated with the property. The values of a computed property are usually computed when code requests it. You can think of a computed property as a function disguised as a property. Let's take a look at how we would define a read-only computed property:

```
var salaryWeek: Double {
get{
  return self.salaryYear/52
  }
}
```

To create a read-only computed property, we begin by defining it as if it were a normal variable with the `var` keyword, followed by the variable name, colon and the variable type. What comes next is different; we add a curly bracket at the end of the declaration and then define a `getter` method that is called when the value of our computed property is requested. In the example, the `getter` method divides the current value of the `salaryYear` property by `52` to get the employee's weekly salary.

We can simplify the definition of the read-only computed property by removing the `get` keyword. We could rewrite the `salaryWeek` function like this:

```
var salaryWeek: Double {
  return self.salaryYear/52
}
```

Computed properties are not limited to being read-only, we can also write to them. To enable the `salaryWeek` property to be writeable, we would need to add a `setter` method. The following example shows how we would add a `setter` method that will set the `salaryYear` property, based on the value being passed into the `salaryWeek` property:

```
var salaryWeek: Double {
  get {
    return self.salaryYear/52
  }
  set (newSalaryWeek){
    self.salaryYear = newSalaryWeek*52
  }
}
```

We can simplify the setter definition by not defining a name for the new value. In this case, the value would be assigned to a default variable name, `newValue`. The `salaryWeek` computed property could be rewritten like this:

```
var salaryWeek: Double {
  get{
    return self.salaryYear/52
  }
  set{
    self.salaryYear = newValue*52
  }
}
```

The `salaryWeek` computed property, as written in the preceding example, could be added to either the `EmployeeClass` class or the `EmployeeStruct` structure without any modifications. Let's see how we would do this by adding the `salaryWeek` property to our `EmployeeClass` class:

```
public class EmployeeClass {
  var firstName = ""
  var lastName = ""
  var salaryYear = 0.0
  var salaryWeek: Double {
    get{
      return self.salaryYear/52
    }
    set (newSalaryWeek){
      self.salaryYear = newSalaryWeek*52
    }
  }
}
```

Now, let's look at how we would add the `salaryWeek` computed property to the `EmployeeStruct` structure:

```
struct EmployeeStruct {
    var firstName = ""
    var lastName = ""
    var salaryYear = 0.0
   .
    var salaryWeek: Double {
        get{
            return self.salaryYear/52
        }
        set (newSalaryWeek){
```

```
                self.salaryYear = newSalaryWeek*52
            }
        }
    }
```

As we can see, the class and structure definitions are the same so far, except for the initial class or `struct` keywords are used to define them as either a structure or a class.

We read and write to a computed property exactly as we would to a stored property. Code that is external to the class or structure should not be aware that the property is a computer property. Let's see this in action by creating an instance of the `EmployeeStruct` structure:

```
var f = EmployeeStruct(firstName: "Jon", lastName: "Hoffman",
  salaryYear: 39000)

print(f.salaryWeek) //prints 750.00 to the console
f.salaryWeek = 1000
print(f.salaryWeek) //prints 1000.00 to the console
print(f.salaryYear) //prints 52000.00 to the console
```

The preceding example starts off by creating an instance of the `EmployStruct` structure with the `salaryYear` value being set to `39,000`. Next, we print the value of the `salaryWeek` property to the `console`. This value is currently `750.00`. We then set the `salaryWeek` property to `1000.00` and print out both the `salaryWeek` and `salaryYear` properties to the console. The values of the `salaryWeek` and `salaryYear` properties are now `1000.00` and `52000` respectively. As we can see, in this example, setting either the `salaryWeek` or `salaryYear` property changes the values returned by both.

Computed properties can be very useful for offering different views of the same data. For example, if we had a value that represented the length of something, we could store the length in centimeters and then use computed properties that calculate the values for meters, millimeters, and kilometers.

Now, let's take a look at property observers.

Property observers

Property observers are called every time the value of the property is set. We can add property observers to any non-lazy stored property. We can also add property observers to any inherited stored or computed property by overriding the property in the subclass. We will look at the *Overriding properties* section a little later in this chapter.

There are two property observers that we can set in Swift—`willSet` and `didSet`. The `willSet` observer is called right before the property is set, and the `didSet` observer is called right after the property is set.

One thing to note about property observers is that they are not called when the value is set during initialization. Let's look at how we would add a property observer to the salary property of our `EmployeeClass` class and `EmployeeStruct` structure:

```
var salaryYear: Double = 0.0 {
  willSet(newSalary) {
    print("About to set salaryYear to \(newSalary)")
  }
  didSet {
    if salaryWeek > oldValue {
      print("\(firstName) got a raise")
    }
    else {
      print("\(firstName) did not get a raise")
    }
  }
}
```

When we add a property observer to a stored property, we need to include the type of the value being stored within the definition of the property. In the preceding example, we did not need to define our `salaryYear` property as a `Double` type; however, when we add property observers the definition is required.

After the property definition, we define a `willSet` observer that simply prints out the new value that the `salaryYear` property will be set to. We also define a `didSet` observer that will check whether the new value is greater than the old value and if so, it will print out that the employee got a raise, otherwise, it will print out that the employee did not get a raise.

As with the getter in computed properties, we do not need to define the name for the new value for the `willSet` observer. If we do not define a name, the new value is put in a constant named `newValue`. The following example shows how we would rewrite the previous `willSet` observer without defining a name for the new value:

```
willSet {
    print("About to set salaryYear to \(newValue)")
}
```

As we have seen, properties are mainly used to store information associated with a class or structure, and methods are mainly used to add the business logic to a class or structure. Let's look at how we would add methods to class or structure.

Methods

Methods are functions that are associated with a class or structure. A method, like a function, will encapsulate the code for a specific task or functionality that is associated with the class or structure. Let's look at how we would define a method in classes and structures. The following code will return the full name of the employee by using the `firstName` and `lastName` properties:

```
func getFullName() -> String {
    return firstName + " " + lastName
}
```

We define this method exactly as we would define any function. A method is simply a function that is associated with a specific class or structure, and everything that we learned about functions in the previous chapters applies to methods. The `getFullName()` function can be added directly to the `EmployeeClass` class or `EmployeeStruct` structure without any modification.

To access a method, we use the same dot syntax we used to access properties. The following code shows how we would access the `getFullName()` method of a class and a structure:

```
var e = EmployeeClass()
var f = EmployeeStruct(firstName: "Jon", lastName: "Hoffman",
  salaryYear: 50000)

e.firstName = "Jon"
e.lastName = "Hoffman"
e.salaryYear = 50000.00

print(e.getFullName()) //Jon Hoffman is printed to the console
print(f.getFullName()) //Jon Hoffman is printed to the console
```

In the preceding example, we initialize an instance of both the `EmployeeClass` class and `EmployeeStruct` structure. We populate the structure and class with the same information and then use the `getFullName()` method to print the full name of the employee to the console. In both cases, `Jon Hoffman` is printed to the console.

There is a difference in how we define methods for classes and structures, which we need to update property values within the method. Let's look at how we would define a method that gives an employee a raise within the `EmployeeClass` class:

```
func giveRaise(amount: Double) {
  self.salaryYear += amount
}
```

If we add the preceding code to our `EmployeeClass`, it works as expected and when we call the method, with an amount, the employee gets a raise. However, if we try to add this method as it is written to the `EmployeeStruct` structure, we receive the `Cannot invoke '+=' with an argument list of type '(Double, Double)'` error. By default, we are not allowed to update property values within a method of a structure. If we want to modify a property, we can opt into mutating behavior for that method by adding the `mutating` keyword before the `func` keyword of the method declaration. Therefore, the following code would be the correct way to define the `giveRaise()` method for the `EmployeeStruct` structure:

```
mutating func giveRase(amount: Double) {
    self.salaryYear += amount
}
```

In the preceding examples, we used the `self` property. Every instance of a type has a property called `self`, which is the instance itself. We use the `self` property to refer to the current instance of the type within the instance itself, so when we write `self.salaryYear`, we ask for the value of the `salaryYear` property of the current instance.

The `self` property can be used to distinguish between a local variable and instance variable that have the same name. Let's look at an example that illustrates this:

```
func compareFirstName(firstName: String) -> Bool {
  return self.firstName == firstName
}
```

In the preceding example, the method accepts an argument with the name, `firstName`. There is also a property that has this name. We use the self property to specify that we want the instance property with the name, `firstName`, and not the local variable with this name.

Other than the `mutating` keyword being required for methods that change the value of the structure's properties, methods can be defined and used exactly as functions are defined and used. Therefore, everything we learned about functions in the previous chapter can be applied to methods.

There are times when we want to initialize properties or perform some business logic when a class or structure is first initialized. For this, we will use an initializer.

Custom initializers

Initializers are called when we initialize a new instance of a particular type (class or structure). Initialization is the process of preparing an instance for use. The initialization process can include setting initial values for stored properties, verifying resources, such as web services, files, and so on are available, or setting up the UI properly. Initializers are generally used to ensure that the instance of the class or structure is properly initialized prior to first use.

Initializers are special methods that are used to create a new instance of a type. We define an initializer exactly as we would define other methods, but we must use the `init` keyword as the name of the initializer to tell the compiler that this method is an initializer. In its simplest form, the initializer does not accept any arguments. Let's look at the syntax used to write a simple initializer:

```
init() {
  //Perform initialization here
}
```

This format works for both classes and structures. By default, all classes and structures have an empty default initializer that we can override if we choose to. We saw these default initializers when we used the `EmployeeClass` class and `EmployeeStruct` structure in the previous section. Structures also have an additional default initializer, which we saw with the `EmployeeStruct` structure that accepts a value for each stored property and initializes them with those values. Let's look at how we would add custom initializers to our `EmployeeClass` class and `EmployeeStruct` structure. In the following code, we create three custom initializers that will work for both the `EmployeeClass` class and `EmployeeStruct` structure:

```
init() {
  self.firstName = ""
  self.lastName = ""
  self.salaryYear = 0.0
}

init(firstName: String, lastName: String) {
  self.firstName = firstName
  self.lastName = lastName
  self.salaryYear = 0.0
}

init(firstName: String, lastName: String, salaryYear: Double) {
  self.firstName = firstName
  self.lastName = lastName
  self.salaryYear = salaryYear
}
```

The first initializer, `init()`, when used, will set all of the stored properties to their default values. The second initializer, `init(firstName: String, lastName: String)`, when used, will populate the `firstName` and `lastName` properties with the values of the arguments. The third initializer, `init(firstName: String, lastName: String, salaryYear: Double)`, will populate all the properties with the values of the arguments.

In the previous example we can see that in Swift, unlike Objective-C, an initializer does not have a return value. This means that we do not have to define the return type for the initializer or have a return statement within the initializer. Let's look at how we would use these initializers:

```
var g = EmployeeClass()
var h = EmployeeStruct(firstName: "Me", lastName: "Moe")
var i = EmployeeClass(firstName: "Me", lastName: "Moe",
  salaryYear: 45000)
```

The variable `g` uses the `init()` initializer to create an instance of the `EmployeeClass` class; therefore, all the properties of this `EmployeeClass` instance contain their default values.

The `h` variable uses the `init(firstName: String, lastName: String)` initializer to create an instance of the `EmployeeStruct` structure; therefore, the `firstName` property of the structure is set to `Me` and the `lastName` property is set to `Moe`, which are the two arguments passed into the initializer. The `salaryYear` property is still set to the default value of 0.0.

The `EmployeeClass` sets the `init(firstName: String, lastName: String, salaryYear: Double)` initializer to create an instance of the `EmployeeClass` class; therefore, the `firstName` property is set to `Me`, the `lastName` property is set to `Moe`, and the `salaryYear` is set to `45000`.

Since all the initializers are identified with the `init` keyword, the parameters and parameter types are used to identify which initializer to use. Therefore, Swift provides automatic external names for all of these parameters. In the previous example. We can see that when we use an initializer that has parameters, we include the parameter names. Let's take a look at internal and external parameter names with initializers.

Internal and external parameter names

Just like functions, the parameters associated with an initializer can have separate internal and external names. Unlike functions, if we do not supply external parameter names for our parameters, Swift will automatically generate them for us. In the previous examples, we did not include external parameter names in the definition of the initializers, so Swift created them for us using the internal parameter name as the external parameter name.

If we wanted to supply our own parameter names, we would do so by putting the external function name before the internal function name, exactly as we do with any normal function. Let's look at how we would define our own external parameter names by redefining one of the initializers within our `EmployeeClass` class:

```
init(employeeWithFirstName firstName: String, lastName lastName:
  String, andSalary salaryYear: Double) {
  self.firstName = firstName
  self.lastName = lastName
  self.salaryYear = salaryYear
}
```

In the preceding example, we created the `init(employeeWithFirstName firstName: String, lastName lastName: String, andSalary salaryYear: Double)` initializer. This initializer will create an instance of the `EmployeeClass` class and populate the instance properties with the value of the arguments. In this example, each of the parameters has both external and internal property names. Let's look at how we would use this initializer, with the external property names, to create an instance of the `EmployeeClass` class:

```
var i = EmployeeClass(employeeWithFirstName: "Me", lastName:
  "Moe", andSalary: 45000)
```

Notice that we are now using the external parameter names as we defined in our initializer. Using external parameter names can help make our code more readable and differentiate between different initializers.

So, what will happen if our initializer fails? For example, what if our class relies on a specific resource, such as web service or a specific file that is not currently available? This is where failable initializers come in.

Failable initializers

A failable initializer is an initializer that may fail to initialize the resources needed for a class or a structure, thereby rendering the instance unusable. When using a failable initializer, the result of the initializer is an optional type, containing either a valid instance of the type or nil.

An initializer can be made failable by adding a question mark (`?`) after the `init` keyword. Let's look at how we would create a failable initializer that will not allow a new employee to be initialized with a salary below `$20,000` a year:

```
init?(firstName: String, lastName: String, salaryYear: Double) {
  self.firstName = firstName
  self.lastName = lastName
  self.salaryYear = salaryYear
  if self.salaryYear < 20000 {
    return nil
  }
}
```

In the previous example, we did not include a `return` statement within the initializer because Swift does not need to return the initialized instance; however, in a failable initializer, if the initialization fails, we will return a `nil`. If the initializer successfully initializes the instance, we do not need to return anything. Therefore, in our example, if the yearly salary that is passed in is below `$20,000` a year, we return `nil`, indicating that the initialization failed, otherwise, nothing will be returned. Let's look at how we would use a failable initializer to create an instance of a class or structure:

```
if let f = EmployeeClass(firstName: "Jon", lastName: "Hoffman",
  salaryYear: 29000) {
  print(f.getFullName())
} else {
  print("Failed to initialize")
}
```

In the previous example, we initialize the instance of the `EmployeeClass` class with a yearly salary greater than $20,000; therefore, the instance gets initialized correctly and the full name of `Jon Hoffman` is printed to the console. Now let's try to initialize an instance of the `EmployeeClass` class with a yearly salary less than $20,000 to see how it fails:

```
if let f = EmployeeClass(firstName: "Jon", lastName: "Hoffman",
  salaryYear: 19000) {
  print(f.getFullName())
  print(f.compareFirstName("Jon"))
```

```
} else {
  print("Failed to initialize")
}
```

In the example, the yearly salary that we are attempting to initialize for our employee is less than $20,000; therefore, the initialization fails and a `Failed to initialize` message is printed to the console.

There are times when we want to restrict access to certain parts of our code. This enables us to hide implementation details and only expose the interfaces we want to expose. This feature is handled with named access controls.

Access control allows us to restrict the access and visibility to parts of our code. This allows us to hide implementation details and only expose the interfaces we want the external code to access. We can assign specific access levels to both classes and structures. We can also assign specific access levels to properties, methods, and initializers that belong to our classes and structures.

In Swift, there are three access levels:

- **Public**: This is the most visible access control level. It allows us to use the property, method, class, and so on anywhere we want to import the module. Basically, anything can use a property, method, class, and so on that has an access control level of public. This level is primarily used by frameworks to expose the framework's public API.
- **Internal**: This is the default access level. This access level allows us to use the property, method, class, and so on in the defining source as well as the module that the source is in (the application or framework). If this level is used in a framework, it lets other parts of the framework use the property, method, class, and so on, but code outside the framework will be unable to access it.
- **Private**: This is the least visible access control level. It only allows us to use the property, method, class, and so on in the source file that defines it.

If we are writing code that will be self-contained within a single application and there is no need for it to be made available outside the application, then we can largely ignore access controls. The default access level of internal already matches this requirement. We may, however, want to hide parts of the implementation, which can be done by setting the access level to private, but that should be an exception and not the rule.

When we are developing frameworks, the access controls really become useful. We would need to mark the public facing interfaces as public, so other modules such as applications that import the framework can use them. We would then use the internal and private access control levels to mark the interfaces that we want to use internally to the framework and the source file, respectively.

To define access levels, we place the name of the level before the definition of the entity. The following code shows examples of how we would add access levels to several entities:

```
private struct EmployeeStruct {}
public class EmployeeClass {}
internal class EmployeeClass2 {}
public var firstName = "Jon"
internal var lastName = "Hoffman"
private var salaryYear = 0.0
public func getFullName() -> String {}
private func giveRaise(amount: Double) {}
```

There are some limitations with access controls, but these limitations are there to ensure that access levels in Swift follow a simple guiding principle—*no entity can be defined in terms of another entity that has a lower (more restrictive) access level*. What this means is we cannot assign a higher (less restrictive) access level to an entity when it relies on another entity that has a lower (more restrictive) access level.

As following examples:

- We cannot mark a method as being public when one of the arguments or the return type has an access level of private because external code would not have access to the private type
- We cannot set the access level of a method or property to public when the class or structure has an access level of private because external code would not be able to access the constructor when the class is private

Inheritance

The concept of inheritance is a basic object-oriented development concept. Inheritance allows a class to be defined as having a certain set of characteristics and then other classes can be derived from that class. The derived class inherits all of the features of the class it is inheriting from (unless the derived class overrides those characteristics) and then usually adds additional characteristics of its own.

With inheritance, we can create what is known as a class hierarchy. In a class hierarchy, the class at the top of the hierarchy is known as the **base class** and the derived classes are known as **subclasses**. We are not limited to only creating subclasses from a base class; we can also create subclasses from other subclasses. The class that a subclass is derived from is known as the parent or superclass. In Swift, a class can have only one parent class, known as single inheritance.

Inheritance is one of the fundamental differences that separate classes from structures. Classes can be derived from a parent or super class, but a structure cannot be.

Subclasses can call and access the properties, methods, and subscripts of their super class. They can also override the properties, methods, and subscripts of their super class. Subclasses can add property observers to properties that they inherit from a super class, so they can be notified when the values of the properties change. Let's look at an example that illustrates how inheritance works in Swift.

We will start off by defining a base class named `Plant`. The `Plant` class will have two properties, `height` and `age`. It will also have one method, `growHeight()`. The `height` property will represent the height of the plant, the `age` property will represent the age of the plant, and the `growHeight()` method will be used to increase the height of the plant. Here is how we would define the `Plant` class:

```
class Plant {
    var height = 0.0
    var age = 0

    func growHeight(inches: Double) {
        self.height +=  inches;
    }
}
```

Now that we have our `Plant` base class, let's see how we would define a subclass of it. We will name this subclass `Tree`. The `Tree` class will inherit the `age` and `height` properties of the `Plant` class and add one additional property named `limbs`. It will also inherit the `growHeight()` method of the `Plant` class and add two additional methods: `limbGrow()`, where a new limbs is grown, and `limbFall()`, where one of the limbs falls off the tree. Let's have a look at the following code:

```
class Tree: Plant {
  private var limbs = 0

  func limbGrow() {
    self.limbs++
  }
  func limbFall() {
    self.limbs--
  }
}
```

We indicate that a class has a super class by adding a colon and the name of the super class to the end of the class definition. In the `Tree` example, we indicated that the `Tree` class has a super class named `Plant`.

Now, let's look at how we could use the `Tree` class that inherited the `age` and `height` properties from the `Plant` class:

```
var tree = Tree()
tree.age = 5
tree.height = 4
tree.limbGrow()
tree.limbGrow()
```

The preceding example begins by creating an instance of the `Tree` class. We then set the `age` and `height` properties to `5` and `4`, respectively, and add two limbs to the tree by calling the `limbGrow()` method twice.

We now have a base class named `Plant` that has a subclass named `Tree`. This means that the super (or parent) class of `Tree` is the `Plant` class. This also means that one of the subclasses (or child classes) of `Plant` is named `Tree`. There are, however, lots of different kinds of trees in the world. Let's create two subclasses from the `Tree` class. These subclasses will be the `PineTree` class and the `OakTree` class:

```
class PineTree: Tree {
  var needles = 0
}

class OakTree: Tree {
  var leaves = 0
}
```

The class hierarchy now looks like this:

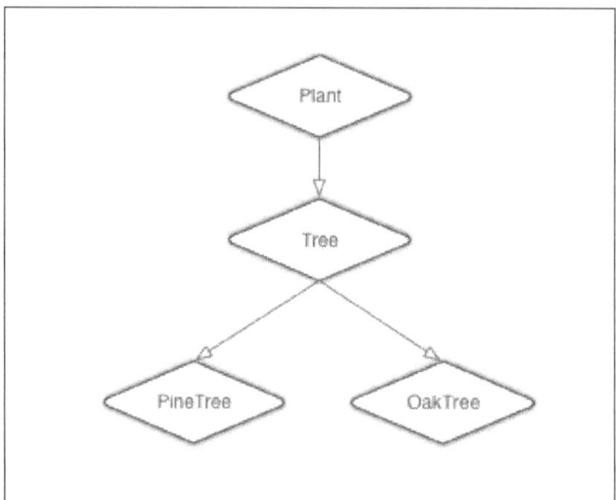

It is important to keep in mind that in Swift, a class can have multiple subclasses; however, a class can have only one super class. There are times when a subclass needs to provide its own implementation of a method or property that it inherited from its super class. This is known as overriding.

Overriding methods and properties

To override a method, property, or subscript, we need to prefix the definition with the `override` keyword. This tells the compiler that we intend to override something in the super class and that we did not make a duplicate definition by mistake. The `override` keyword does prompt the Swift compiler to verify that the super class (or one of its parents) has a matching declaration that can be overridden. If it cannot find a matching declaration in one of the super classes, an error will be thrown.

Overriding methods

Let's look at how we would override a method. We will start by adding a `getDetails()` method to the `Plant` class that we will then override in the child classes. The following code shows how the new Plant class looks similar to with the `getDetails()` method added:

```
class Plant {
  var height = 0.0
  var age = 0

  func growHeight(inches: Double) {
    self.height +=  inches;
  }

  func getDetails() -> String {
    return "Plant Details"
  }
}
```

Now let's see how we would override the `getDetails()` method in the `Tree` class:

```
class Tree: Plant {
  private var limbs = 0

  func limbGrow() {
    self.limbs++
  }
  func limbFall() {
```

```
        self.limbs--
      }

      override func getDetails() -> String {
        return "Tree Details"
      }
    }
```

The thing to note here is that we do not use the `override` keyword in the `Plant` class because it is the first class to implement this method; however, we do include it in the `Tree` class since we are overriding the `getDetails()` method from the `Plant` class. Now, let's see what happens if we call the `getDetails()` method from an instance of the `Plant` and `Tree` classes:

```
var plant = Plant()
var tree = Tree()
print("Plant: \(plant.getDetails())")
print("Tree: \(tree.getDetails())")
```

The previous example would print the following two lines to the console:

```
Plant: Plant Details
Tree: Tree Details
```

As we can see, the `getDetails()` method in the `Tree` subclass overrides the `getDetails()` of its parent `Plant` class.

Inside the `Tree` class, we can still call the `getDetails()` method (or any overridden method, property, or subscript) of its super class by using the `super` prefix. Let's see how we would call the `getDetails()` method of the `Plant` class from an instance of the `Tree` class. We will begin by replacing the `getDetails()` method in the `Plant` class with the following method that will generate a string containing the values of the `height` and `age` properties. Let's take a look at the following code:

```
func getDetails() -> String {
    return "Height:  \(height)  age:  \(age)"
}
```

In the preceding code, we are changing the `getDetails()` method to return a string that contains the `height` and `age` of the plant. Now let's replace the `getDetails()` method for the `Tree` class with the following method:

```
override func getDetails() -> String {
  var details = super.getDetails()
  return "\(details)  limbs:  \(limbs)"
}
```

In the preceding example, we begin by calling the `getDetails()` method of the super class (the `Plant` class in this case) to get a string containing the tree's `height` and `age`. We then build a new string object that contains the results of the `getDetails()` method from the super class, adds the number of limbs to it and then returns it. Let's look at what happens if we call the `getDetails()` method of the `Tree` class:

```
var tree = Tree()
tree.age = 5
tree.height = 4
tree.limbGrow()
tree.limbGrow()
print(tree.getDetails())
```

If we run the preceding code, the following line would be printed to the console:

```
Height:  4.0  age:  5  limbs:  2
```

As we can see, the string that is returned contains the `height` and `age` information from the `Plant` class and the limbs information from the `Tree` class.

We can also chain the overridden methods. Let's see what happens if we add the following method to the `OakTree` class:

```
override func getDetails() -> String {
  let details = super.getDetails()
  return "\(details)  Leaves:  \(leaves)"
}
```

When we call the `getDetails()` method of an instance of the `OakTree` class, it calls the `getDetails()` method of its super class (the `Tree` class). The `getDetails()` method of the `Tree` class also calls the `getDetails()` method of its super class (the `Plant` class). The `getDetails()` method of the `Tree` class will finally create a string object that contains the `height` and `age` from the `Plant` class, the `limbs` from the `Tree` class, and the `leaves` from the `OakTree` class. Let's look at an example of this:

```
var tree = OakTree()
tree.age = 5
tree.height = 4
tree.leaves = 50
tree.limbGrow()
tree.limbGrow()
print(tree.getDetails())
```

If we run the preceding code, we would see the following line printed to the console:

```
Height:  4.0  age:  5  limbs:  2  Leaves:  50
```

Overriding properties

We can provide custom `getter` and `setter` to override any inherited property. When we override a property, we must provide the name and the type of property we are overriding, so the compiler can verify one of the classes in the class hierarchy has a matching property to override. While overriding properties are not as common as overriding methods, it is good for us to know how to do this when we need.

Let's see how we would override a property by adding the following method to our `Plant` class:

```
var description: String {
  get {
    return "Base class is Plant."
  }
}
```

The `description` property is a basic read-only property. This property returns the string, `Base class is Plant.`. Now let's override this property by adding the following property to the `Tree` class:

```
override var description: String {
  return "\(super.description)  I am a Tree class."
}
```

When we override a property, we use the same `override` keyword that we use when we override a method. The `override` keyword tells the compiler that we want to override a property, so the compiler can verify that another class in the class hierarchy contains a matching property to override. We then implement the property as we would any other property. Calling the `description` property of the tree would result in the `Base class is Plant. I am a Tree class.` string being returned.

There are times when we want to prevent a subclass from overriding the properties and methods. There are also times when we want to prevent an entire class from being subclassed. Let's see how we do this.

Preventing overrides

To prevent overrides or subclassing, we use the `final` keyword. To use the `final` keyword, we add it before the item's definition. Examples are `final func`, `final var`, and `final class`.

Any attempt to override an item marked final will throw a compile-time error.

Protocols

There are times when we would like to describe the implementations (methods, properties, and other requirements) of a class without actually providing the implementation. For this, we would use protocols.

Protocols define a blueprint of methods, properties, and other requirements for a class or a structure. A class or a structure can then provide an implementation that conforms to those requirements. The class or structure that provides the implementation is said to conform to the protocol.

Protocol syntax

The syntax to define a protocol is very similar to how we define a class or a structure. The following example shows the syntax used to define a protocol:

```
protocol MyProtocol {
  //protocol definition here
}
```

We state that a class or structure conforms to a particular protocol by placing the name of the protocol after the class or structure's name, separated by a colon. Here is an example of how we would state that a class conforms to the `MyProtocol` protocol:

```
class myClass: MyProtocol {
  //class implementation here
}
```

A class or a structure can conform to multiple protocols. We would list the protocols that the class or structure conforms to by separating them with commas. The following example shows how we would state that our class conforms to multiple protocols:

```
class MyClass: MyProtocol, AnotherProtocol, ThirdProtocol {
  // class implementation here
}
```

When we need a class to inherit from a super class and implement a protocol, we would list the super class first, followed by the protocols. The following example illustrates this:

```
Class MyClass: MySuperClass, MyProtocol, MyProtocol2 {
  // Class implementation here
}
```

Property requirements

A protocol can require that the conforming class or structure provide certain properties with a specified name and type. The protocol does not say if the property should be a stored or computed property because the implementation details are left up to the conforming class or structure.

When defining a property within a protocol, we must specify whether the property is a read-only or a read-write property by using the `get` and `set` keywords. Let's look at how we would define properties within a protocol by creating a `FullName` protocol:

```
protocol FullName {
  var firstName: String {get set}
  var lastName: String {get set}
}
```

The `FullName` protocol defines two properties, which any class or structure that conforms to the protocol must implement. These are the `firstName` and `lastName` properties. Both these properties in the `FullName` protocol are read-write properties. If we wanted to specify that the property is read-only, we would define it with only the `get` keyword, like this:

```
var readOnly: String {get}
```

Let's see how we would create a `Scientist` class that conforms to this protocol:

```
class Scientist: FullName {
  var firstName = ""
  var lastName = ""
}
```

If we had forgotten to include either the `firstName` or `lastName` property, we would have received a `Scientist does not conform to protocol 'FullName'` error message. We also need to make sure that the type of the property is the same. For example, if we changed the `lastName` definition in the `Scientist` class to `var lastName = 42`, we would also receive a `Scientist does not conform to protocol 'FullName'` error message because the protocol specifies that we must have a `lastName` property of the string type.

Method requirements

A protocol can require that the conforming class or structure provide certain methods. We define a method within a protocol exactly as we do within a normal class or structure, except without the curly braces or method body. Let's add a `getFullName()` method to our `FullName` protocol and `Scientist` class.

The following example shows how the `FullName` protocol would look with the `getFullName()` method added:

```
protocol FullName {
  var firstName: String {get set}
  var lastName: String {get set}

  func getFullName() -> String
}
```

Now, we will need to add a `getFullName()` method to our Scientist class so that it will properly conform to the `FullName` protocol:

```
class Scientist: FullName {
  var firstName = ""
  var lastName = ""
  var field = ""

  func getFullName() -> String {
    return "\(firstName) \(lastName) studies \(field)"
  }
}
```

Structures can conform to Swift protocols exactly as classes do. The following example shows how we can create a `FootballPlayer` structure that conforms to the `FullName` protocol:

```
struct FootballPlayer: FullName {
    var firstName = ""
    var lastName = ""
    var number = 0

    func getFullName() -> String {
        return "\(firstName) \(lastName) has the number \(number)"
    }
}
```

When a class or structure conforms to a Swift protocol, we can be sure that it has implemented the required properties and methods. This can be very useful when we want to ensure that certain properties or methods are implemented over various classes, as our preceding examples show.

Protocols are also very useful when we want to decouple our code from requiring specific classes or structures. The following code shows how we would decouple our code using the `FullName` protocol, the `Scientist` class, and the `FootballPlayer` structure that we have already built:

```
var scientist = Scientist()
scientist.firstName = "Kara"
scientist.lastName = "Hoffman"
scientist.field = "Physics"

var player = FootballPlayer();
player.firstName = "Dan"
player.lastName = "Marino"
player.number = 13

var person: FullName
person = scientist
print(person.getFullName())
person = player
print(player.getFullName())
```

In the preceding code, we begin by creating an instance of the `Scientist` class and the `FootballPlayer` structure. We then create a `person` variable that is of the `FullName` (protocol) type and set it to the `scientist` instance that we just created. We then call the `getFullName()` method to retrieve our description. This will print out the `Kara Hoffman studies Physics` message to the console.

We then set the `person` variable equal to the `player` instance and call the `getFullName()` method again. This will print out the `Dan Marino has the number 13` message to the console.

As we can see, the `person` variable does not care what the actual implementation class or structure is. Since we defined the `person` variable to be of the `FullName` type, we can set the `person` variable to an instance of any class or structure that conforms to the `FullName` protocol.

Optional requirements

There are times when we want protocols to define optional requirements, that is, methods or properties that are not required to be implemented. To use optional requirements, we need to start off by marking the protocol with the `@objc` attribute. To mark a property or method as optional, we use the `optional` keyword.

One very important thing to note about using the `@objc` attribute is that only classes can adopt protocols marked with it; structures cannot adopt these protocols.

Let's look at how we would use the `optional` keyword to define optional properties and methods:

```
@objc protocol Phone {
  var phoneNumber: String {get set}
  optional var emailAddress: String {get set}

  func dialNumber()
  optional func getEmail()
}
```

In the `Phone` protocol we just created, we defined a required property named `phoneNumber`, and an optional property named `emailAddress`. Also, in the `Phone` protocol, we defined a required function named `dialNumber()` and an optional function named `getEmail()`. This means that a class that adopts the `Phone` protocol must provide a `phoneNumber` property and a `dialNumber()` method. A class that adopts the Phone protocol can also optionally provide an `emailAddress` property and a `getEmail()` method, but it is not required too.

Swift 2 adds protocol extensions to Swift. This is a very exciting and important feature in the Swift language. To read about protocol extensions, please refer to *Chapter 6, Using Protocols and Protocol Extensions.*

There are times when we need to add additional functionality to an existing class or structure. To do this, we use extensions.

Extensions

With extensions, we can add new properties, methods, initializers, and subscripts, or make an existing class or structure conform to a protocol. One thing to note is that extensions cannot override the existing functionality.

To define an extension, we use the `extension` keyword, followed by the type that we are extending. The following example shows how we would create an extension that extends the string class:

```
extension String {
  //add new functionality here
}
```

Let's see how extensions work by adding a `reverse()` method and a `firstLetter` property to Swift's standard string class:

```
extension String {
    var firstLetter: Character {
        get {
            return self.characters.first
        }
    }

    func reverse() -> String {
        var reverse = ""
        for letter in self.characters {
            reverse = "\(letter)" + reverse
        }
        return reverse
    }
}
```

When we extend an existing class or structure, we define properties, methods, initializers, subscripts, and protocols in exactly the same way as we would normally define them in a standard class or structure. In the string extension example, we see that we define the `reverse()` method and the `firstLetter` property exactly as we would define them in a normal class.

Extensions are very useful for adding additional functionality to classes and structures from external frameworks, even for Apple's frameworks, as demonstrated in the examples. It is preferred to use extensions to add additional functionality to classes from external frameworks rather than subclassing because it allows us to use the classes provided by the frameworks throughout our code.

Memory management

As I mentioned at the start of this chapter, structures are value types and classes are reference types. What this means is that when we pass an instance of a structure within our application, such as a parameter of a method, we create a new instance of the structure in the memory. This new instance of the structure is only valid while the application is in the scope where the structure was created. Once the structure goes out of scope, the new instance of the structure is destroyed and the memory is released. This makes memory management of structures pretty easy and somewhat painless.

Classes, on the other hand, are of the reference type. This means that we allocate the memory for the instance of the class only once when it is initially created. When we want to pass an instance of the class within our application, as either a function argument or by assigning it to a variable, we really pass a reference to where the instance is stored in the memory. Since the instance of a class may be referenced in multiple scopes (unlike a structure), it cannot be automatically destroyed, and memory is not released when it goes out of scope if it is referenced in another scope. Therefore, Swift need some form of memory management to track and release the memory used by instances of classes when the class is no longer needed. Swift uses **Automatic Reference Counting (ARC)** to track and manage memory usage.

With ARC, for the most part, memory management in Swift simply works. ARC will automatically track the references to instances of classes, and when an instance is no longer needed (no references pointing to it), ARC will automatically destroy the instance and release the memory. There are a few instances where ARC requires additional information about relationships to properly manage the memory. Before we look at the instances where ARC needs help, let's look at how memory management and ARC work.

Reference versus value types

Let's look at an example that illustrates how a reference type (instance of a class) and a value type (instance of a structure or a variable) are passed to a function. We will begin by defining a new class named `MyClass` and a new structure named `MyStruct`. The `MyClass` class and the `MyStruct` structure each contain one property named `name`:

```
class MyClass {
  var name = ""
}

struct MyStruct {
  var name = ""
}
```

We will now create a function that will accept, as parameters, one instance of the `MyClass` class and one instance of the `MyStruct` struct. Within the function, we will change the value of the `name` property of both the `MyClass` class and the `MyStruct` structure. Then, by examining the value of that property once the function exits, we will be able to see how instances of a class and structure are passed to functions. Here is the code for the `showPass()` function:

```
func showPass(myc: MyClass, var mys: MyStruct) {
    print("Received Class: \(myc.name) Struct: \(mys.name)")
    myc.name = "Set in function - class"
```

```
        mys.name = "Set in function - struct"
        print("Set  Class: \(myc.name) Struct: \(mys.name)")
    }
```

In the `showPass()` function, we print the values of the named properties for both the `MyClass` and `MyStruct` instances to the console. We then change the values of the named properties and reprint the values to the console again. This will show us the value of the properties when the function first begins and the value after the properties were changed (just before the function exits).

Now, to see how a reference type and a value type are passed to a function, we will create an instance of both the `MyClass` class and the `MyStruct` structure, set the values of the `name` properties, and pass those instances to the `showPass()` function. The function will then change the values of the `name` properties and then return control back to the code that calls it. Finally, we will examine the value of the name properties after the `showPass()` function exits to see whether they have their original value or the value set in the function. Here is the code to do this:

```
var mci = MyClass()
mci.name = "set in main - class"

var msi = MyStruct()
msi.name = "set in main - struct"

print("Main  Class: \(mci.name) Struct: \(msi.name)")

showPass(mci, msi)
print("Main  Class: \(mci.name) Struct: \(msi.name)")
```

If we run this code, we see the following output:

```
Received Class: set in main - class Struct: set in main - struct
Set Class: Set in function - class Struct: Set in function -
struct
Main Class: Set in function - class Struct: set in main - struct
```

As we can see from the output, the `showPass()` function receives the instance of the class and structure with the name properties set to `set in main - class` and `set in main - struct`, respectively. Next, just before the function exits we see, that the `name` property of the class is set to `Set in function - class` and the `name` property of the structure is set to `Set in function - struct`. Finally, when the function exits and we are back to the main part of the code, we see that the `name` property of the class is set to `Set in function - class`, which was set in the `showPass()` function. However, the `name` property of the structure has the value that was originally set prior to calling the function, `set in main - struct`.

This example illustrates that when we pass a reference type (instance of a class) to a function, we are passing a reference to the original class that means any changes we make are kept when the function exits. When we pass a value type (instance of a structure or a variable) to a function, we are passing the value (copy of the instance), which means any changes that we make are made to the local copy and are lost once the function exits.

The working of ARC

Whenever we create a new instance of a class, ARC allocates the memory needed to store that class. This ensures that there is enough memory to store the information associated with that instance of the class, and also locks the memory so that nothing overwrites it. When the instance of the class is no longer needed, ARC will release the memory allocated for the class so that it can be used for other purposes. This ensures that we are not tying up memory that is no longer needed.

If ARC were to release the memory for an instance of a class that we still needed, it would not be possible to retrieve the class information from memory. If we did try to access the instance of the class after the memory was released, there is a possibility that our application would crash. To ensure memory is not released for an instance of a class that is still needed, ARC counts how many times the instance is referenced (how many active properties, variables, or constants are pointing to the instance of the class). Once the reference count for an instance of a class equals zero (nothing is referencing the instance), the memory is released.

All of the previous examples run properly in a Playground, the following examples will not. When we run sample code in a Playground, ARC does not release objects that we create; this is by design so that we can see how the application runs and also the state of the objects at each step. Therefore, we will need to run these samples as an iOS or OS X project. Let's look at an example of how ARC works.

We begin by creating a `MyClass` class with the following code:

```
class MyClass {
  var name = ""
  init(name: String) {
    self.name = name
    print("Initializing class with name \(self.name)")
  }
  deinit {
   print("Releasing class with name \(self.name)")
  }
}
```

This class is very similar to our previous `MyClass` class, except that we add a deinitializer that is called just before an instance of the class is destroyed and removed from memory. This deinitializer prints out a message to the console that lets us know that the instance of the class is about to be removed.

Now, let's look at the code that shows how ARC creates and destroys instances of a class:

```
var class1ref1: MyClass? = MyClass(name: "One")
var class2ref1: MyClass? = MyClass(name: "Two")
var class2ref2: MyClass? = class2ref1

print("Setting class1ref1 to nil")
class1ref1 = nil

print("Setting class2ref1 to nil")
class2ref1 = nil

print("Setting class2ref2 to nil")
class2ref2 = nil
```

In the example, we begin by creating two instances of the `MyClass` class named `class1ref1` (which stands for class 1 reference 1) and `class2ref1` (which stands for class 2 reference 1). We then create a second reference to `class2ref1` named `class2ref2`. Now, in order to see how ARC works, we need to begin setting the references to nil. We start out by setting the `class1ref1` to `nil`. Since there is only one reference to `class1ref1`, the deinitializer will be called. Once the deinitializer completes its task, in our case, it prints a message to the console letting us know that the instance of the class has been destroyed and the memory has been released.

We then set the `class2ref1` to nil, but there is a second reference to this class (`class2ref2`) that prevents ARC from destroying the instance so that the deinitializer is not called. Finally, we set `class2ref2` to nil, which allows ARC to destroy this instance of the `MyClass` class.

If we run this code, we will see the following output, which illustrates how ARC works:

```
Initializing class with name One
Initializing class with name Two
Setting class1ref1 to nil
Releasing class with name One
Setting class2ref1 to nil
Setting class2ref2 to nil
Releasing class with name Two
```

From the example, it seems that ARC handles memory management very well. However, it is possible to write code that will prevent ARC from working properly.

Strong reference cycles

A strong reference cycle is where the instance of two classes holds a strong reference to each other, preventing ARC from releasing either instance. Strong reference cycles are a lot easier to understand with an example, so let's create one. Once again, we are not able to use a Playground for this example, so we need to create an Xcode project. In the project, we start off by creating two classes named `MyClass1` and `MyClass2` with the following code:

```
class MyClass1 {
  var name = ""
  var class2: MyClass2?

  init(name: String) {
    self.name = name
    print("Initializing class with name \(self.name)")
  }
  deinit {
    print("Releaseing class with name \(self.name)")
  }

}

class MyClass2 {
  var name = ""
  var class1: MyClass1?

  init(name: String) {
    self.name = name
    print("Initializing class2 with name \(self.name)")
  }
  deinit {
    print("Releaseing class2 with name \(self.name)")
  }

}
```

As we can see from the code, `MyClass1` contains an instance of `MyClass2`; therefore, the instance of `MyClass2` cannot be released until `MyClass1` is destroyed. We can also see from the code that `MyClass2` contains an instance of `MyClass1`; therefore, the instance of `MyClass1` cannot be released until `MyClass2` is destroyed. This creates a cycle of dependency in which neither instance can be destroyed until the other one is destroyed. Let's see how this works by running the following code:

```
var class1: MyClass1? = MyClass1(name: "Class1")
var class2: MyClass2? = MyClass2(name: "Class2")
//class1 and class2 each have a reference count of 1
      .
class1?.class2 = class2
//Class2 now has a reference count of 2
class2?.class1 = class1
//class1 now has a reference count of 2
      .
print("Setting classes to nil")
class2 = nil
//class2 now has a reference count of 1, not destroyed
class1 = nil
//class1 now has a reference count of 1, not destroyed
```

As we can see from the comments in the example, the reference counters for each instance never reaches zero; therefore, ARC cannot destroy the instances, thereby creating a memory leak. A memory leak is where an application continues to use memory but does not properly release it. This can cause an application to eventually crash.

To resolve a strong reference cycle, we need to prevent one of the classes from keeping a strong hold on the instance of the other class, thereby allowing ARC to destroy them both. Swift provides two ways of doing this by letting us define the properties as either a weak reference or an unowned reference.

The difference between a weak reference and an unowned reference is that the instance which a weak reference refers to can be nil, whereas the instance that an unowned reference is referring to cannot be nil. This means that when we use a weak reference, the property must be an optional property since it can be nil. Let's see how we would use unowned and weak references to resolve a strong reference cycle. Let's start by looking at the unowned reference.

We begin by creating two more classes, `MyClass3` and `MyClass4`:

```
class MyClass3 {
    var name = ""
    unowned let class4: MyClass4
```

```
    init(name: String, class4: MyClass4) {
        self.name = name
        self.class4 = class4
        print("Initializing class3 with name \(self.name)")
    }
    deinit {
        print("Releasing class3 with name \(self.name)")
    }

}

class MyClass4{
    var name = ""
    var class3: MyClass3?

    init(name: String) {
        self.name = name
        print("Initializing class4 with name \(self.name)")
    }
    deinit {
        print("Releasing class4 with name \(self.name)")
    }
}
```

The `MyClass4` class looks pretty similar to the `MyClass1` and `MyClass2` classes in the preceding example. What is different here is the `MyClass3` class. In the `MyClass3` class, we set the `class4` property to `unowned`, which means it cannot be nil and it does not keep a strong reference to the `MyClass4` instance that it is referring to. Since the `class4` property cannot be `nil`, we also need to set it when the class is initialized.

Now let's see how we can initialize and deinitialize the instances of these classes with the following code:

```
var class4 = MyClass4(name: "Class4")
var class3: MyClass3? = MyClass3(name: "class3", class4: class4)

class4.class3 = class3

print("Classes going out of scope")
```

In the preceding code, we create an instance of the `MyClass4` class and then use that instance to create an instance of the `MyClass3` class. We then set the `class3` property of the `MyClass4` instance to the `MyClass3` instance we just created. This creates a reference cycle of dependency between the two classes again, but this time, the `MyClass3` instance is not keeping a strong hold on the `MyClass4` instance, allowing ARC to release both instances when they are no longer needed.

If we run this code, we see the following output, showing that both the `MyClass3` and `MyClass4` instances are released and the memory is freed:

```
Initializing class4 with name Class4
Initializing class3 with name class3
Classes going out of scope.
Releasing class4 with name Class4
Releasing class3 with name class3
```

Now let's look at how we would use a weak reference to prevent a strong reference cycle. We begin by creating two new classes:

```
class MyClass5 {
  var name = ""
  var class6: MyClass6?
  init(name: String) {
    self.name = name
    print("Initializing class5 with name \(self.name)")
  }
  deinit {
    print("Releasing class5 with name \(self.name)")
  }
}

class MyClass6 {
  var name = ""
  weak var class5: MyClass5?
  init(name: String) {
    self.name = name
    print("Initializing class6 with name \(self.name)")
  }
  deinit {
    print("Releasing class6 with name \(self.name)")
  }
}
```

The `MyClass5` and `MyClass6` classes look very similar to the `MyClass1` and `MyClass2` classes we created earlier to show how a strong reference cycle works. The big difference is that we define the `class5` property in the `MyClass6` class as a weak reference.

Now, let's see how we can initialize and deinitialize instances of these classes with the following code:

```
var class5: MyClass5? = MyClass5(name: "Class5")
var class6: MyClass6? = MyClass6(name: "Class6")

class5?.class6 = class6
class6?.class5 = class5

print("Classes going out of scope ")
```

In the preceding code, we create instances of the `MyClass5` and `MyClass6` classes and then set the properties of those classes to point to the instance of the other class. Once again, this creates a cycle of dependency, but since we set the `class5` property of the `MyClass6` class to weak, it does not create a strong reference, allowing both instances to be released.

If we run the code, we will see the following output, showing that both the `MyClass5` and `MyClass6` instances are released and the memory is freed:

```
Initializing class5 with name Class5
Initializing class6 with name Class6
Classes going out of scope.
Releasing class5 with name Class5
Releasing class6 with name Class6
```

It is recommended that we avoid creating circular dependencies, as shown in this section, but there are times when we need them. For those times, remember that ARC does need some help to release them.

Summary

As this chapter ends, we end the introduction to the Swift programming language. At this point, we have enough knowledge of the Swift language to begin writing our own applications; however, there is still much to learn.

In the following chapters, we will look in more depth at some of the concepts that we already discussed, such as optionals and subscripts. We will also show how we would perform common tasks with Swift, such as parsing common file formats and handling concurrency. Finally, we will also have some chapters that will help us write better code like a sample Swift style guide, and a chapter on design patterns.

6
Using Protocols and Protocol Extensions

While watching the presentations from WWDC 2015 about protocol extensions and protocol-oriented programming, I will admit that I was very skeptical. I have worked with object-oriented programming for so long that I was unsure if this new programming paradigm would solve all of the problems that Apple was claiming it would. Since I am not one to let my skepticism get in the way of trying something new, I set up a new project that mirrored the one I was currently working on, but wrote the code using Apple's recommendations for protocol-oriented programming and used protocol extensions extensively in the code. I can honestly say that I was amazed with how much cleaner the new project was compared to the original one. I believe that protocol extensions is going to be one of those defining features that set one programming language apart from the rest. I also believe that many major languages will soon have similar features.

In this chapter, you will learn:

- How protocols are used as a type
- How to implement polymorphism in Swift using protocols
- How to use protocol extensions
- Why we would want to use protocol extensions

Protocol extensions are the backbone for Apple's new protocol-oriented programming paradigm and are arguably one of the most important additions to the Swift programming language. With protocol extensions, we are able to provide method and property implementations to any type that conforms to a protocol. To really understand how useful protocols and protocol extensions are, let's get a better understanding of protocols.

> While classes, structs, and enums can all conform to protocols in Swift, for this chapter, we will be focusing on classes and structs. Enums are used when we need to represent a finite number of cases and while there are valid use cases where we would have an enum conform to a protocol, they are very rare in my experience. Just remember that anywhere that we refer to a class or struct, we can also use an enum.

Let's begin exploring protocols by seeing how they are full-fledged types in Swift.

Protocols as types

Even though no functionality is implemented in a protocol, they are still considered a full-fledged type in the Swift programming language and can be used like any other type. What this means is we can use protocols as a parameter type or a return type in a function. We can also use them as the type for variables, constants, and collections. Let's take a look at some examples. For these few examples, we will use the `PersonProtocol` protocol:

```
protocol PersonProtocol {
    var firstName: String {get set}
    var lastName: String {get set}
    var birthDate: NSDate {get set}
    var profession: String {get}

    init (firstName: String, lastName: String, birthDate: NSDate)
}
```

In this first example, we will see how we would use protocols as a parameter type or return type in functions, methods, or initializers:

```
func updatePerson(person: PersonProtocol) -> PersonProtocol {
    // Code to update person goes here
    return person
}
```

In this example, the `updatePerson()` function accepts one parameter of the `PersonProtocol` protocol type and then returns a value of the `PersonProtocol` protocol type. Now let's see how we can use protocols as a type for constants, variables, or properties:

```
var myPerson: PersonProtocol
```

In this example, we create a variable of the `PersonProtocol` protocol type that is named `myPerson`. We can also use protocols as the item type to store in collection such as arrays, dictionaries, or sets:

```
var people: [PersonProtocol] = []
```

In this final example, we create an array of `PersonProtocol` protocol types. As we can see from these three examples, even though the `PersonProtocol` protocol does not implement any functionality, we can still use protocols when we need to specify a type. We cannot, however, create an instance of a protocol. This is because no functionality is implemented in a protocol. As an example, if we tried to create an instance of the `PersonProtocol` protocol, we would be receiving the `error: protocol type 'PersonProtocol' cannot be instantiated error`, as shown in the following example:

```
var test = PersonProtocol(firstName: "Jon", lastName: "Hoffman",
 birthDate: bDateProgrammer)
```

We can use the instance of any class or struct that conforms to our protocol anywhere that the protocol type is required. As an example, if we defined a variable to be of the `PersonProtocol` protocol type, we could then populate that variable with any class or struct that conforms to the `PersonProtocol` protocol. For this example, let's assume that we have two types named `SwiftProgrammer` and `FootballPlayer`, which conform to the `PersonProtocol` protocol:

```
var myPerson: PersonProtocol

myPerson = SwiftProgrammer(firstName: "Jon", lastName: "Hoffman",
birthDate: bDateProgrammer)
print("\(myPerson.firstName) \(myPerson.lastName)")

myPerson = FootballPlayer(firstName: "Dan", lastName: "Marino",
birthDate: bDatePlayer)
print("\(myPerson.firstName) \(myPerson.lastName)")
```

In this example, we start off by creating the `myPerson` variable of the `PersonProtocol` protocol type. We then set the variable with an instance of the `SwiftProgrammer` type and print out the first and last names. Next, we set the `myPerson` variable to an instance of the `FootballPlayer` type and print out the first and last names again. One thing to note is that Swift does not care if the instance is a class or struct. It only matters that the type conforms to the `PersonProtocol` protocol type. Therefore, if our `SwiftProgrammer` type was a struct and the `FootballPlayer` type was a class, our previous example would be perfectly valid.

As we saw earlier, we can use our `PersonProtocol` protocol as the type for an array. This means that we can populate the array with instances of any type that conforms to the `PersonProtocol` protocol. Once again, it does not matter if the type is a class or a struct as long as it conforms to the `PersonProtocol` protocol. Here is an example of this:

```
var programmer = SwiftProgrammer(firstName: "Jon", lastName:
"Hoffman", birthDate: bDateProgrammer)

var player = FootballPlayer(firstName: "Dan", lastName: "Marino",
birthDate: bDatePlayer)

var people: [PersonProtocol] = []
people.append(programmer)
people.append(player)
```

In this example, we create an instance of the `SwiftProgrammer` type and an instance of the `FootballPlayer` type. We then add both instances to the `people` array.

Polymorphism with protocols

What we were seeing in the previous examples is a form of polymorphism. The word polymorphism comes from the Greek roots *Poly*, meaning many and *morphe*, meaning form. In programming languages, polymorphism is a single interface to multiple types (many forms). In the previous example, the single interface was the `PersonProtocol` protocol and the multiple types were any type that conforms to that protocol.

Polymorphism gives us the ability to interact with multiple types in a uniform manner. To illustrate this, we can extend our previous example where we created an array of the `PersonProtocol` types and loop through the array. We can then access each item in the array using the properties and methods define in the `PersonProtocol` protocol, regardless of the actual type. Let's see an example of this:

```
for person in people {
    print("\(person.firstName) \(person.lastName):
    \(person.profession)")
}
```

If we ran this example, the output would look similar to this:

```
Jon Hoffman: Swift Programmer
Dan Marino: Football Player
```

We have mentioned a few times in this chapter that when we define the type of a variable, constant, collection type, and so on to be a protocol type, we can then use the instance of any type that conforms to that protocol. This is a very important concept to understand and it is what makes protocols and protocol extensions so powerful.

When we use a protocol to access instances, as shown in the previous example, we are limited to using only properties and methods that are defined in the protocol. If we want to use properties or methods that are specific to the individual types, we would need to cast the instance to that type.

Type casting with protocols

Type casting is a way to check the type of the instance and/or to treat the instance as a specified type. In Swift, we use the `is` keyword to check if an instance is a specific type and the `as` keyword to treat the instance as a specific type.

To start with, let's see how we would check the instance type using the `is` keyword. The following example shows how would we do this:

```
for person in people {
  if person is SwiftProgrammer {
     print("\(person.firstName) is a Swift Programmer")
}
}
```

In this example, we use the `if` conditional statement to check whether each element in the people array is an instance of the `SwiftProgrammer` type and if so, we print that the person is a Swift programmer to the console. While this is a good method to check whether we have an instance of a specific class or struct, it is not very efficient if we wanted to check for multiple types. It is a lot more efficient to use the `switch` statement, as shown in the next example, if we want to check for multiple types:

```
for person in people {
    switch (person) {
    case is SwiftProgrammer:
        print("\(person.firstName) is a Swift Programmer")
    case is FootballPlayer:
        print("\(person.firstName) is a Football Player")
    default:
        print("\(person.firstName) is an unknown type")
    }
}
```

In the previous example, we showed how to use the `switch` statement to check the instance type for each element of the array. To do this check, we use the `is` keyword in each of the `case` statements in an attempt to match the instance type.

In *Chapter 4, Control Flow and Functions*, we saw how to filter conditional statements with the `where` statement. We can also use the `where` statement with the `is` keyword to filter the array, as shown in the following example:

```
for person in people where person is SwiftProgrammer {
    print("\(person.firstName) is a Swift Programmer")

}
```

Now let's look at how we can cast an instance of a class or struct to a specific type. To do this, we can use the `as` keyword. Since the cast can fail if the instance is not of the specified type, the `as` keyword comes in two forms: `as?` and `as!`. With the `as?` form, if the casting fails, it returns a nil, and with the `as!` form, if the casting fails, we get a runtime error; therefore, it is recommended to use the `as?` form unless we are absolutely sure of the instance type or we perform a check of the instance type prior to doing the cast.

Let's look at how we would use the `as?` keyword to cast an instance of a class or struct to a specified type:

```
for person in people {
    if let p = person as? SwiftProgrammer {
        print("\(person.firstName) is a Swift Programmer")
    }
}
```

Since the `as?` keyword returns an optional, we can use optional binding to perform the cast, as shown in this example. If we are sure of the instance type, we can use the `as!` keyword. The following example shows how to use the `as!` keyword when we filter the results of the array to only return instances of the `SwiftProgrammer` type:

```
for person in people where person is SwiftProgrammer {
  let p = person as! SwiftProgrammer
}
```

Now that we have covered the basics of protocols, that is, how polymorphism works and type casting, let's dive into one of the most exciting new features of Swift protocol extensions.

Protocol extensions

Protocol extensions allow us to extend a protocol to provide method and property implementations to conforming types. They also allow us to provide common implementations to all the confirming types eliminating the need to provide an implementation in each individual type or the need to create a class hierarchy. While protocol extensions may not seem too exciting, once you see how powerful they really are, they will transform the way you think about and write code.

Let's begin by looking at how we would use protocol extension with a very simplistic example. We will start off by defining a protocol called `DogProtocol` as follows:

```
protocol DogProtocol {
    var name: String {get set}
    var color: String {get set}
}
```

With this protocol, we are saying that any type that conforms to the `DogProtocol` protocol, must have the two properties of the String type, namely, `name` and `color`. Now let's define the three types that conform to this protocol. We will name these types `JackRussel`, `WhiteLab`, and `Mutt` as follows:

```
struct JackRussel: DogProtocol {
    var name: String
    var color: String
}

class WhiteLab: DogProtocol {
    var name: String
    var color: String

    init(name: String, color: String) {
        self.name = name
        self.color = color
    }
}

struct Mutt: DogProtocol {
    var name: String
    var color: String
}
```

We purposely created the `JackRussel` and `Mutt` types as structs and the `WhiteLab` type as a class to show the differences between how the two types are set up and to illustrate how they are treated in the same way when it comes to protocols and protocol extensions. The biggest difference that we can see in this example is the struct types provide a default initiator, but in the class, we must provide the initiator to populate the properties.

Now let's say that we want to provide a method named `speak` to each type that conforms to the `DogProtocol` protocol. Prior to protocol extensions, we would start off by adding the method definition to the protocol, as shown in the following code:

```
protocol DogProtocol {
    var name: String {get set}
    var color: String {get set}
   func speak() -> String
}
```

Once the method is defined in the protocol, we would then need to provide an implementation of the method in every type that conforms to the protocol. Depending on the number of types that conformed to this protocol, this could take a bit of time to implement. The following code sample shows how we might implement this method:

```
struct JackRussel: DogProtocol {
    var name: String
    var color: String
     func speak() -> String {
        return "Woof Woof"
    }
}

class WhiteLab: DogProtocol {
    var name: String
    var color: String

    init(name: String, color: String) {
        self.name = name
        self.color = color
    }
    func speak() -> String {
        return "Woof Woof"
    }

}

struct Mutt: DogProtocol {
```

```
    var name: String
    var color: String
    func speak() -> String {
        return "Woof Woof"
    }

}
```

While this method works, it is not very efficient because anytime we update the protocol, we would need to update all the types that conform to it and we may be duplicating a lot of code, as shown in this example. Another concern is, if we need to change the default behavior of the `speak()` method, we would have to go in each implementation and change the `speak()` method. This is where protocol extensions come in.

With protocol extensions, we could take the `speak()` method definition out of the protocol itself and define it with the default behavior, in protocol extension. The following code shows how we would define the protocol and the protocol extension:

```
protocol DogProtocol {
    var name: String {get set}
    var color: String {get set}
}

extension DogProtocol {
    func speak() -> String {
        return "Woof Woof"
    }
}
```

We begin by defining `DogProtocol` with the original two properties. We then create a protocol extension that extends `DogProtocol` and contains the default implementation of the `speak()` method. With this code, there is no need to provide an implementation of the `speak()` method in each of the types that conform to `DogProtocol` because they automatically receive the implementation as part of the protocol. Let's see how this works by setting our three types that conform to `DogProtocol` back to their original implementations and they should receive the `speak()` method from the protocol extension:

```
struct JackRussel: DogProtocol {
    var name: String
    var color: String
}
class WhiteLab: DogProtocol {
    var name: String
```

```
    var color: String

    init(name: String, color: String) {
        self.name = name
        self.color = color
    }
}

struct Mutt: DogProtocol {
    var name: String
    var color: String
}
```

We can now use each of the types as shown in the following code:

```
let dash = JackRussel(name: "Dash", color: "Brown and White")
let lily = WhiteLab(name: "Lily", color: "White")
let buddy = Mutt(name: "Buddy", color: "Brown")
let dSpeak = dash.speak()  // returns "woof woof"
let lSpeak = lily.speak()  // returns "woof woof"
let bSpeak = buddy.speak() // returns "woof woof"
```

As we can see in this example, by adding the `speak()` method to the `DogProtocol` protocol extension, we are automatically adding that method to all the types that conform to `DogProtocol`. The `speak()` method in the `DogProtocol` protocol extension can be considered a default implementation of the `speak()` method because we are able to override it in the type implementations. As an example, we could override the `speak()` method in the `Mutt` struct, as shown in the following code:

```
struct Mutt: DogProtocol {
    var name: String
    var color: String
    func speak() -> String {
        return "I am hungry"
    }
}
```

When we call the `speak()` method for an instance of the `Mutt` type, it will return the string, `"I am hungry"`.

Now that we have seen how we would use protocols and protocol extensions, let's look at a more real-world example. In numerous apps across multiple platforms (iOS, Android, and Windows), I have had the requirement to validate user input as it is entered. This validation can be done very easily with regular expressions; however, we do not want various regular expressions littered throughout our code. It is very easy to solve this problem by creating different classes or structs that contains the validation code; however, we would have to organize these classes to make them easy to use and maintain. Prior to protocol extensions in Swift, I would use protocols to define the validation requirements and then create a struct that would conform to the protocol for each validation that I needed. Let's take a look at this preprotocol extension method.

A regular expression is a sequence of characters that define a particular pattern. This pattern can then be used to search a string to see whether the string matches the pattern or contains a match of the pattern. Most major programming languages contain a regular expression parser, and if you are not familiar with regular expressions, it may be worthwhile to learn more about them.

The following code shows the `TextValidationProtocol` protocol that defines the requirements for any type that we want to use for text validation:

```
protocol TextValidationProtocol {

    var regExMatchingString: String {get}
    var regExFindMatchString: String {get}
    var validationMessage: String {get}

    func validateString(str: String) -> Bool
    func getMatchingString(str: String) -> String?
}
```

In this protocol, we define three properties and two methods that any type that conforms to `TextValidationProtocol` must implement. The three properties are:

- `regExMatchingString`: This is a regular expression string used to verify that the input string contains only valid characters.
- `regExFindMatchString`: This is a regular expression string used to retrieve a new string from the input string that contains only valid characters. This regular expression is generally used when we need to validate the input in real time, as the user enters information, because it will find the longest matching prefix of the input string.

- `validationMessage`: This is the error message to display if the input string contains non-valid characters.

The two methods for this protocol are as follows:

- `validateString`: This method will return `true` if the input string contains only valid characters. The `regExMatchingString` property will be used in this method to perform the match.
- `getMatchingString`: This method will return a new string that contains only valid characters. This method is generally used when we need to validate the input real time as the user enters information because it will find the longest matching prefix of the input string. We will use the `regExFindMatchString` property in this method to retrieve the new string.

Now let's see how we would create a struct that conforms to this protocol. The following struct would be used to verify that the input string contains only alpha characters:

```
struct AlphaValidation1: TextValidationProtocol {
    static let sharedInstance = AlphaValidation1()
    private init(){}

    let regExFindMatchString = "^[a-zA-Z]{0,10}"
    let validationMessage = "Can only contain Alpha characters"

    var regExMatchingString: String { get {
        return regExFindMatchString + "$"
        }
    }

    func validateString(str: String) -> Bool {
        if let _ = str.rangeOfString(regExMatchingString, options:
        .RegularExpressionSearch) {
            return true
        } else {
            return false
        }
    }
    func getMatchingString(str: String) -> String? {
        if let newMatch = str.rangeOfString(regExFindMatchString,
        options: .RegularExpressionSearch) {
            return str.substringWithRange(newMatch)
        } else {
            return nil
        }
    }
}
```

In this implementation, the `regExFindMatchString` and `validationMessage` properties are stored properties, and the `regExMatchingString` property is a computed property. We also implement the `validateString()` and `getMatchingString()` methods within the struct.

Normally, we would have several different types that conform to `TextValidationProtocol` where each one would validate a different type of input. As we can see from the `AlphaValidation1` struct, there is a bit of code involved with each validation type. A lot of the code would also be duplicated in each type. The code for both methods (`validateString()` and `getMatchingString()`) and the `regExMatchingString` property would be duplicated in every validation class. This is not ideal, but if we wanted to avoid creating a class hierarchy with a super class that contains the duplicate code (I personally prefer using value types over classes), we would have no other choice. Now let's see how we would implement this using protocol extensions.

With protocol extensions, we need to think about the code a little differently. The big difference is, we neither need, nor want to define everything in the protocol. With standard protocols or when we use class hierarchy, all the methods and properties that you would want to access using the generic superclass or protocol would have to be defined within the superclass or protocol. With protocol extensions, it is preferable for us not to define a property or method in the protocol if we are going to be defining it within the protocol extension. Therefore, when we rewrite our text validation types with protocol extensions, `TextValidationProtocol` would be greatly simplified to look similar to this:

```
protocol TextValidationProtocol {
    var regExFindMatchString: String {get}
    var validationMessage: String {get}
}
```

In original `TextValidationProtocol`, we defined three properties and two methods. As we can see in this new protocol, we are only defining two properties. Now that we have our `TextValidationProtocol` defined, let's create the protocol extension for it:

```
extension TextValidationProtocol {

    var regExMatchingString: String { get {
        return regExFindMatchString + "$"
        }
    }

    func validateString(str: String) -> Bool {
        if let _ = str.rangeOfString(regExMatchingString, options:
        .RegularExpressionSearch) {
```

```
            return true
        } else {
            return false
        }
    }
    func getMatchingString(str: String) -> String? {
        if let newMatch = str.rangeOfString(regExFindMatchString,
        options: .RegularExpressionSearch) {
            return str.substringWithRange(newMatch)
        } else {
            return nil
        }
    }
}
```

In the `TextValidationProtocol` protocol extension, we define the two methods and the third property that were defined in original `TextValidationProtocol`, but were not defined in the new one. Now that we have created our protocol and protocol extension, we are able to define our text validation types. In the following code, we define three structs that we will use to validate text when a user types it in:

```
struct AlphaValidation: TextValidationProtocol {
    static let sharedInstance = AlphaValidation()
    private init(){}

    let regExFindMatchString = "^[a-zA-Z]{0,10}"
    let validationMessage = "Can only contain Alpha characters"
}

struct AlphaNumericValidation: TextValidationProtocol {
    static let sharedInstance = AlphaNumericValidation()
    private init(){}

    let regExFindMatchString = "^[a-zA-Z0-9]{0,15}"
    let validationMessage = "Can only contain Alpha Numeric
    characters"
}


struct DisplayNameValidation: TextValidationProtocol {
    static let sharedInstance = DisplayNameValidation()
    private init(){}

    let regExFindMatchString = "^[\\s?[a-zA-Z0-9\\-_\\s]]{0,15}"
    let validationMessage = "Display Name can contain only contain
    Alphanumeric Characters"
}
```

In each one of the text validation structs, we create a static constant and a private initiator so that we can use the struct as a singleton. For more information on the singleton pattern, please see the *The Singleton design pattern* section of *Chapter 17, Adopting Design Patterns in Swift*.

After we define the singleton pattern, all we do in each type is set the values for the `regExFindMatchString` and `validationMessage` properties. Now, we have not duplicated the code virtually because even if we could, we would not want to define the singleton code in the protocol extension because we would not want to force that pattern on all the conforming types.

To use the text validation classes, we would want to create a dictionary object that would map the `UITextField` objects to the validation class to use it like this:

```
var validators = [UITextField: TextValidationProtocol]()
```

We could then populate the `validators` dictionary as shown here:

```
validators[alphaTextField] = AlphaValidation.sharedInstance

validators[alphaNumericTextField] =
AlphaNumericValidation.sharedInstance

validators[displayNameTextField] =
DisplayNameValidation.sharedInstance
```

We can now set the `EditingChanged` event of the text fields to a single method named `keyPressed()`. To set the edition changed event for each field, we would add the following code to the `viewDidLoad()` method of our view controller:

```
alphaTextField.addTarget(self,   action:Selector("keyPressed:"),
forControlEvents: UIControlEvents.EditingChanged)
alphaNumericTextField.addTarget(self, action:
Selector("keyPressed:"), forControlEvents:
UIControlEvents.EditingChanged)
displayNameTextField.addTarget(self, action:
Selector("keyPressed:"), forControlEvents:
UIControlEvents.EditingChanged)
```

Now let's create the `keyPressed()` method that each text field calls when a user types a character into the field:

```
@IBAction func keyPressed(textField: UITextField) {
        if let validator = validators[textField] where
        !validator.validateString(textField.text!) {
            textField.text =
            validator.getMatchingString(textField.text!)
```

```
            messageLabel?.text = validator.validationMessage
        }
    }
```

In this method, we use the `if let validator = validators[textField]` statement to retrieve the validator for the particular text field and then we use the `where !validator.validateString(textField.text!)` statement to validate the string that the user has entered. If the string fails validation, we use the `getMatchingString()` method to update the text in the text field by removing all the characters from the input string, starting with the first invalid character and then displaying the error message from the text validation class. If the string passes validation, the text in the text field is left unchanged.

In the downloadable code for this book, you will find a sample project that demonstrates how to use the text validation types.

Summary

In this chapter, we saw that protocols are treated as full-fledged types by Swift. We also saw how polymorphism can be implemented in Swift with protocols. We concluded this chapter with an in-depth look at protocol extensions and saw how we would use them in Swift.

Protocols and protocol extensions are the backbone of Apple's new protocol-oriented programming paradigm. This new model for programming has the potential to change the way we write and think about code. While we did not specifically cover protocol-oriented programming in this chapter, understanding the topics in this chapter gives us the solid understanding of protocols and protocol extensions needed to learn about this new programming model.

7
Writing Safer Code with Availability and Error Handling

When I first started writing iOS and OS X applications with Objective-C, one of the most noticeable *deficiencies* was the lack of exception handling when working with the Cocoa and Cocoa Touch frameworks. Most modern programming languages such as Java and C# use `try-catch` blocks or something similar to handle exceptions. While Objective-C did have the `try-catch` block, it wasn't used within the Cocoa frameworks themselves and it never felt like a true part of the language. I do have significant experience with C, so I was able to understand how the Cocoa and Cocoa Touch frameworks received and responded to errors, and to be honest, I actually preferred this method, even though I had grown accustom to exception handling with Java and C#. When Swift was first introduced, I was hoping that Apple would put true error handling into the language, so we would have the option of using it; however, it was not in the initial release of Swift. Now with Swift 2, Apple has added error handling to Swift. While this error handling may look similar to exception handling in Java and C#, there are some very significant differences.

We will cover the following topics in this chapter:

- How to use the `do-catch` block in Swift
- How to represent errors
- How to use the availability attribute

Error handling prior to Swift 2.0

Error handling is the process of responding to and recovering from error conditions within our applications. Prior to Swift 2.0, error reporting followed the same pattern as Objective-C; however, with Swift, we did have the added benefit of using optional return values, where returning a nil would indicate an error within the function.

In the simplest form of error handling, the return value from the function would indicate whether it was successful or not. This return value could be something as simple as a Boolean true/false value or something more complex such as an enum, whose values indicated what actually went wrong if the function was unsuccessful. If we needed to report additional information about the error that occurred, we could add an `NSError` out parameter of the `NSErrorPointer` type, but this wasn't the easiest of approaches and these errors tended to be ignored by developers. The following example illustrates how errors were generally handled prior to Swift 2.0:

```
var str = "Hello World"
var error: NSError

var results = str.writeToFile(path, atomically: true, encoding:
NSUTF8StringEncoding, error: &error)

if results {
  // successful code here
} else {
    println("Error writing filer:  \(error)")
}
```

While handling errors in this manner works well and can be modified to suit most needs, it definitely is not the perfect solution. There are a couple of issues with this solution, with the biggest being that it is easy for developers to ignore both the value that is returned and the error itself. While most experienced developers will be very careful to check all the errors, sometimes, it is hard for novice developers to understand what and when to check, especially if the function does not contain an `NSError` parameter.

In addition to using `NSError`, we could also raise and catch exceptions using the `NSException` class; however, very few developers actually use this method. Even within the Cocoa and Cocoa Touch frameworks, this method of exception handling was rarely ever used.

While using the `NSError` class and return values to handle errors does work well, there were many people, including me, who were disappointed that Apple did not include additional error handling when Swift was originally released. Well, now with Swift 2.0, we do have native error handling.

Error handling in Swift 2

Languages such as Java and C# generally refer to the error handling process as *exception handling*; within the Swift documentation, Apple refers to this process as *error handling*. While on the outside, the Java and C# exception handling may look very similar to Swift's error handling, there are some significant differences that those familiar with exception handling in the other language will notice throughout this chapter.

Representing errors

Before we can really understand how error handling works in Swift, we must first see how we would represent an error. In Swift, errors are represented by values of types that conform to the `ErrorType` protocol. Swift's enums are very well-suited to modeling the error conditions because generally, we have a finite number of error conditions to represent.

Let's look at how we would use an enum to represent an error. For this, we will define a fictitious error named `MyError` with three error conditions: `Minor`, `Bad`, and `Terrible`:

```
enum MyError: ErrorType {
    case Minor
    case Bad
    case Terrible
}
```

In this example, we define that the `MyError` enum conforms to the `ErrorType` protocol. We then define the three error conditions: `Minor`, `Bad`, and `Terrible`. We can also use the associated values with our error conditions. Let's say that we wanted to add a description to one of the error conditions; we would do it like this:

```
enum MyError: ErrorType {
    case Minor
    case Bad
    case Terrible (description: String)
}
```

Those who are familiar with exception handling in Java and C# can see that representing errors in Swift is a lot cleaner and easier. Another advantage that we have is it is very easy to define multiple error conditions and group them together, so all the related error conditions are of one type.

Now let's see how we would model errors in Swift. For this example, let's look at how we would assign numbers to players in a baseball team. In a baseball team, every new player who is called up is assigned a unique number for that team. This number also must be within a certain range of numbers. In this case, we would have three error conditions: number is too large, number is too small, or number is not unique. The following example shows how we might represent these error conditions:

```
enum PlayerNumberError: ErrorType {
    case NumberTooHigh(description: String)
    case NumberTooLow(description: String)
    case NumberAlreadyAssigned
}
```

With the `PlayerNumberError` type, we define three very specific error conditions that tell us exactly what was wrong. These error conditions are also grouped together in one type since they are all related to assigning player's numbers.

This method of defining errors allows us to define very specific errors that let our code know exactly what went wrong if an error condition occurs and, as we see in our example, it also lets us group our errors, so all of the related errors can be defined in the same type.

Now that we know how to represent errors, let's look at how we would throw errors.

Throwing errors

When an error occurs in a function, the code that called the function must be made aware of it; this is called **throwing the error**. When a function throws an error, it assumes that the code that called the function, or some code further up the chain, will catch and recover appropriately from the error.

To throw an error from a function we use the `throws` keyword. This keyword lets the code that called it know that an error may be thrown from the function. Unlike exception handling in other languages, we do not list the specific errors types that may be thrown.

Since we do not list the specific error types that may be thrown from a function within the function's definition, it would be good practice to list them in the documentation and comment for the function so that other developers who use our function know what error types to catch.

Let's look at how we would throw errors, but first, let's add a fourth error to our `PlayerNumberError` type that we defined earlier. This error condition is thrown if we are trying to retrieve a player by his or her number but no player is assigned that number. The new `PlayerNumberError` type will now look similar to this:

```
enum PlayerNumberError: ErrorType {
    case NumberTooHigh(description: String)
    case NumberTooLow(description: String)
    case NumberAlreadyAssigned
    case NumberDoesNotExist
}
```

To demonstrate how to throw errors, we will begin by creating a `BaseballTeam` struct that will contain a list of player for a given team. These players will be stored in a dictionary object named `players` and will use the player's number as the key. The `BaseballPlayer` type, which will be used to represent a single player, will be a `typealias` for a tuple type and is defined like this:

```
typealias BaseballPlayer = (firstName: String, lastName: String,
number: Int)
```

In this `BaseballTeam` struct, we will have two methods. The first one will be named `addPlayer()`. This will have one parameter of the `BaseballPlayer` type and will attempt to add the player to the team. This method could throw one of the three error conditions: `NumberTooHigh`, `NumberTooLow`, or `NumberAlreadyExists`. Here is how we would write this method:

```
    mutating func addPlayer(player: BaseballPlayer) throws {

        guard player.number < maxNumber else {
            throw PlayerNumberError.NumberTooHigh(description: "Max
number is \(maxNumber)")
        }

        guard player.number > minNumber else {
            throw PlayerNumberError.NumberTooLow(description: "Min
number is \(minNumber)")
        }

        guard players[player.number] == nil else {
            throw PlayerNumberError.NumberAlreadyAssigned
        }
        players[player.number] = player
    }
```

In the method's definition, we see that the `throws` keyword is added. The `throws` keyword lets any code that calls this method know that it may throw an error and the errors must be handled. We then use the three `guard` statements. These `guard` statements are used to verify that the number is not too large, not too small, and is unique in the `players` dictionary. If any of the conditions are not met, we throw the appropriate error using the `throw` keyword.

If we make it through all the three checks, the player is added to the `players` dictionary.

The second method that we will be adding to the `BaseballTeam` struct is the `getPlayerByNumber()` method. This method will attempt to retrieve the baseball player that is assigned a given number. If no player is assigned that number, this method will throw a `PlayerNumberError.NumberDoesNotExist` error. The `getPlayerByNumber()` method will look similar to this:

```
func getPlayerByNumber(number: Int) throws -> BaseballPlayer {
    if let player = players[number] {
        return player
    } else {
        throw PlayerNumberError.NumberDoesNotExist
    }
}
```

In this method definition, we see that it can throw an error because we use the `throws` keyword within the definition. The `throws` keyword must be placed before the `return` type in the method definition.

Within the method, we attempt to retrieve the baseball player with the number that is passed into the method. If we are able to retrieve the player, we return it; otherwise, we throw the `PlayerNumberError.NumberDoesNotExist` error. Notice that if we throw an error from a method that has a `return` type, we do not need to return a value.

Now let's see how we would catch an error with Swift.

Catching errors

When an error is thrown from a function, we need to catch it in the code that called the function; this is done using the `do-catch` block. The `do-catch` block takes the following syntax:

```
do {
    try [Some function that throws]
```

```
    [Any additional code]
} catch [pattern] {
    [Code if function threw error]
}
```

If an error is thrown, it is propagated out until it is handled by a `catch` clause. The `catch` clause consists of the `catch` keyword, followed by a pattern to match the error against. If the error matches the pattern, the code within the `catch` block is executed.

Let's look at how we would use the `do-catch` block by calling both the `getPlayerByNumber()` and `addPlayer()` methods of the `BaseballTeam` struct. Let's look at the `getPlayerByNumber()` method first since it only throws one error condition:

```
do {
    let player = try myTeam.getPlayerByNumber(34)
    print("Player is \(player.firstName) \(player.lastName)")
} catch PlayerNumberError.NumberDoesNotExist {
    print("No player has that number")
}
```

Within this example, the `do-catch` block calls the `getPlayerByNumber()` method of the `BaseballTeam` struct. This method will throw the `PlayerNumberError.NumberDoesNotExist` error condition if no player on the team has been assigned this number; therefore, we attempt to match that error in our `catch` statement.

Anytime an error is thrown within a `do-catch` block, the remainder of the code within the block is skipped and the code within the `catch` block, which matches the error, is executed. Therefore, in our example, if the `PlayerNumberError.NumberDoesNotExist` error is thrown by the `getPlayerByNumber()` method, then the `print()` function is never reached.

We do not have to include a pattern after the `catch` statement. If a pattern is not included after the `catch` statement or we put an underscore, the `catch` statement will match all error conditions. For example, either one of the following two `catch` statements will catch all errors:

```
do {
    // our statements
} catch {
    // our error conditions
}

do {
```

```
    // our statements
} catch _ {
    // our error conditions
}
```

If we want to capture the error, we can use the `let` keyword, as shown in the following example:

```
do {
    // our statements
} catch let error {
    print("Error:  \(error)")
}
```

Now let's look at how we could use the `catch` statement, similar to a `switch` statement, to catch different error conditions. For this, we will call the `addPlayer()` method of our `BaseballTeam` struct:

```
do {
    try myTeam.addPlayer(("David", "Ortiz", 34))
} catch PlayerNumberError.NumberTooHigh(let description) {
    print("Error: \(description)")
} catch PlayerNumberError.NumberTooLow(let description) {
    print("Error: \(description)")
} catch PlayerNumberError.NumberAlreadyAssigned {
    print("Error: Number already assigned")
}
```

In this example, we have three `catch` statements. Each `catch` statement has a different pattern to match; therefore, they will each match a different error condition. If we recall, the `PlayerNumberError.NumberToHigh` and `PlayerNumberError.NumberToLow` error conditions have associated values. To retrieve the associated value, we use the `let` statement within the parentheses, as shown in the example.

It is always good practice to make your last `catch` statement an empty `catch` so that it will `catch` any error that did not match any of the patterns in the previous `catch` statements. Therefore, the previous example should be rewritten like this:

```
do {
    try myTeam.addPlayer(("David", "Ortiz", 34))
} catch PlayerNumberError.NumberTooHigh(let description) {
    print("Error: \(description)")
} catch PlayerNumberError.NumberTooLow(let description) {
    print("Error: \(description)")
```

```
} catch PlayerNumberError.NumberAlreadyAssigned {
    print("Error: Number already assigned")
} catch {
    print("Error: Unknown Error")
}
```

We can also let the errors propagate out rather than immediately catch them. To do this, we just need to add the `throws` keyword to the function definition. For instance, in the following example, rather than catching the error, we let it propagate out to the code that calls the function rather than handling the error within the function:

```
func myFunc() throws {
    try myTeam.addPlayer(("David", "Ortiz", 34))
}
```

If we are certain that an error will not be thrown, we can call the function using a forced-try expression, which is written as `try!`. The forced-try expression disables error propagation and wraps the function call in a runtime assertion that no error will be thrown from this call. If an error is thrown, we will get a runtime error, so be very careful when using this expression.

When I am working with exceptions in languages such as Java and C#, I see a lot of empty `catch` blocks. This is where we need to catch the exception because one might be thrown; however, we do not want to do anything with it. In Swift, the code would look something like this:

```
do {
    let player = try myTeam.getPlayerByNumber(34)
    print("Player is \(player.firstName) \(player.lastName)")
} catch {}
```

Seeing code like this is one of the things that I dislike about exception handling. Well, the Swift developers have an answer for this: the `try?` keyword. The `try?` keyword attempts to perform an operation that may throw an error. If the operation succeeds, the results are returned in the form of an optional; however, if the operation fails with an error being thrown, the operation returns a nil and the error is discarded.

Since the results of the `try?` keyword are returned in the form of an optional, we would normally want to use this keyword with optional binding. We could rewrite the previous example like this:

```
if let player = try? myTeam.getPlayerByNumber(34) {
    print("Player is \(player.firstName) \(player.lastName)")
}
```

As we can see, the `try?` keyword makes our code much cleaner and easier to read.

If we need to perform some clean up action, regardless of if we had any errors or not, we can use the `defer` statement. We use the `defer` statement to execute a block of code just before code execution leaves the current scope. The following example shows how we would use the `defer` statement:

```
func deferFunction()  {
    print("Function started")
    var str: String?

    defer {
    print("In defer block")
        if let s = str {
            print("str is \(s)")
        }
    }

    str = "Jon"
    print("Function finished")
}
```

If we called this function, the first line that is printed to the console is—`Function started`. The execution of the code would skip over the `defer` block and `Function finished` would be printed to the console next. Finally, the `defer` block of code would be executed just before we leave the function's scope, and we would see the message, `In defer block`. The following is the output from this function:

```
Function started
Function finished
In defer block
str is Jon
```

The `defer` block will always be called before execution leaves the current scope, even if an error is thrown. The `defer` block is very useful when we need to perform some clean up functions prior to leaving a function.

The `defer` statement is very useful when we want to make sure we perform all the necessary clean up, even if an error is thrown. For example, if we successfully open up a file to write to, we will always want to make sure we close that file, even if we have an error during the write operation. We could then put the file closed functionality in a `defer` block to make sure that the file is always closed prior to leaving the current scope.

Now let's look at how we would use the new availability attribute with Swift.

The availability attribute

Using the latest SDK gives us access to all of the latest features for the platform that we are developing for; however, there are times when we want to also target older platforms. Swift allows us to use the availability attribute to safely wrap code to run only when the correct version of the operating system is available. The availability was first introduced in Swift 2.

The availability blocks essentially lets us say, "If we are running the specified version of the operating system or higher, run this code. Otherwise, run some other code." There are two ways in which we can use the `availability` attribute. The first way allows us to execute a specific block of code and can be used with an `if` or `guard` statement. The second way allows us to mark a method or type as available only on certain platforms.

The `availability` attribute accepts up to five comma-separated arguments that allow us to define the minimum version of the operating system or application extension needed to execute our code. These arguments are:

- `iOS`: This is the minimum iOS version that is compatible with our code
- `OSX`: This is the minimum OS X version that is compatible with our code
- `watchOS`: This is the minimum watchOS version that is compatible with our code
- `iOSApplicationExtension`: This is the minimum iOS application extension that is compatible with our code
- `OSXApplicationExtension`: This is the minimum OS X application extension that is compatible with our code

After the argument, we specify the minimum version that is required. We only need to include the arguments that are compatible with our code. As an example, if we are writing an iOS application, we only need to include the `iOS` argument in the `available` attribute. We end the argument list with an `*` (asterisk). Let's look at how we would execute a specific block of code only if we meet the minimum requirements:

```
if #available(iOS 9.0, OSX 10.10, watchOS 2, *) {
     // Available for iOS 9, OSX 10.10, watchOS 2 or above
    print("Minimum requirements met")
} else {
    //  Block on anything below the above minimum requirements
    print("Minimum requirements not met")
}
```

In this example, the `if #available(iOS 9.0, OSX 10.10, watchOS 2, *)` line of code prevents the block of code form executing when the application is run on a system that does not meet the specified minimum operating system version. In this example, we also use the `else` statement to execute a separate block of code if the operating system did not meet the minimum requirements.

We can also restrict access to a function or a type. In the previous code, the `available` attribute was prefixed with the `#` (pound) character. To restrict access to a function or type, we prefix the available attribute with an `@` (at) character. The following example shows how we would restrict access to a type and function:

```
@available(iOS 9.0, *)
func testAvailability() {
    // Function only available for iOS 9 or above
}

@available(iOS 9.0, *)
struct TestStruct {
  // Type only available for iOS 9 or above
}
```

In the previous example, we specify that the `testAvailability()` function and the `testStruct()` type can only be accessed if the code is run on a device that has iOS version 9 or above. In order to use the `@available` attribute to block access to a function or type, we must wrap the code that calls that function or type with the `#available` attribute. The following example shows how we would call the `testAvailability()` function:

```
if #available(iOS 9.0, *) {
    testAvailability()
} else {
     // Fallback on earlier versions
}
```

In this example, the `testAvailability()` function is only called if the application is running on a device that has iOS version 9 or above.

Summary

In this chapter, we looked at the new error-handling features and `availability` attribute that were added in Swift 2. These two features can help us write safer code and make our applications more stable.

The error-handling feature of Swift 2 significantly changes the way Swift programmers handle errors. While we are not required to use this new feature in our custom types, it does give us a uniform manner to handle and respond to error. Apple has also started to use this error handling in the Cocoa and Cocoa Touch frameworks.

The new `availability` attribute allows us to develop applications that take advantage of the latest features of our target operating systems while still allowing our applications to run on older versions.

In the next chapter, we will look at how to create and parse XML and JSON documents.

8

Working with XML and JSON Data

For years, I used **Extensible Markup Language** (**XML**) as the format of choice to exchange data between systems. Its simplicity, readability, and ease of use made it an easy choice. The only real drawback with XML, in my opinion, is the large size of XML documents. Mobile devices, such as iOS devices, rely on exchanging data over mobile networks when they are not connected to a Wi-Fi network. These mobile networks are generally slower than a standard Wi-Fi or cabled networks. Most mobile devices also have data plans that limit the amount of data a user can use in a given month. That was when I really started looking at using **JavaScript Object Notation** (**JSON**) to exchange data between systems. Now, I almost exclusively use JSON to exchange data, especially with mobile devices. Even though, for mobile development, JSON seems to be becoming the format of choice, XML is still very widely used because it is generally easier to read and use than JSON. As a developer, it is a good idea to have a working knowledge of both formats.

In this chapter, we will cover:

- Parsing XML documents
- Building XML documents
- Parsing JSON documents
- Building JSON documents

XML and JSON

It was not that long ago that most consumer-based applications were self-contained and did not need to exchange data with external services. However, in today's age of smartphones and data-driven applications, it is now rare to develop applications that do not need to exchange data with external services. This makes it essential for application developers to know how to exchange data in standard formats.

These days, API designers tend to favor one of the two formats to exchange data—XML or JSON. There have been a number of other data exchange formats that have been promoted over the years, but XML and JSON are, by far, the current leaders. The primary reason for this is that the openness and interoperability of XML and JSON are unmatched by the other data exchange formats. It would be hard to find a public web API that does not offer XML and/or JSON to exchange data.

Apple has provided simple and efficient APIs to work with both XML and JSON data. While there are a number of third-party libraries and frameworks that offer certain advantages and disadvantages over Apple's APIs, in this chapter we will stick with Apple's APIs. Let's look at how we will parse XML and JSON documents with Swift, but first let's create some common files that we will use for the XML and JSON examples in the chapter.

Common files

Let's start by creating a structure that will be used to define the tags that are valid for our XML and JSON documents. These tags will be:

- `books`: This is the root element that encloses all the other elements
- `book`: This element encloses all the information about a particular book
- `author`: This element contains the author's name
- `publisher`: This element contains the publisher's name
- `category`: This element contains the category of the book
- `description`: This element contains the description of the book
- `name`: This is an attribute of the book element in the XML example and a standard element in the JSON example. This element contains the name of the book

The `DocTags` structure will define the seven static properties that will contain the names of these seven tags. This following code shows how to define this structure:

```
struct DocTags {
  static let BOOKS_TAG = "books"
  static let BOOK_TAG = "book"

  static let AUTHOR_TAG = "author"
  static let PUBLISHER_TAG = "publisher"
  static let NAME_TAG = "name"
  static let CATEGORY_TAG = "category"
  static let DESCRIPTION_TAG = "description"
}
```

Rather than using a structure, we could define our document tags in an enum instead. Which one we use is really a matter of preference.

Each of the seven properties defined in the `DocTags` structure is defined with the `static` and `let` keywords. The `static` keyword defines the properties as `static` properties. A `static` property is one that is not associated with any given instances of the structure, and any changes to a `static` property are reflected in all the instances of the structure. The advantage a `static` property has over an `instance` property is that we do not need to create an instance of the structure to use it.

Next, we will need to create a class that will contain the information about each book. We will name this class `Book`:

```
class Book {
  var name = ""
  var author = ""
  var publisher = ""
  var category = ""
  var description = ""
}
```

While Apple recommends that we use value types (structs and enums) over reference types (classes), in the examples for this chapter a reference type is preferred so we can pass the actual instance of our book type as we build it rather than the value.

As we can see, the `Book` class contains five properties. These properties will contain information about each book.

While we are parsing the XML and JSON documents, we will be able to retrieve each element of the document and the value stored within the element; therefore, we will need a way to take that information and set the values of the `Book` properties. With this in mind, let's create a helper function that will take the name of the element and the value associated with it as parameters. We will then set the appropriate property, based on the name of the element. Let's name this function `addValue` and add it to our `Book` class:

```
func addValue(tagName: String, withValue value: String) {
  switch tagName {
  case DocTags.NAME_TAG:
    self.name = value
  case DocTags.AUTHOR_TAG:
    self.author = value
  case DocTags.PUBLISHER_TAG:
    self.publisher = value
  case DocTags.CATEGORY_TAG:
    self.category = value
  case DocTags.DESCRIPTION_TAG:
    self.description = value
  default:
    break
  }
}
```

The `addValue` function will use a `switch` statement to compare the element name to each of the tags defined in the `DocTags` structure. If a match is found, it will set the value of the appropriate property. If no match is found, it will skip that element; normally, we should be able to simply ignore the extra tags.

Generally, the parser code, which we will see next, is not too bad when we are dealing with one class as in this example. When you start to work with more complex XML and JSON documents, which might require multiple classes, having helper methods such as the `addValue` method can significantly clean up the parsing code and make it much easier to read. These helper functions can be in their own class or part of the data storage class (as shown in the preceding example), depending on what works best for your particular application. Usually, I prefer the helper functions separated from the data storage class.

XML and the NSXMLParser class

To parse XML documents in Swift, we will use Apple's `NSXMLParser` class. While there are several alternatives to `NSXMLParser`, each with its own advantages and disadvantages, I have always found `NSXMLParser` to be simple to understand and use. It is also designed in a way that is consistent with Apple's other APIs, which means if we are familiar with Apple's other APIs, `NSXMLParser` will seem pretty straightforward.

The `NSXMLParser` class is a **Simple API for XML (SAX)** parser. SAX parsers provide a mechanism to parse XML documents sequentially. Unlike **Document Object Model (DOM)** parsers, which read the entire document into the memory and then parse it, a SAX parser reports on each parsing event as it happens. This allows for a much smaller memory footprint while parsing. It also means that we need to have code to handle each parsing event that is needed to parse the XML document.

The `NSXMLParser` class can parse XML documents from a URL, an `NSData` object, or through a stream. To parse XML documents from various sources, we initiate the `NSXMLParser` class with the appropriate initializer:

- `Init(contentsOfURL:)`: This initiates the `NSXMLParser` class with the content referenced by the provided URL
- `Init(data:)`: This initiates the `NSXMLParser` class with the content of the `NSData` object
- `Init(stream:)`: This initiates the `NSXMLParser` class with the content from the supplied stream

For this chapter's XML example, we will be using the `init(data:)` initializer to parse a string representation of an XML document. The `NSData` class is designed to work with binary data. The initializer can be easily replaced by any of the other initializers to parse an XML document from a URL or stream. The XML parsing example will be designed to parse the following XML document:

```
<?xml version="1.0"?>
<books>
  <book name="iOS and OS X Network Development Cookbook">
    <author>Jon Hoffman</author>
    <publisher>PacktPub</publisher>
    <category>Programming</category>
    <description>Network development for iOS and OS
      X</description>
  </book>
  <book name="Mastering Swift">
    <author>Jon Hoffman</author>
```

```
        <publisher>PacktPub</publisher>
        <category>Programming</category>
        <description>Learning Swift</description>
      </book>
    </books>
```

Using the NSXMLParserDelegate protocol

The `NSXMLParserDelegate` protocol defines several optional methods that can be defined by the `NSXMLParser` delegate. These methods are called when certain parsing events occur while `NSXMLParser` is parsing XML documents. The `NSXMLParserDelegate` method may also define several optional methods that are used to handle the **Document Type Definition** (**DTD**) markup. The DTD markup defines the legal document structure of an XML document by defining a list of valid elements and attributes.

We will be implementing the following delegate methods for the XML example in this chapter:

- `parserDidStartDocument(_:)`: This method is called when the parser begins parsing the XML document
- `parserDidEndDocument(_:)`: This method is called after the parser has successfully parsed the entire XML document
- `parser(_: didStartElement: namespaceURI: qualifiedName: attributes:)`: This method is called when the parser encounters a start tag for an element
- `parser(_: didEndElement: namespaceURI: qualifiedName:)`: This method is called when the parser encounters an end tag for an element
- `parser(_:parseErrorOccurred:)`: This method is called when the parser encounters a critical error and is unable to parse the document
- `parser(_:foundCharacters:)`: This method is called to provide a string representation of all or part of the characters of the data for the current element

Let's take a look at how we will parse XML documents with `NSXMLParser` and `NSXMLParserDelegate`.

Parsing XML documents

To parse an XML document we begin by creating a class or struct that conforms to the `NSXMLParaseDelegate` protocol. In our example, we will name the class `MyXMLParser`. Our `MyXMLParser` class definition will look like this:

```
class MyXMLParser: NSObject, NSXMLParserDelegate {

   }
```

Within the `MyXMLParser` class, we will add three properties that will be used by the parser while it is parsing the document. These three properties are:

- `books`: This property will be an optional array that will contain the list of books defined in the XML document
- `book`: This will be an optional instance of the `Book` class that represents the current book being parsed within the XML document
- `elementData`: This will be an instance of the string class that contains the value of the current element that is being parsed

These properties will be defined like this:

```
var books: [Book]?
var book: Book?
var elementData = ""
```

Now we need to add the `NSXMLParserDelegate` methods. The first one we add will be the `parseXmlString` method, which will be used to start the `NSXMLParser` class:

```
func parseXmlString(xmlString: String) {
   let xmlData = xmlString.dataUsingEncoding(NSUTF8StringEncoding)
   let parser = NSXMLParser(data: xmlData!)
   parser.delegate = self
   parser.parse()
}
```

We begin the `parseXmlString()` method by converting the `xmlString` variable to an `NSData` object using the `dataUsingEncoding()` method. The `dataUsingEncoding()` method comes from the `NSString` class, but we can use it with our Swift string type because Swift automatically bridges Swift string types to the `NSString` classes.

We then use the `init(data:)` initializer to initialize `NSXMLParser`. This initializer is called like this:

```
NSXMLParser(data: xmlData!)
```

We then set the NSXMLParser delegate to the current instance of the MyXmlParser class. We can do this because the MyXmlParser class conforms to the NSXMLParserDelegate protocol. This allows the current instance of the class to receive alerts as the document is being parsed.

Finally, the parse() method is called to begin parsing the XML document.

Now let's add the parserDidStartDocument() method. This method will be called when NSXMLParser begins parsing the XML document:

```
func parserDidStartDocument(parser: NSXMLParser!) {
  println("Started XML parser")
}
```

In our example, we do not need to perform any setup prior to parsing the document; therefore, the parserDidStartDocument() method just prints the Started XML Parser message to the console.

Now, let's look at the parser(_: didStartElement: namespaceURI: qualifiedName: attributes:) delegate method. Before we implement this delegate method, we need to figure out which elements require us to perform tasks when we encounter their start tags. In our example, we will need to check for the starting tags of two elements—books and book.

The books element is the root element that encloses all the items in the XML document. When we encounter the books element start tag, we will need to initialize the books array. This books array will contain a list of book instances that are generated as we parse the XML document.

When we encounter the start tag for the book element, we will need to create a new instance of the Book class because the start tag means we are starting a new book. We might think that we should also save the current instance of the book property to the books array prior to creating a new instance, but we will do that when we encounter the book end tag rather than the start tag. The implementation always seems to be much cleaner when we save information based on an end tag rather than a start tag.

Here is the code for the parser(_: didStartElement: namespaceURI: qualifiedName: attributes:) delegate method:

```
func parser(parser: NSXMLParser, didStartElement elementName: String,
namespaceURI: String?, qualifiedName qName: String?, attributes
attributeDict: [String : String]) {
    if elementName == DocTags.BOOKS_TAG {
        books = []
    } else if elementName == DocTags.BOOK_TAG {
        book = Book()
```

```
            if let name = attributeDict[DocTags.NAME_TAG] {
                book!.addValue(DocTags.NAME_TAG, withValue: name as!)
            }

        }
    }
```

We begin this method by seeing whether the `elementName` parameter is equal to the `books` tag and, if so, we create a new array that will contain the books defined in the XML document. If the `elementName` parameter is not equal to the `books` tag, we check to see whether it is equal to the `Book` tag. If it is equal to the `book` tag, we set the `book` property to a new instance of the `book` class, clearing any previous saved information. We then check whether the element has an attribute with the `name` key (`name`) and, if so, we set the `name` property of the `book` instance to the value of that attribute. This instance of the `Book` class will contain the information about the book.

The next delegate method that we will implement is the `parser(_:foundCharacters:)` delegate method. This method receives the value or partial value of the element that is being parsed.

```
    func parser(parser: NSXMLParser, foundCharacters string: String) {
      elementData += string
    }
```

Since the value of any given element may be quite large, we may receive the value in pieces rather than in one chunk. This means that the `parser(_:foundCharacters:)` method may be called multiple times for the same element. In our example, we use the `elementData` property to keep track of the value of the current element; thus, in the `parser(_:foundCharacters:)` method, we simply append the value of the string parameter to the `elementData` property. We will clear the `elementData` property when we encounter an end tag for an element.

Next, let's see how to use the `parser(_: didEndElement: namespaceURI: qualifiedName:)` delegate method when the parser encounters the end tag of an element. Before we implement this method, we need to figure out what elements we require to perform a task when we encounter their end tag. In our example, we will need to check whether we encountered the end tag of a `book` element. If we encountered any other tag besides the end of the `book` element, we will use the `addValue()` method of the `book` instance to determine what to do with the value.

When we encounter the end tag for the `book` element, we will need to add the current instance of the `book` property to the `books` array. If this is an end tag for any other element, we will call the `addValue()` method of the current book instance, remembering that the `addValue()` method will ignore any element if it does not recognize the element's name.

We will also need to clear the `elementData` property each time we encounter the end of an element so that the information from the previous element does not corrupt the next element.

The following example shows how we will implement the `parser(_: didEndElement: namespaceURI: qualifiedName:)` delegate method:

```
func parser(parser: NSXMLParser, didEndElement elementName: String,
namespaceURI: String?, qualifiedName qName: String?) {
    if elementName == DocTags.BOOK_TAG {
        if let myBook = book {
            if var _ = books {
                books!.append(myBook)
            }
        }
        book = Book()
    } else if let myBook = book {
        myBook.addValue(elementName, withValue: elementData)
    }
    elementData = ""
}
```

When the parser has completed parsing the document, it will call the `parser(_:parseErrorOccurred:)` delegate method. In our example, we will use this method to simply print the name of the book and author to the screen for each book in the `books` array, as shown in the following code:

```
func parserDidEndDocument(parser: NSXMLParser) {
  if let myBooks = books {
    for myBook in myBooks {
      println("Found - \(myBook.name) \(myBook.author)")
    }
  }
}
```

If an error is encountered while parsing the document, the `parser:parseErrorOccurred:` delegate method is called to handle the error. In our example, we will print the error to the console, but normally we would need to properly handle the error:

```
func parser(parser: NSXMLParser parseErrorOccurred parseError:
  NSError {
  print"Parse Error occurred (parseError)")
}
```

To parse an XML document, we will use the `MyXmlParser` class like this:

```
var xmlParser = MyXMLParser()
xmlParser.parseXmlString(xmlString)
```

Now that we have seen how to parse an XML document, let's take a look at how we create one.

XML and NSXMLDocument

The `NSXMLDocument` class and its related classes make it very easy to create XML documents from our custom object; however, they are only available to OS X-based projects at the time of writing this book. Hopefully, someone at Apple will realize that we need a good way to build XML documents for iOS projects without using third-party frameworks or manually creating the document.

To build an XML document with Swift for OS X-based applications, we will need to use three foundation classes. These classes are as follows:

- `NSNode`: This class is the superclass of the `NSXMLDocument` and `NSXMLElement` classes. This will be used to add attributes to an instance of the `NSXMLElement` class.
- `NSXMLDocument`: This class is the top-level object for the XML document.
- `NSXMLElement`: All the elements in the XML document are instances of the `NSXMLElement` class.

Let's see how to use these three classes to build an XML document. For this, we will create a function named `buildXMLString(books:)`, which takes an array of the `Book` objects as its only parameter:

```
func buildXMLString(books: [Book]?)] -> String {
  if let myBooks = books {
    let xmlRoot = NSXMLElement(name: DocTags.BOOKS_TAG)
    let xmlData = NSXMLDocument(rootElement: xmlRoot)
    for book in myBooks {
      let bookElement = NSXMLElement(name: DocTags.BOOK_TAG)
      xmlRoot.addChild(bookElement)
      let nameAttribute =
        NSXMLNode.attributeWithName(DocTags.NAME_TAG,
          stringValue:book.name) as NSXMLNode
      bookElement.addAttribute(nameAttribute)
      bookElement.addChild(NSXMLElement(name: DocTags.AUTHOR_TAG,
        stringValue: book.author))
      bookElement.addChild(NSXMLElement(name:
        DocTags.CATEGORY_TAG, stringValue: book.category))
```

```
            bookElement.addChild(NSXMLElement(name:
              DocTags.DESCRIPTION_TAG, stringValue: book.description))
            bookElement.addChild(NSXMLElement(name:
              DocTags.PUBLISHER_TAG, stringValue: book.publisher))
          }
          return xmlData.XMLString
        }
        else {
          return ""
        }
      }
```

Since the `books` parameter is defined as optional, we begin the `buildXMLString()` function by verifying it is not null using the `if let myBooks = books` line. If it is null, we return an empty string; otherwise, we begin building the XML document.

The initializer that we are using for the `NSXMLDocument` class requires the root element for the XML document; therefore, we will begin by creating the `xmlRoot` constant using the `BOOKS_TAG` constant and then using it to create an instance of the `NSXMLDocument` class. Next, we loop through each instance of the `Book` class in the `books` array.

For each instance of the `Book` class, we create a new instance of the `NSXMLElement` class with the book name, which will contain the information about the book. This element will be the `<Book></Book>` element in our XML document. All the information about the book will either be an attribute of this element or a child element of this element.

The name of the book is an attribute of the `book` element; therefore, we need to create an instance of the `NSXMLNode` class that contains the attribute's name and value. We do this with the `NXMLNode.attributeWithName()` function. We then add that attribute to the `book` element using the `addAttribute()` function.

Next, we add the remaining information about the book (`author`, `category`, `description`, and `publisher`) as child nodes to the `book` element using the `addChild()` function.

Finally, we convert the `NSXMLDocument` class to a string using the `XMLString` property and return that string to the code that called the function.

XML and manually building XML documents

Since we are unable to use the `NSXMLNode`, `NSXMLDocument`, and `NSXMLElement` classes in iOS projects, we generally need to manually build the XML string or use third-party libraries. This method is error-prone and it requires us to have a very good knowledge of how XML documents are built but, if we are careful, we can create simple XML documents this way.

Let's see how to manually create an XML document. For this, we will create a function named `builXMLString()`, which takes an array of `Book` objects as its only parameter. We will also create a helper class named `getElementString()` that will create a string representation of an XML element. The `getElementString()` function will accept two elements: the element name and value. Let's have a look at the following code:

```
func buildXMLString(books: [Book]?) -> String {
  var xmlString = ""
  if let myBooks = books {
    xmlString = "<\(DocTags.BOOKS_TAG)>"
    for book in myBooks {
      xmlString += "<\(DocTags.BOOK_TAG)
        \(DocTags.NAME_TAG)=\"\(book.name)\">"
      xmlString += getElementString(DocTags.AUTHOR_TAG,
        elementValue: book.author)
      xmlString += getElementString(DocTags.CATEGORY_TAG,
        elementValue: book.category)
      xmlString += getElementString(DocTags.DESCRIPTION_TAG,
        elementValue: book.description)
      xmlString += getElementString(DocTags.PUBLISHER_TAG,
        elementValue: book.publisher)
      xmlString += "<\\\(DocTags.BOOK_TAG)>"
    }
    xmlString += "<\\\(DocTags.BOOKS_TAG)>"
  }
  return xmlString
}
func getElementString(elementName: String, elementValue: String)
  ->String {
  return "<\(elementName)>\"\(elementValue)\"<\\\(elementName)>"
}
```

Since the `books` parameter is defined as optional, we begin the `buildXMLString()` function by verifying it is not null with the `if let myBooks = books` line. If it is null, the function will return an empty string; otherwise, we begin building the XML document.

In this class, we simply create strings that represent the XML tags and append them to the `xmlString` variable. The `xmlString` variable will contain the XML document at the end of the function.

The `getElementString()` function creates a string that contains the start tag for the element, followed by the value of the element and the end tag for the element. This function is used to add most of the XML elements in this example.

As we can see, without an intimate knowledge of the syntax of XML documents, it would be virtually impossible to build complex documents with this method. We also need to be very careful to not to forget the closing tags at the end of an element.

JSON and NSJSONSerialization

To serialize and deserialize JSON documents, we will use the `NSJSONSerialization` class. As we will see, it is much easier to use the `NSJSONSerialization` class with JSON documents than it is to use the `NSXMLParser` class with XML documents; however, it can be more error-prone when we try to access the information. Just remember to always check values that are defined as optional for null prior to accessing them.

The `NSJSONSerialization` class, unlike the `NSXMLParser` class, will parse the entire JSON document memory and then return a JSON object; therefore, there is a lot less code to write but it is more memory-intensive, however.

The `NSJSONSerialization` class can parse JSON documents from an `NSData` object or through a stream. To parse JSON documents from the various sources, we use the `NSJSONSerialization` class with the appropriate static method:

- `JSONObjectWithData(_: options: error:)`: This initializer will parse a JSON document stored as an `NSData` object
- `JSONObjectWithStream(_: options: error:)`: This initializer will parse a JSON document from a stream

The documentation for these two methods says that they return an optional of the `AnyObject` type. Generally, the results of these methods are in an instance of the `NSDictionary` or an `NSArray` class, depending on the JSON document. If you are unsure what type of object is being created, you can insert the following code, where the `jsonResponse` variable is the result returned from the two static methods:

```
switch jsonResponse {
case is NSDictionary:
  // Code to parse a NSDictionary
case is NSArray:
```

```
        // Code to parse an NSArray
    default:
        // Code to handle unknown type
    }
```

In the preceding code, we use the `is` operator to check whether the response is of the `NSDictionary` or `NSArray` type.

Unlike the `NSXMLParser` class, the `NSJSONSerialization` class can be used to also create JSON documents from a collection object. To do this, we will use the `dataWithJSONObject(_: options: error:)` initializer, which will serialize a JSON document from a collection object. While it is possible to use other objects besides collection objects to create the JSON document, a proper JSON document is usually in the format of a dictionary or an array.

In the JSON examples in this chapter, we will show you how to parse the following JSON document. This document contains the same information that was in the XML example, but it is stored as a JSON document now, as shown in the following code:

```
{
  "books": [
    {
      "name": "iOS and OS X Network Development Cookbook",
      "author": "Jon Hoffman",
      "publisher": "PacktPub",
      "category": "Programming",
      "description": "Network development for iOS and OS X"
    },
    {
      "name": "Mastering Swift",
      "author": "Jon Hoffman",
      "publisher": "PacktPub",
      "category": "Programming",
      "description": "Learning Swift"
    }
  ]
}
```

Let's see how to parse a JSON document that is stored as a string.

Parsing a JSON document

In this section, we will use the `NSJSONSerialization` class to parse the previously shown JSON documents. The `jsonString` variable in this function represents the JSON document that was previously shown. This function will create an array of `Book` objects based on the information in the JSON document. At the end of the function, we will print out the information about the books to show that they were correctly parsed from the document, as well as return the array of books, as shown in the following code:

```
func parseJson() throws {
    var myBooks: [Book] = []
    let jsonData = jsonString.dataUsingEncoding(NSUTF8StringEncoding)
    if let data = jsonData {

        let jsonDoc : AnyObject = try NSJSONSerialization.
JSONObjectWithData(data, options: NSJSONReadingOptions.AllowFragments)

        if let books = jsonDoc.objectForKey(DocTags.BOOKS_TAG) as?
NSArray {
            for var i=0; i < books.count; i++ {
                if let dict = books.objectAtIndex(i) as? NSDictionary
{
                    let book = Book()
                    addValueToBook(book, elementName: DocTags.AUTHOR_
TAG, elementValue: (dict.objectForKey(DocTags.AUTHOR_TAG) as? String))
                    addValueToBook(book, elementName: DocTags.
CATEGORY_TAG, elementValue: (dict.objectForKey(DocTags.CATEGORY_TAG)
as? String))
                    addValueToBook(book, elementName: DocTags.
DESCRIPTION_TAG, elementValue: (dict.objectForKey(DocTags.DESCRIPTION_
TAG) as? String))
                    addValueToBook(book, elementName: DocTags.NAME_
TAG, elementValue: (dict.objectForKey(DocTags.NAME_TAG) as? String))
                    addValueToBook(book, elementName: DocTags.
PUBLISHER_TAG, elementValue: (dict.objectForKey(DocTags.PUBLISHER_TAG)
as? String))
                    myBooks.append(book)
                }
            }

            for book in myBooks {
                print("Found - \(book.name) \(book.author)")
            }
        }
    }
}
```

The `parseJson()` function starts off by converting the `jsonString` variable that contains the JSON document to an `NSData` object so that we can parse it with the `NSJSONSerialization` object. Since the conversion results in an optional value, we need to verify that it is not null. We do this with the following line of code:

```
if let data = jsonData
```

If the conversion was successful, we can then use the `JSONObjectWithData()` method of the `NSJSONSerialization` class to create the JSON object from the `NSData` object we just created.

Knowing that in our JSON document, the root tag of `books` contains an array of books, we use the following line to attempt to retrieve the array from the JSON object we just created:

```
if let books = jsonDoc.objectForKey(DocTags.BOOKS_TAG) as? NSArray
```

This line of code checks that the object is not null and is also an instance of the `NSArray` class. If the JSON object is supposed to contain an `NSDictionary` object, we would simply replace the `as? NSArray` with `as? NSDictionary`.

If we were able to successfully retrieve the `NSArray` class from the JSON object, then we loop through each item of the `NSArray` class. In our example, each item of the `NSArray` class is in an instance of the `NSDictionary` class; however, it is always a good idea to verify this. To verify that each item is an instance of the `NSDictionary` class, we use the following code:

```
if let dict = books[i] as? NSDictionary
```

Once we have the `NSDictionary` object, we use the `addValueToBook()` function (that we will see in just a minute) to populate the properties of the `Book` class.

Finally, we end the function by printing out the name and author of each book that we extracted from the JSON document. Let's take a look at the `addValueToBook()` function that we use to populate the properties of the `Book` class:

```
func addValueToBook(book: Book, elementName: String, elementValue:
  String?) {
    if let value = elementValue {
      book.addValue(elementName, withValue: value)
    }
}
```

If we attempt to extract a value from an `NSDictionary` object where the key does not exist, the `NSDictionary` object will return a null object. In this case, we need to verify that the value is not null prior to assigning it to a property that does not accept a null value. The `addValueToBook()` function verifies that the values are not null prior to adding them to the instance of the `Book` class.

When using the `NSJSONSerialization` class, it is better to have too many checks rather than not enough. Just remember if we try to set a non-optional variable to nil or use an object that is nil, our application will crash. JSON documents are not type-safe; therefore, it is also advisable to check the types of the values returned to make sure they are of the expected type.

Now, let's see how to create a JSON document with the `NSJSONSerialization` class.

Creating a JSON document

Creating a JSON document using the `NSJSONSerialization` class is incredibly easy but, once again, we need to do several checks to make sure nothing goes wrong. The following code will create a valid JSON document from any object that can be converted to JSON data, such as dictionaries and/or arrays:

```
func buildJSON(value: AnyObject) throws -> String {
    if NSJSONSerialization.isValidJSONObject(value) {
        let data = try NSJSONSerialization.dataWithJSONObject(value, 
options: [])
        if let string = NSString(data: data, encoding: 
NSUTF8StringEncoding) {
            return string as String
        }
    }
    return ""
}
```

The first thing we do in the `buildJSON()` function is to verify that the `value` parameter is of a type that can be converted to a JSON object. We do this using the `isValidJSONObject()` function of the `NSJSONSerialization` class. This function will return a Boolean `true` value if the `value` parameter can be converted; otherwise, it will return a Boolean `false` value.

If the `value` parameter can be converted to a JSON object, then we use the `dataWithJSONObject()` function of the `NSJSONSerialization` class to convert the value parameter to JSON data. If there is an issue with the conversion, the `dataWithJSONObject()` function throws an error, which is thrown back to the code that called the `buildJSON()` function..

Finally, we convert the JSON data to a `String` object and return it to the code that called the function. If anything goes wrong, we return an empty string.

Summary

In this chapter, we saw that it takes a lot less code to parse/build JSON objects with the `NSJSONSerialization` class as compared to parsing/building XML objects. However, we do have a lot more control on how the document is parsed using the `NSXMLParser` class. The key thing to keep in mind with both the `NSJSONSerialization` class and the `NSXMLParser` class is that we need to remember to check that optional variables do not contain a nil value, before attempting to use them.

While it seems that the majority of newer services are using the JSON format over XML, it is good to have a working knowledge of both formats because there is still a large percentage of services that use XML.

9
Custom Subscripting

Custom subscripts were added to Objective-C in 2012. At that time, Chris Lattner was already 2 years into developing Swift and like other good features of Objective-C, subscripts became a part of the Swift language. I did not frequently use custom subscripts in Objective-C, but I did know that they were a part of the language when I needed them. Subscripts in Swift seem, to me, to be a more natural part of the language, possibly because they were part of the language when it was released and not added in later.

In this chapter, you will learn the following topics:

- What are custom subscripts
- How to add custom subscripts to classes, structures, or enums
- How to create read/write and read-only subscripts
- How to use external names without custom subscripts
- How to use multidimensional subscripts

Introducing subscripts

Subscripts are shortcuts for accessing elements of a collection, list, or sequence. They are used to set or retrieve the values by index rather than using getter and setter methods. Subscripts, if used correctly, can significantly enhance the usability and readability of our custom types.

We can define multiple subscripts for a single type, and the appropriate subscript will be chosen, based on the type of index passed into the subscript. We can also set external parameter names for our subscripts that can help distinguish between subscripts that have the same type.

Using a custom subscript is similar to using subscripts for arrays and dictionaries. For example, to access an element in an array, we will use the `anArray[index]` syntax, and to access an element of a dictionary, we will use the same syntax, that is, `aDictionary[key]`. When we define a custom subscript for our custom types, we also access them with the same syntax, `ourType[key]`.

When creating custom subscripts, we should try to make them feel like they are a natural part of the class, structure, or enum. As mentioned earlier, subscripts can significantly enhance the usability and readability of our code, but if we try to overuse subscripts, they will not feel natural and will be hard to use.

In this chapter, we will look at several examples of how we can create and use custom subscripts. We will also show an example of how not to use a subscript. Before we show how to use custom subscripts, let's review how subscripts are used with Swift arrays to see how subscripts are used within the Swift language. We should use subscripts in a similar manner to how Apple uses them within the language itself to make our custom subscripts easy to understand and use.

Subscripts with Swift arrays

The following example shows how to use subscripts to access and change the values of an array:

```
var arrayOne = [1,2,3,4,5,6]
print(arrayOne[3])  //Displays '4'
arrayOne[3] = 10
print(arrayOne[3])  //Displays '10'
```

In the preceding example, we create an array of integers and then use the subscript syntax to display and change the item of element number `3` in the array. Subscripts are mainly used to get or retrieve information from a collection. We generally do not use subscripts when specific logic needs to be applied to determine which item to select. As examples, we will not use subscripts to append an item to the end of the array or to retrieve the number of items in the array. To append an item to the end of an array, or to get the number of items in an array, we will use functions or properties like this:

```
arrayOne.append(7)  //append 7 to the end of the array
arrayOne.count  //returns the number of items in an array
```

Subscripts in our custom types should follow the same standard set by the Swift language itself, so other developers that use our types are not confused by the implementation. The key to knowing when to use subscripts, and when not to, is to understand how the subscript will be used.

Read and write custom subscripts

Let's see how to define a subscript that is used to read and write to a backend array. Reading and writing to a backend storage class is one of the most common uses of custom subscripts, but, as we will see in this chapter, we do not need to have a backend storage class. The following code is a subscript to read and write an array:

```
class MyNames {
    private var names:[String] = ["Jon", "Kim", "Kailey", "Kara"]
    subscript(index: Int) -> String {
        get {
            return names[index]
        }
        set {
            names[index] = newValue
        }
    }
}
```

As we can see, the syntax is similar to how we can define properties within a class using the `get` and `set` keywords. The difference is that we declare the subscript using the `subscript` keyword. We then specify one or more inputs and the return type.

We can now use the custom subscript, just like we used subscripts with arrays and dictionaries. The following code shows how to use the subscript in the preceding example:

```
var nam = MyNames()
print(nam[0])  //Displays 'Jon'
nam[0] = "Buddy"
print(nam[0])  //Displays 'Buddy'
```

In the preceding code, we create an instance of the `MyNames` class. We then display the original name at index `0`, change the name at index `0`, and redisplay it. In this example, we use the subscript that we defined in the `MyNames` class to retrieve and set elements of the `names` array within the `MyNames` class.

While we could just make the `names` array property available for external code to read and write directly to, this would lock our code into using an array to store the data. If we ever want to change the backend storage mechanism to a dictionary object, or even an SQLite database, we will be unable to do so because all of the external code would also have to be changed. Subscripts are very good at hiding how we store information within our custom types; therefore, external code that uses our custom type does not rely on any specific storage implementations.

We would also be unable to verify that the external code was inserting valid information into the array if we gave direct access to it. With subscripts, we can add validation to our setters to verify that the data being passed in is correct before adding it to the array. This can be very useful whether we are creating a framework or a library.

Read-only custom subscripts

We can also make the subscript read-only by either not declaring a setter method within the subscript or by not implicitly declaring a getter or setter method. The following code shows how to declare a read-only property by not declaring a setter method:

```
//No getter/setters implicitly declared
subscript(index: Int) ->String {
  return names[index]
}
```

The following example shows how to declare a read-only property by only declaring a getter method:

```
//Declaring only a getter
subscript(index: Int) ->String {
  get {
    return names[index]
  }
}
```

In the first example, we do not define either a getter or setter method. So, Swift sets the subscript as read-only and the code acts as if it was in a getter definition. In the second example, we specifically set the code in a getter definition. Both examples are valid read-only subscripts.

Calculated subscripts

While the preceding example is very similar to using the stored properties in a class or structure, we can also use subscripts in a similar manner to the computed properties. Let's see how to do this:

```
struct MathTable {
    var num: Int
```

```
        subscript(index: Int) -> Int {
            return num * index
        }
    }
```

In the preceding example, we used an array as the backend storage mechanism for the subscript. In this example, we use the value of the subscript to calculate the return value. We will use this subscript as follows:

```
var table = MathTable(num: 5)
print(table[4])
```

This example will display the calculated value of `5` (the number defined in the initialization) times `4` (the subscript value), which is equal to 20.

Subscript values

In the preceding subscript examples, all of the subscripts accepted integers as the value for the subscript; however, we are not limited to integers. In the following example, we will use a string type as the value for the subscript. The subscript will also return a string type:

```
struct Hello {
  subscript (name: String) ->String {
    return "Hello \(name)"
  }
}
```

In this example, the subscript takes a string as the value within the subscript and returns a message, saying `Hello`. Let's see how to use this subscript:

```
var hello = Hello()
print(hello["Jon"])
```

This example will display the message, `Hello Jon`, to the console.

Subscripts with ranges

Similar to how we use `range` operators with arrays, we can also let our custom subscripts use the `range` operator. Let's expand the `MathTable` structure that we created earlier to include a second subscript that will take a range operator and see how it works:

```
struct MathTable {
  var num: Int
```

```
    subscript(index: Int) -> Int {
      return num * index
    }
    subscript(aRange: Range<Int>) -> [Int] {
      var retArray: [Int] = []
      for i in aRange {
        retArray.append(self[i])
      }
        return retArray

    }
  }
```

The new subscript in our example takes a range as the value for the subscript and then returns an array of integers. Within the subscript, we generate an array, which will be returned to the calling code by using the other subscript method that we previously created to multiply each value of the range by the `num` property.

The following example shows how to use this new subscript:

```
var table = MathTable(num: 5)
print(table[2...5])
```

If we run the example, we will see an array that contains the value, `10`, `15`, `20`, and `25`.

External names for subscripts

As we mentioned earlier in this chapter, we can have multiple subscript signatures for our custom types. The appropriate subscript will be chosen, based on the type of index passed into the subscript. There are times when we may wish to define multiple subscripts that have the same type. For this, we could use external names similar to how we define external names for the parameters of a function.

Let's rewrite the original `MathTable` structure to include two subscripts that each accept an integer as the subscript type; however, one will perform a multiplication operation, and the other will perform an addition operation:

```
struct MathTable {
  var num: Int
  subscript(multiply index: Int) -> Int {
    return num * index
  }
  subscript(addition index: Int) -> Int {
    return num + index
  }
}
```

As we can see, in this example we define two subscripts and each subscript is an integer type. The difference between the two subscripts is the external name within the definition. In the first subscript, we define an external name of `multiply` because we multiply the value of the subscript by the `num` property within this subscript. In the second subscript, we define an external name of `addition` because we add the value of the subscript to the `num` property within the subscript.

Let's see how to use these two subscripts:

```
var table = MathTable(num: 5)
print(table[multiply: 4])  //Displays 20 because 5*4=20
print(table[addition: 4])  //Displays 9 because 5+4=9
```

If we run this example, we will see that the correct subscript is used, based on the external name within the subscript.

Using external names within our subscript is very useful if we need multiple subscripts of the same type; I would not recommend using external names unless they are needed to distinguish between multiple subscripts.

Multidimensional subscripts

While the most common subscripts are the ones that take a single parameter, subscripts are not limited to single parameters. They can take any number of input parameters, and these parameters can be of any type.

Let's see how we could use a multidimensional subscript to implement a Tic-Tac-Toe board. A Tic-Tac-Toe board looks similar to this:

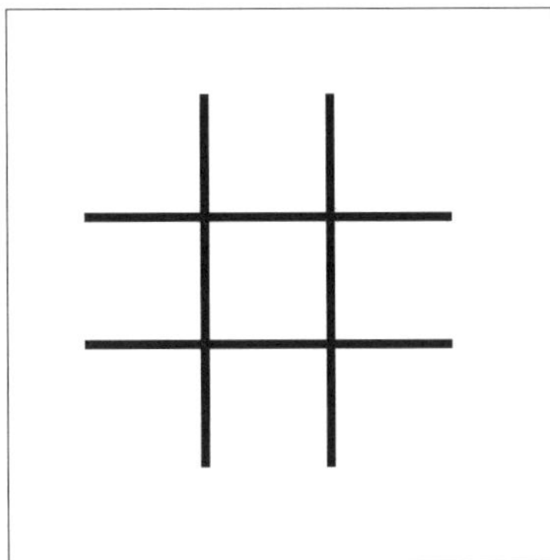

The board can be represented by a two-dimensional array where each dimension has three elements. Each player will then take a turn placing his/her pieces (typically, X or O) within the board until one player has three pieces in a row or the board is full.

Let's see how we could implement a Tic-Tac-Toe board using a multidimensional array and multidimensional subscripts:

```
struct TicTacToe {
  var board = [["","",""],["","",""],["","",""]]
  subscript(x: Int, y: Int) -> String {
    get {
      return board[x][y]
    }
    set {
      board[x][y] = newValue
    }
  }
}
```

We start the Tic-Tac-Toe structure by defining a 3x3 array that will represent the game board. We then define a subscript that can be used to set and retrieve player pieces on the board. The subscript will accept two integer values. Multiple types are defined by putting the value types between parentheses. In our example, we are defining the subscript with the parameters, `(x: Int, y: Int)`. We can then use the `x` and `y` variable names within our subscripts to access the values that are passed in.

Let's see how to use this subscript to set the user's pieces on the board:

```
var board = TicTacToe()
board[1,1] = "x"
board[0,0] = "o"
```

If we run this code, we will see that we added the player `x` piece to the center square and player `o` piece to the upper-left square, so our game board will look similar to this:

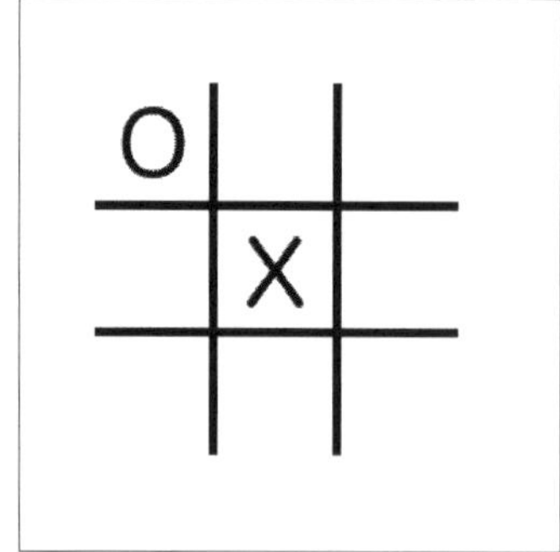

We are not limited to using only one type in our multidimensional subscripts, so we can use multiple types. For example, we could have a subscript of the `(x: Int, y:Double, z: String)` type.

We can also add external names for our multidimensional subscript types to help identify what values are used for and to distinguish between the subscripts that have the same types. Let's take a look at how to use multiple types and external names with subscripts by creating a subscript that will return an array of string instances, based on the values of the subscript:

```
struct SayHello {
  subscript(messageText message:String, messageName name:String,
number number:Int) -> [String]{
  var retArray: [String] = []
    for var i=0; i < number; i++ {
      retArray.append("\(message) \(name)")
    }
    return retArray
  }
}
```

In the `SayHello` structure, we define our subscript like this:

```
subscript(messageText message:String,messageName name:String, number
number:Int) -> [String]
```

This defines a subscript with three elements. Each element has an external name (`message`, `name`, and `number`) and an internal name (`message`, `name`, and `number`). The first two elements are of the string type and the last one is an int type. We use the first two elements to create a message for the user that will repeat the number of times defined by the last (`number`) element. We will use this subscript as follows:

```
var message = SayHello()
var ret = message[messageText:"Bonjour",messageName:"Jon",number:5]
```

If we run this code, we will see that the `ret` variable contains an array of five strings, where each string equals `Bonjour Jon`.

When not to use a custom subscript

As we have seen in this chapter, creating custom subscripts can really enhance our code; however, we should avoid overusing them or using them in a way that is not consistent with the standard subscript usage. The way to avoid overusing subscripts is to examine how subscripts are used in Swift's standard libraries.

Let's take a look at the following example:

```
class MyNames {
  private var names:[String] = ["Jon", "Kim", "Kailey", "Kara"]
  var number: Int {
    get {
      return names.count
    }
  }
  subscript(add name: String) -> String {
    names.append(name)
    return name
  }
  subscript(index: Int) -> String {
    get {
      return names[index]
    }
    set {
      names[index] = newValue
    }
  }
}
```

In the preceding example, within the `MyNames` class, we define an array of names that is used within our application. As an example, let's say that within our application, we display this list of names and allow users to add names to it. Within the `MyNames` class, we then define the following subscript that allows us to append a new name to the array:

```
subscript(add name: String) -> String {
  names.append(name)
  return name
}
```

This will be a poor use of subscript syntax because its usage is not consistent with how subscripts are used within the Swift language. This might cause confusion when the class is used in the future. It will be more appropriate to rewrite this subscript as a function like this:

```
func append(name: String) {
  names.append(name)
}
```

Remember, when you are using custom subscripts make sure that you are using them appropriately.

Summary

As we saw in this chapter, adding support for subscripts to our custom types can greatly enhance their readability and usability. We saw that subscripts can be used to add an abstraction layer between our backend storage class and external code. Subscripts can also be used in a similar manner to computed properties where the subscript is used to calculate a value. As we noted, the key with subscripts is to use them appropriately and in a manner that is consistent with subscripts in the Swift language.

10 Using Optional Types

When I first started using Swift, the concept that I had the most trouble with was optional types. Coming from an Objective-C, C, Java, and Python background, I was able to relate to most of Swift's features to how things worked in one of the other languages that I knew, but optionals were different. There really was nothing like optionals in the other languages that I used, so it took a lot of reading to fully understand them. While I briefly covered optionals in *Chapter 2, Learning about Variables, Constants, Strings, and Operators*, which gave enough of an overview to get started with, we need to cover a lot more information to really understand what optionals are, how to properly use them, and why they are so important in the Swift language.

In this chapter, we will cover the following topics:

- An introduction to optional types
- The need for optional types in Swift
- Unwrapping an optional
- Optional binding
- Optional chaining

Introducing optionals

When we declare variables in Swift, they are, by default, non-optional, which means that they must contain a valid, non-nil value. If we try to set a non-optional variable to nil, it will result in a `Type '{type}' does not conform to protocol 'NilLiteralConvertible'` error, where `{type}` is the type of the variable.

For example, the following code will throw an error when we attempt to set the `message` variable to `nil` because `message` is a non-optional type:

```
var message: String = "My String"
message = nil
```

It is very important to understand that nil in Swift is very different from nil in Objective-C. In Objective-C, nil is a pointer to non-existent object; however, in Swift, nil is the absence of a value. This concept is very important to fully understand optionals in Swift.

A variable defined as an optional can contain a valid value or it can indicate an absence of a value. We indicate an absence of a value by assigning it a special nil value. Optionals of any type can be set to nil, whereas in Objective-C, only objects can be set to nil.

To really understand the concept behind optionals, let's look at a line of code that defines an optional:

```
var myString: String?
```

The question mark at the end indicates that the `myString` variable is an optional. When we look at this code, it would be wrong to read this line of code as "the `myString` variable is a string type that is optional". We should actually read this line of code as "the `myString` variable is an optional type, which may contain a string type or may contain no value". The subtle difference between the two lines actually makes a big difference in understanding how optionals work.

Optionals are a special type in Swift. When we defined the `myString` variable, we actually defined it as an optional type. To understand this, let's look at some more code:

```
var myString1: String?
var myString2: Optional<String>
```

These two declarations are equivalent. Both lines declare an optional type that may contain a string type or may be absent of a value. In Swift, we can think of the absence of a value as being set to nil, but always remember that this is different than setting something to nil in Objective-C. In this book, when we refer to nil, we are referring to how Swift uses nil and not how Objective-C uses nil.

The optional type is an enumeration with two possible values, `None` and `Some(T)`, where `T` is the associated value of the appropriate type. If we set the optional to `nil`, then it will have a value of `None`, and if we set a value, then the optional will have a value of `Some` with an associated value of the appropriate type. In *Chapter 2, Learning about Variables, Constants, Strings, and Operators*, we explained that an enum in Swift may have associated values. Associated values allow us to store additional information along with the enum's member value.

Internally, an optional is defined as follows:

```
enum Optional<T> {
  case None
  case Some(T)
}
```

Here, `T` is the type to associate with the optional. The `T` symbol is used to define a generic. We can read more about generics in *Chapter 11, Working with Generics*.

The need for optional types in Swift

Now, the burning question is why does Swift need optionals? To understand why Swift has optionals, we should examine what problems optionals are designed to solve.

In most languages, it is possible to create a variable without giving it an initialized value. For example, in Objective-C, both lines of code are valid:

```
int i;
MyObject *m;
```

Now, let's say that the `MyObject` class has the following method:

```
-(int)myMethodWithValue:(int)i {
    return i*2;
}
```

This method takes the value passed in from the `i` parameter, multiplies it by 2, and returns the results. Let's try to call this method using the following code:

```
MyObject *m;
NSLog(@"Value: %d",[m myMethodWithValue:5]);
```

Our first thought might be that this code would display `Value: 10`; however, this would be wrong. In reality, this code would display `Value: 0` because we did not initialize the `m` object prior to using it.

When we forget to initialize an object or set a value for a variable, we can get unexpected results at runtime, as we just demonstrated. The unexpected results can be, at times, very difficult to track down.

With optionals, Swift is able to detect problems like this at compile time and alert us at runtime. If we expect a variable or object to always contain a value prior to using it, we will declare the variable as a non-optional (this is the default declaration). Then, at compile time, we would receive an error if we try to use it prior to initializing it. Let's look at an example of this. The following code would display an error at compile time because we are attempting to use a non-optional variable prior to initialize it:

```
var myString: String
print(myString)
```

If a variable is declared as an optional, it is good programming practice to verify that it contains a valid value before attempting to use it. We should only declare a variable as an optional if there is a valid reason for the variable to contain no value. This is the reason Swift declares variables a non-optional by default.

Now that we (hopefully) have a good understanding of what optionals are and what types of problems they are designed to solve, let's look at how to use them.

Defining an optional

Typically, to define an optional type, we put a question mark after the type in the variable declaration. Keep in mind that the type we define in the variable's declaration is actually the associated value in the optional enum. The following code shows us how we would typically declare an optional:

```
var myOptional: String?
```

This code declares an optional variable that might contain a string or no value (nil). When a variable is declared like this, by default, it is set to no value.

Using optionals

There are a number of ways that we can use optionals within our code. The key to using optionals is to always verify that they contain a valid value prior to accessing it. We use the unwrapping term to refer to retrieve the value of an optional.

Forced unwrapping an optional

To unwrap or retrieve the value of an optional, we place an exclamation mark (`!`) after the variable name. Forced unwrapping, in this manner, can be very dangerous and should be used only if we are certain that the value is not nil.

When we use the exclamation mark to unwrap an optional, we are telling the compiler that we know the optional does not contain a nil value, so go ahead and give us the value. Let's look at how to do this:

```
var myString1: String?
myString1 = "test"
var test: String = myString1!
```

This code will work as we expect it to, where the `test` variable will contain the `test` string; however, if the line that set the `myString1` optional to `test` was removed, we would receive a runtime error when we run the application. Note that the compiler will not alert us of an issue because we are using the exclamation point to unwrap the optional; therefore, the compiler assumes that we know what we are doing and will happily compile the code for us. We should verify that the `myString1` optional contains a valid value prior to unwrapping it. The following example is one way to do this:

```
var myString1: String?
myString1 = "test"
if myString1 != nil {
    var test:String = myString1!
}
```

Now, if the line that sets the `myString1` optional to `test` was removed, we would not receive a runtime error because we are only unwrapping the `myString` optional, if it contains a valid (non-nil) value.

Unwrapping optionals, as we just described, is not the most optimal way, and it is not recommended that we unwrap optionals in this manner. We can combine the verification and unwrapping into one step called **optional binding**.

Optional binding

Optional binding is the recommended way to unwrap an optional. With optional binding, we perform a check to see whether the optional contains a valid value and, if so, unwrap it into a temporary variable or constant. This is all performed in one step.

Optional binding is performed with the `if` or `while` conditional statements. It takes the following format if we want to put the value of the optional in a constant:

```
if let constantName = optional {
   statements
}
```

If we need to put the value in a variable, instead of a constant, we can use the `var` keyword instead of the `let` keyword, as shown in the following example:

```
if var variableName = optional {
   statements
}
```

The following example shows how to perform optional binding:

```
var myString3: String?
myString3 = "Space"
if let tempVar = myString3 {
    print(tempVar)
} else {
    print("No value")
}
```

In the example, we define the `myString3` variable as an optional type. If the `myString3` optional contains a valid value, then we set the new variable named `tempvar` to the value of the `myString3` optional and print the value to the console. If the `myString3` optional does not contain a value, then we print `No` value to the console.

Starting with Swift 1.2, we are able to use optional binding to unwrap multiple optionals within the same optional binding line. For example, if we had three optionals named `optional1`, `optional2` and `optional3`, we could use the following code to attempt to unwrap all the three at once:

```
If let tmp1 = optional1, tmp2 = optional2, tmp3 = optional3 {
}
```

If any of the three optionals failed to unwrap, the whole optional binding statement fails.

It is perfectly acceptable with optional binding to assign the value to a variable of the same name. The following code illustrates this:

```
if let myOptional = myOptional {
  print(myOptional)
} else {
  print("myOptional was nil")
}
```

One thing to note is that the `temp` variable is scoped only for the conditional block and cannot be used outside the conditional block. To illustrate the scope of the temporary variable, let's take a look at the following code:

```
var myOptional: String?
myOptional = "test"
if var tmp = myOptional {
    print("Inside:  \(tmp)")
}
// This next line will cause a compile time error
print("Outside: \(tmp)")
```

This code would not compile because the `tmp` variable is only valid within the conditional block and we are attempting to use it outside of the conditional block.

Using optional binding is a lot cleaner and easier than manually verifying that the optional has a value and then forcing the unwrapping of the optional.

Returning optionals from functions, methods, and subscripts

We can set the return type of a function or a method to the optional type. This allows us to return a nil (no value) from the function or method. To set the return type to an optional type, we will insert a question mark after the name of the type in the function or method declaration.

The following example shows us how we will return an optional from a function or method:

```
func getName(index: Int) -> String? {
    let names = ["Jon", "Kim", "Kailey", "Kara"]
    if index >= names.count || index < 0 {
        return nil
    } else {
        return names[index]
    }
}
```

In the example, we defined the return type as an optional that can be either a string value or no value. Inside the function, we will return the name if the index is within the bounds of the array, or `nil` if it is outside the bounds of the array.

The following code shows how to call this function where the return value is an optional:

```
var name = getName(2)
var name2 = getName(5)
```

In the previous code, the name variable will contain Kailey, while the name2 variable will contain nil (no value). Note that we do not have to define the variable as an optional (with a question mark) since Swift knows it is an optional type because that is the return type defined by the function.

We can also define a subscript that returns an optional type. We define a subscript as an optional exactly like we defined functions. Here is an example template of a subscript that returns an optional:

```
subscript(index: Int) -> String? {
   //some statements
}
```

With this definition, we are able to return a nil (no value) from our subscript.

Using optionals as a parameter in a function or method

We can also accept an optional as a parameter to a function or a method. This allows us to have the option of passing a nil (no value) into a function or method if required. The following example shows how to define an optional parameter for a function:

```
func optionalParam(myString: String?) {
  if let temp = myString {
    print("Contains value \(temp)")
  }
  else {
    print("Does not contain value")
  }
}
```

To define a parameter as an optional type, we use the question mark within the parameter definition. Within this example, we use optional binding to check whether the optional contains a value or not. If it contains a value, we print Contains value to the console; otherwise, we print Does not contain value.

Optional types with tuples

We can define a whole tuple as an optional or any of the elements within a tuple as an optional. It is especially useful to use optionals with tuples when we return a tuple from a function or method. This allows us to return part (or all) of the tuples as nil. The following example shows how to define a tuple as an optional, and also how to define individual elements of a tuple as an optional type:

```
var tuple1: (one: String, two: Int)?
var tuple2: (one: String, two: Int?)
```

The first line defines the whole tuple as an optional type. The second line defines the second value within the tuple as an optional, while the first value is a non-optional.

Optional chaining

Optional binding allows us to unwrap one optional at a time, but what would happen if we had optional types embedded within other optional types? This would force us to have optional binding statements embedded within other optional binding statements. There is a better way to handle this by using optional chaining. Before we look at optional chaining, let's see how this would work with optional binding:

```
class Collar {
    var color: String
    init(color: String) {
        self.color = color
    }
}

class Pet {
    var name: String
    var collar: Collar?
    init(name: String) {
        self.name = name
    }
}

class Person {
    var name: String
    var pet: Pet?
    init(name: String) {
        self.name = name
    }
}
```

In this example, we begin by defining a `Collar` class, which has one property defined. This property is named `color`, which is of the type string. We can see that the `color` property is not an optional; therefore, we can safely assume that it will always have a valid value.

Next, we define a `Pet` class that has two properties defined. These properties are named `name` and `collar`. The `name` property is of the string type and the `collar` property is an optional that may contain a `Collar` type object.

Finally, we define the `Person` class that also has two properties. These properties are named `name` and `pet`. The `name` property is of the string type and the `pet` property is an optional that may contain a `Pet` type object.

For the examples that follow, let's use the following code to initialize the classes:

```
var jon = Person(name: "Jon")
var buddy = Pet(name: "Buddy")
jon.pet = buddy
var collar = Collar(color: "red")
buddy.collar = collar
```

Now, let's say that we want to get the color of the collar for a person's pet; however, the person may not have a pet (the `pet` property is `nil`) or the pet may not have a collar (the `collar` property is `nil`). We could use optional binding to drill down through each layer, as shown in the following example:

```
if let tmpPet = jon.pet, tmpCollar = tmpPet.collar {
   print("The color of the collar is \(tmpCollar.color)")
  }
else {
    print("Cannot retrieve color")
}
```

While this example is perfectly valid and would print out the message, `The color of the collar is red`, the code is rather messy and hard to follow because we have optional binding statements embedded within other optional binding statements.

Optional chaining allows us to drill down through multiple optional type layers of properties, methods, and subscripts in one line of code. These layers can be chained together and if any layer returns a `nil`, the entire chain gracefully fails and returns nil. If none of the values return `nil`, the last value of the chain is returned. Since the results of optional chaining may be a `nil` value, the results are always returned as an optional type, even if the final value we are retrieving is a non-optional type.

To specify optional chaining, we will place a question mark (`?`) after each of the optional values within the chain. The following example shows how to use optional chaining to make the preceding example much cleaner and easier to read:

```
if let color = jon.pet?.collar?.color {
    print("The color of the collar is \(color)")
} else {
    print("Cannot retrieve color")
}
```

In this example, we put a question mark after the `pet` and `collar` properties to signify that they are of the optional type and if either value is `nil`, the whole chain will return `nil`. This code would also print out the message, `The color of the collar is red`; however, it is much easier to read than the preceding example that used optional binding.

The nil coalescing operator

The nil coalescing operator is similar to the ternary operator that we discussed in *Chapter 2, Learning about Variables, Constants, Strings, and Operators*, of this book. The ternary operator assigns a value to a variable, based on the evaluation of a comparison operator or a Boolean value. The nil coalescing operator unwraps an optional, and if it contains a value, it will return that value, or a default value if the optional is `nil`.

Let's look at a prototype for the nil coalescing operator:

```
optionalA ?? defaultValue
```

In this example, we demonstrate the nil coalescing operator when the optional contains a nil and also when it contains a value:

```
var defaultName = "Jon"

var optionalA: String?
var optionalB: String?

optionalB = "Buddy"

var nameA = optionalA ?? defaultName
var nameB = optionalB ?? defaultName
```

In this example, we begin by initializing our `defaultName` variable to `Jon`. We then define two optionals that are named `optionalA` and `optionalB`. The `optionalA` variable will be set to `nil` while the `optionalB` variable is set to `Buddy`.

The nil coalescing operator is used in the final two lines. Since the `optionalA` variable contains a `nil`, the `nameA` variable will be set to the value of the `defaultName` variable, which is `Jon`. The `nameB` variable will be set to the value of the `optionalB` variable as it contains a value.

Summary

While the concept of optional types, as used in the Swift language, might seem a little foreign at first, the more you use them, the more they will make sense. One of the biggest advantages with optional types is we get additional compile time checks that alert us if we forget to initialize non-optionals prior to using them.

The one thing to take away from this chapter is the concept of what optionals are. To reinforce this concept, let's review a couple of paragraphs from this chapter.

It is very important to understand that nil in Swift is very different than nil in Objective-C. In Objective-C, nil is a pointer to a non-existent object; however, in Swift nil is an absence of a value. This concept is very important to fully understand optionals in Swift.

A variable defined as an optional can contain a valid value or it can be absent of a value. We set a variable to a valueless state by assigning it Swift's special nil value. Optionals of any type can be set to nil, whereas in Objective-C, only objects could be set to nil.

The optional type is an enumeration with two possible values, `None` and `Some (T)`, where `T` is the associated value of the appropriate type. If we set the optional to `nil`, it will have a value of `None`, and if we set a value, the optional will have a value of `Some` with an associated value of the appropriate type. In *Chapter 2, Learning about Variables, Constants, Strings, and Operators*, we explained that an enum in Swift may have associated values. Associated values allow us to store additional information along with the enum's member value.

11

Working with Generics

My first experience with generics was back in 2004, when they were first introduced in the Java programming language. I can still remember picking up my copy of *The Java Programming Language, Fourth edition*, which covered Java 5, and reading about Java's implementation of generics. Since then, I have used generics in a number of projects, not only in Java but in other languages as well. If you are familiar with generics in other languages, such as Java, the syntax that Swift uses will be familiar to you. Generics allow us to write very flexible and reusable code; however, just like with subscripts, we need to make sure that we use them properly and do not overuse them.

In this chapter, we will cover the following topics:

- An introduction to generics
- Creating and using generic functions
- Creating and using generic classes
- Using associated types with protocols

An introduction to generics

The concept of generics has been around for a while, so it should not be a new concept to developers coming from languages such as Java or C#. Swift's implementation of generics is very similar to these languages. For those developers coming from other languages such as Objective-C, which do not have generics, they might seem a bit foreign at first.

Generics allow us to write very flexible and reusable code that avoids duplication. With a type safe language, such as Swift, we often need to write functions or types that are valid for multiple types. For example, we might need to write a function that swaps the values of two variables; however, we may use this function to swap two string types, two int types, and two double types. Without generics, we will need to write three separate functions; however, with generics, we can write one generic function to provide the swap functionality for multiple types. Generics allow us to tell a function or type—I know Swift is a type-safe language, but I do not know the type that will be needed yet. I will give you a placeholder for now and will let you know what type to enforce later.

In Swift, we have the ability to define both generic functions and generic types. Let's look at generic functions first.

Generic functions

Let's begin by examining the problem that generics try to solve and then we will see how generics solve this problem. Let's say that we wanted to create functions that swapped the values of two variables (as described in the introduction); however, for our application, we have a need to swap two ints, two doubles, and two strings. Without generics, this would require us to write three separate functions. The following code shows what these functions would look similar to:

```
func swapInts (inout a: Int, inout b: Int) {
    let tmp = a
    a = b
    b = tmp
}

func swapDoubles(inout a: Double, inout b: Double) {
    let tmp = a
    a = b
    b = tmp
}

func swapStrings(inout a: String, inout b: String) {
    let tmp = a
    a = b
    b = tmp
}
```

With these three functions, we can swap the original values of two ints, two doubles, and two strings. Now, let's say, as we develop our application further, we find out that we also need to swap the values of two UInt32, two floats, or even a couple of custom types. We might easily end up with eight or nine swap functions. The worst part is that each of these functions contains duplicate code. The only difference between these functions is the type of variable change. While this solution does work, generics offer a much more elegant and simple solution that eliminates the duplication of code. Let's see how we would condense all these three preceding functions into a single generic function:

```
func swap<T>(inout a: T, inout b: T) {
    let tmp = a
    a = b
    b = tmp
}
```

Let's look at how we defined the `swap()` function. The function itself looks pretty similar to a normal function, except for the capital `T`. The capital `T`, as used in the `swap()` function, is a placeholder type and tells Swift that we will be defining the type later. When we do define the type, the type we define will replace all the placeholders.

To define a generic function, we include the placeholder type between two angular brackets (`<T>`) after the function's name. We can then use that placeholder type in place of any type definition within the parameter definitions, the return type, or the function itself. The big thing to keep in mind is that, once the placeholder is defined as a type, all the other placeholder assume that type. Therefore, any variable or constant defined with that placeholder must conform to that type.

There is nothing special about the capital `T`, we could use any valid identifier in place of `T`. The following definitions are perfectly valid:

```
func swap<G>(inout a: G, inout b: G) {
  //Statements
}

func swap<xyz>(inout a: xyz, inout b: xyz) {
  //Statements
}
```

In most documentation, generic placeholders are defined with either `T` (for type) or `E` (for element). For standard purposes, we will use `T` to define generic placeholders in this book. It is also good practice to use `T` to define a generic placeholder within our code so that the placeholder is easily recognized when we are looking at the code at a later time.

If we need to use multiple generic types, we can create multiple placeholders by separating them with commas. The following example shows how to define multiple placeholders for a single function:

```
func testGeneric<T,E>(a:T, b:E) {

}
```

In this example, we are defining two generic placeholders, `T` and `E`. In this case, we can set the `T` placeholder to one type and the `E` placeholder to a different type.

Let's look at how to call a generic function. The following code will swap two integers using the `swapGeneric<T>(inout a: T, inout b: T)` function:

```
var a = 5
var b = 10
swap(&a, b: &b)

print("a:  \(a) b:  \(b)")
```

If we run this code, the `a:  10  b:  5` line will be printed to the console. We can see that we do not have to do anything special to call a generic function. The function infers the type from the first parameter and then sets all the remaining placeholders to that type. Now, if we need to swap the values of two strings, we will call the same function like this:

```
var c = "My String 1"
var d = "My String 2"
swapGeneric(&c, b: &d)

print("c:  \(c) d:  \(d)")
```

We can see that we call the function in exactly the same way as we called it when we wanted to swap two integers. One thing that we cannot do is pass two different types into the `swap()` function because we defined only one generic placeholder. If we attempt to run the following code, we will receive an error:

```
var a = 5
var c = "My String 1"
swapGeneric(&a, b: &c)
```

The error that we will receive is `cannot invoke 'swap' with an argument list of type '(inout Int, b: inout String`, which tells us that we are attempting to use a string value with an int value when the function wants only type. The reason the function is looking for an Int value is that the first parameter that we pass into the function is an Int value; therefore, all the generic types in the function became Int types.

Now, let's say we have the following function that has multiple generic types defined:

```
func testGeneric<T,E>(a:T, b:E) {
    print("\(a)  \(b)")
}
```

This function would accept parameters of different types; however; since they are of different types, we would be unable to swap the values because the types are different. There are also other limitations on generics. For example, we may think that the following generic function would be valid; however, we would receive an error if we tried to implement it:

```
func genericEqual<T>(a: T, b: T) -> Bool{
    return a == b
}
```

The error that we receive is `binary operator '==' cannot be applied to two 'T' operands`. Since the type of the arguments is unknown at the time the code is compiled, Swift does not know if it is able to use the equal operator on the types; therefore, the error is thrown. We might think that this is a limit that will make generics hard to use; however, we have a way to tell Swift that we expect the type, represented by the placeholder will have a certain functionality. This is done with type constraints.

A type constraint specifies that a generic type must inherit from a specific class or conform to a particular protocol. This allows us to use the methods and properties defined by the parent class or protocol within the generic function. Let's look at how to use type constraints by rewriting the `genericEqual()` function to use the comparable protocol:

```
func testGenericComparable<T: Comparable>(a: T, b: T) -> Bool{
    return a >= b
}
```

To specify the type constraint, we put the class or protocol constraint after the generic placeholder, where the generic placeholder and the constraint are separated by a colon. This new function works as we might expect, and it will compare the values of the two parameters and return `true` if they are equal or `false` if they are not.

We can declare multiple constraints just like we declare multiple generic types. The following example shows how to declare two generic types with different constraints:

```
func testFunction<T: MyClass, E: MyProtocol>(a: T, b: E) {
}
```

In this function, the type defined by the `T` placeholder must inherit from the `MyClass` class, and the type defined by the `E` placeholder must implement the `MyProtocol` protocol. Now that we have looked at generic functions, let's take a look at generic types.

Generic types

We have already had a general introduction to how generic types work when we looked at Swift arrays and dictionaries. A generic type is a class, structure, or enum that can work with any type, just like the way the Swift arrays and dictionaries work. As we recall, Swift arrays and dictionaries are written so that they can contain any type. The catch is we cannot mix-and-match different types within an array or dictionary. When we create an instance of our generic type, we define the type that the instance will work with. After we define that type, we cannot change the type for that instance.

To demonstrate how to create a generic type, let's create a simple `List` class. This class will use a Swift array as the backend storage for the list and will let us add items to the list or retrieve values from the list.

Let's begin by seeing how to define our generic list type:

```
class List<T> {
}
```

The preceding code defines the generic list type. We can see that we use the `<T>` tag to define a generic placeholder, just like we did when we defined a generic function. This `T` placeholder can then be used anywhere within the type instead of a concrete type definition.

To create an instance of this type, we would need to define the type of items that our list will hold. The following examples show how to create instances of the generic list type for various types:

```
var stringList = List<String>()
var intList = List<Int>()
var customList = List<MyObject>()
```

The preceding example creates three instances of the `List` class. The `stringList` instance can be used with String types, the `intList` instance can be used with Int types, and the `customList` instance can be used with instances of the `MyObject` type.

We are not limited to using generics only with classes. We can also define structures and enums as generics. The following examples show how to define a generic structure and a generic enum:

```
struct GenericStruct<T> {

}

enum GenericEnum<T> {

}
```

The next step in our `List` class is to add the backend storage array. The items stored in this array need to be of the same type as we define when we initiate the class; therefore, we will use the `T` placeholder when we define the type for the array. The following code shows the `List` class with an array named `items`. The `items` array will be defined using the `T` placeholder, so it will hold the same types as we defined for the class:

```
class List<T> {
    var items = [T]()
}
```

This code defines our generic list type and uses `T` as the type placeholder. We can then use the `T` placeholder anywhere in the class to define the type of an item. That item will then be of the same type that we defined when we created the instance of the `List` class. Therefore, if we create an instance of the list type like this `var stringList = List<String>()`, the items array will be an array of string instances. If we created an instance of the list type like this `var intList = List<Int>()`, the item array will be an array of Int instances.

Now, we will need to add the `addItems()` method that will be used to add an item to the list. We will use the `T` placeholder within the method declaration to define that the item parameter will be of the same type as we declared when we initiated the class. Therefore, if we create an instance of the list type to use the string type, we would be required to use the string type as the parameter for the `addItems()` method. However, if we create an instance of the list type to use the int type, we would be required to use the int type as the parameter for the `addItems()` method.

Here is the code for the `addItems()` function:

```
func addItem(item: T) {
    items.append(item)
}
```

To create a standalone generic function, we add the `<T>` declaration after the function name to declare that it is a generic function; however, when we use a generic method within a generic type, we do not need the `<T>` declaration. Instead, all we need to do is to use the type that we defined in the class declaration. If we wanted to introduce another generic type, we could define it with the method declaration.

Now, let's add the `getItemAtIndex()` method that will return the item from the backend array, at the specified index:

```
func getItemAtIndex(index: Int) -> T? {
    if items.count > index {
        return items[index]
    } else {
        return nil
    }
}
```

The `getItemAtIndex()` method accepts one argument that is the index of the item we want to retrieve. We then use the `T` placeholder to specify that our return type is an optional that might be of type `T` or `nil`. If the backend storage array contains an item at the specified index, we will return that item; otherwise, we return no value.

Now, let's look at our entire generic list class:

```
class List<T> {
    var items = [T]()

    func addItem(item: T) {
        items.append(item)
    }
```

```
        func getItemAtIndex(index: Int) -> T? {
            if items.count > index {
                return items[index]
            } else {
                return nil
            }
        }
    }
```

As we can see, we initially defined the generic `T` placeholder type in the class declaration. We then used this placeholder type within our class. In our `List` class, we use this placeholder in three places. We use it as the type for our items array, as the parameter type for our `addItem()` method, and as the associated value for the optional return type in the `getItemAtIndex()` method.

Now, let's look at how to use the `List` class. When we use a generic type, we define the type to be used within the class between angle brackets, such as `<type>`. The following code shows how to use the `List` class to store string types:

```
var list = List<String>()
list.addItem("Hello")
list.addItem("World")
print(list.getItemAtIndex(1))
```

In this code, we start off by creating an instance of the list type called `list` and set it to store `String` types. We then use the `addItem()` method twice to store two items in the list instance. Finally, we use the `getItemAtIndex()` method to retrieve the item at index number `1`, which will display `Optional(World)` to the console.

We can also define our generic types with multiple placeholder types, similar to how we use multiple placeholders in our generic methods. To use multiple placeholder types, we would separate them with commas. The following example shows how to define multiple placeholder types:

```
class MyClass<T,E>{

}
```

We then create an instance of the `MyClass` type that uses the `String` and `Int` types, such as:

```
var mc = MyClass<String, Int>()
```

We can also use type constraints with generic types. Once again, using a type constraint for a generic type is exactly the same as using one with a generic function. The following code shows how to use a type constraint to ensure that the generic type conforms to the comparable protocol:

```
class MyClass<T: Comparable>{}
```

So far, in this chapter, we have seen how to use placeholder types with functions and types. At times, it can be useful to declare one or more placeholder types in a protocol. These types are known as **associated types**.

Associated types

An associated type declares a placeholder name that can be used instead of a type within a protocol. The actual type to be used is not specified until the protocol is adopted. While creating generic functions and types, we used a very similar syntax. Defining associated types for a protocol, however, is very different. We specify an associated type using the `typealias` keyword.

Let's see how to use associated types when we define a protocol. In this example, we will define the `QueueProtocol` protocol that will define the capabilities that need to be implemented by the queue that implements it:

```
protocol QueueProtocol {
    typealias QueueType
    mutating func addItem(item: QueueType)
    mutating func getItem() -> QueueType?
    func count() -> Int
}
```

In this protocol, we define one associated type named `QueueType`. We then used this associated type twice within the protocol—once as the parameter type for the `addItem()` method and once when we define the return type of the `getItem()` method as an optional type that might return the associated type of `QueueType` or a `nil`.

Any type that implements the `QueueProtocol` protocol must be able to specify the type to use for the `QueueType` placeholder and must also ensure that only items of that type are used where the protocol uses the `QueueType` placeholder.

Let's look at how to implement `QueueProtocol` in a non-generic class called `IntQueue`. This class will implement the `QueueProtocol` protocol using the `Int` type:

```
class IntQueue: QueueProtocol {
  var items = [Int]()

  func addItem(item: Int) {
    items.append(item)
  }

  func getItem() -> Int? {
    if items.count > 0 {
      return items.removeAtIndex(0)
    }
    else {
      return nil
    }
  }

  func count() -> Int {
    return items.count
  }
}
```

In the `IntQueue` class, we begin by defining our backend storage mechanism to be an array of `Int` types. We then implement each of the methods defined in the `QueueProtocol` protocol, replacing the `QueueType` placeholder defined in the protocol with the Int type. In the `addItem()` method, the parameter type is defined to be an `Int` type, and in the `getItem()` method the return type is defined to be an optional that might return an `Int` type or no value.

We use the `IntQueue` class as we would use any other class. The following code shows this:

```
var intQ = IntQueue()
intQ.addItem(2)
intQ.addItem(4)
print(intQ.getItem())
intQ.addItem(6)
```

We begin by creating an instance of the IntQueue class named intQ. We then call the addItem() method twice to add two values of the int type to the intQ instance. We then retrieve the first item in the intQ instance by calling the getItem() method. This line will print the number Optional(2) to the console. The final line of code adds another int type to the intQ instance.

In the preceding example, we implemented the QueueProtocol protocol in a non-generic way. This means that we replaced the placeholder types with an actual type (QueueType was replaced by the Int type). We can also implement the QueueProtocol protocol with a generic type. Let's see how to implement the QueueProtocol protocol in a generic type called GenericQueue:

```
class GenericQueue<T>: QueueProtocol {
    var items = [T]()

    func addItem(item: T) {
        items.append(item)
    }

    func getItem() -> T? {
        if items.count > 0 {
            return items.removeAtIndex(0)
        } else {
            return nil
        }
    }

    func count() -> Int {
        return items.count
    }
}
```

As we can see, the GenericQueue implementation is very similar to the IntQueue implementation, except that we define the type to use as the generic placeholder T. We can then use the GenericQueue class as we would use any generic class. Let's take a look at how to use the GenericQueue class:

```
var intQ2 = GenericQueue<Int>()
intQ2.addItem(2)
intQ2.addItem(4)
print(intQ2.getItem())
intQ2.addItem(6)
```

We begin by creating an instance of the `GenericQueue` class that will use the `Int` type. This instance is named `intQ2`. Next, we call the `addItem()` method twice to add two Int types to the `intQ2` instance. We then retrieve the first `Int` type that was added using the `getItem()` method and print the value to the console. This line will print the number `2` to the console.

One of the things that we should watch out for while using generics is to avoid using them when we should be using protocols. This is, in my opinion, one of the most common misuses of generics in other languages. Let's take a look at an example so that we know what to avoid.

Let's say that we define a protocol called `WidgetProtocol`, which is as follows:

```
protocol WidgetProtocol {
    //Code
}
```

Now, let's say that we want to create a custom type (or function) that will use various implementations of the `WidgetProtocol` protocol. I have seen a couple of instances where developers have used generics with a type constraint to create custom types like this:

```
class MyClass<T: WidgetProtocol> {
    var myProp: T?
    func myFunc(myVar: T) {
        //Code
    }
}
```

While this is a perfectly valid use of generics, it is recommended that we avoid implementations like this. It is a lot cleaner and easier to read if we use `WidgetProtocol` without generics. For example, we can write a non-generic version of the `MyClass` type like this:

```
class MyClass {
    var myProp: WidgetProtocol?
    func myFunc(myVar: WidgetProtocol) {

    }
}
```

The second non-generic version of the `MyClass` type is a lot easier to read and understand; therefore, this should be the preferable way to implement the class. However, there is nothing preventing us from using either implementation of the `MyClass` type.

Summary

Generic types can be incredibly useful, and they are also the basis of the Swift standard collection types (array and dictionary); however, as mentioned in the introduction to this chapter, we have to be careful to use them correctly.

We have seen a couple of examples in this chapter that show how generics can make our lives easier. The `swapGeneric()` function that was shown at the beginning of the chapter is a good use of a generic function because it allows us to swap the two values of any type we choose while only implementing the swap code once.

The generic list type is also a good example of how to make custom collection types that can be used to hold any type. How we implemented the generic list type in this chapter is similar to how Swift implements the array and dictionary with generics.

12
Working with Closures

Today, most major programming languages have functionalities similar to what closures offer. Some of these implementations are really hard to use (Objective-C blocks), while others are easy (Java lambda and C# delegates). I found that the functionality that closures provide is especially useful when developing frameworks. I have also used them extensively when communicating with remote services over a network connection. While blocks in Objective-C are incredibly useful (and I used them quite a bit), their syntax used to declare a block was absolutely horrible. Luckily, when Apple was developing the Swift language, they made the syntax of closures much easier to use and understand.

In this chapter, we will cover the following topics:

- An introduction to closures
- Defining a closure
- Using a closure
- Several useful examples of closures
- How to avoid strong reference cycles with closures

An introduction to closures

Closures are self-contained blocks of code that can be passed around and used throughout our application. We can think of an int type as a type that stores an integer and a string type as a type that stores a string. In this context, a closure can be thought of as a type that holds a block of code. What this means is that we can assign closures to a variable, pass them as arguments to functions, and also return functions from them.

Closures have the ability to capture and store references to any variable or constant from the context in which they were defined. This is known as closing over the variables or constants, and the best thing is, for the most part, Swift will handle the memory management for us. The only exception is when we create a strong reference cycle, and we will look at how to resolve this in the *Creating strong reference cycles with closures* section of this chapter.

Closures in Swift are similar to blocks in Objective-C; however, closures in Swift are a lot easier to use and understand. Let's look at the syntax used to define a closure in Swift:

```
{
(parameters) -> return-type in
  statements
}
```

As we can see, the syntax used to create a closure looks very similar to the syntax we use to create functions in Swift, and actually, in Swift, global and nested functions are closures. The biggest difference in the format between closures and functions is the `in` keyword. The `in` keyword is used in place of curly brackets to separate the definition of the closure's parameter and return types from the body of the closure.

There are many uses for closures and we will go over a number of them later in this chapter, but first we need to understand the basics of closures. Let's start by looking at some very basic uses for closures so that we can get a better understanding of what they are, how to define them, and how to use them.

Simple closures

We will begin by creating a very simple closure that does not accept any arguments and does not return any value. All it does is print `Hello World` to the console. Let's take a look at the following code:

```
let clos1 = {
  () -> Void in

  print("Hello World")
}
```

In this example, we create a closure and assign it to the constant `clos1`. Since there are no parameters defined between the parentheses, this closure will not accept any parameters. Also, the return type is defined as `Void`; therefore, this closure will not return any value. The body of the closure contains one line that prints `Hello World` to the console.

There are many ways to use closures; in this example, all we want to do is execute it. We would execute this closure like this:

```
clos1()
```

When we execute the closure, we will see that `Hello World` is printed to the console. At this point, closures may not seem that useful, but as we get further along in this chapter, we will see how useful and powerful they can be.

Let's look at another simple closure example. This closure will accept one string parameter named `name`, but will still not return a value. Within the body of the closure, we will print out a greeting to the name passed into the closure through the `name` parameter. Here is the code for this second closure:

```
let clos2 = {
  (name: String) -> Void in

  print("Hello \(name)")
}
```

The big difference between `clos2` defined in this example and the previous `clos1` closure is that we define a single string parameter between the parentheses in this closure. As we can see, we define parameters for closures just like we define parameters for functions.

We can execute this closure in the same way in which we executed `clos1`. The following code shows how this is done:

```
clos2("Jon")
```

This example, when executed, will print the message `Hello Jon` to the console. Let's look at another way we can use the `clos2` closure.

Our original definition of closures stated, "Closures are self-contained blocks of code that can be passed around and used throughout our application code". What this tells us is that we can pass our closure from the context that they were created in other parts of our code. Let's look at how to pass our `clos2` closure into a function. We will define the function that accepts our `clos2` closure like this:

```
func testClosure(handler:(String)->Void) {
  handler("Dasher")
}
```

We define the function just like we would any other function; however, in our parameter list, we define a parameter named `handler`, and the type defined for the handler parameter is `(String)->Void`. If we look closely, we can see that the `(String)->Void` definition of the `handler` parameter matches the parameter and return types that we defined for `clos2` closure. This means that we can pass the `clos2` closure into the function. Let's look at how to do this:

```
testClosure(clos2)
```

We call the `testClosure()` function just like any other function and the closure that is being passed in looks like any other variable. Since the `clos2` closure executed in the `testClosure()` function, we will see the message, `Hello Dasher`, printed to the console when this code is executed.

As we will see a little later in this chapter, the ability to pass closures to functions is what makes closures so exciting and powerful.

As the final piece to the closure puzzle, let's look at how to return a value from a closure. The following example shows this:

```
let clos3 = {
  (name: String) -> String in

  return "Hello \(name)"
}
```

The definition of the `clos3` closure looks very similar to how we defined the `clos2` closure. The difference is that we changed the `Void` return type to a `String` type. Then, in the body of the closure, instead of printing the message to the console, we used the return statement to return the message. We can now execute the `clos3` closure just like the previous two closures or pass the closure to a function like we did with the `clos2` closure. The following example shows how to execute `clos3` closure:

```
var message = clos3("Buddy")
```

After this line of code is executed, the message variable will contain the `Hello Buddy` string.

The previous three examples of closures demonstrate the format and how to define a typical closure. Those who are familiar with Objective-C can see that the format of closures in Swift is a lot cleaner and easier to use. The syntax for creating closures that we have shown so far in this chapter is pretty short; however, we can shorten it even more. In this next section, we will look at how to do this.

Shorthand syntax for closures

In this section, we will look at a couple of ways to shorten the definition of closures.

> Using the shorthand syntax for closures is really a matter of personal preference. There are a lot of developers that like to make their code as small and compact as possible and they take great pride in doing so. However, at times, this can make code hard to read and understand by other developers.

The first shorthand syntax for closures that we are going to look at is one of the most popular and is the syntax we saw when we were using algorithms with arrays in *Chapter 3, Using Collections and Cocoa Data Types*. This format is mainly used when we want to send a really small (usually one line) closure to a function, like we did with the algorithms for arrays. Before we look at this shorthand syntax, we need to write a function that will accept a closure as a parameter:

```
func testFunction(num: Int, handler:()->Void) {
  for var i=0; i < num; i++ {     handler()
  }
}
```

This function accepts two parameters—the first parameter is an integer named `num`, and the second parameter is a closure named `handler` that does not have any parameters and does not return any value. Within the function, we create a `for` loop that will use the `num` integer to define how many times it loops. Within the `for` loop, we call the `handler` closure that was passed into the function.

We can create a closure and pass it to the `testFunction()` like this:

```
let clos = {
    () -> Void in
    print("Hello from standard syntax")
}
testFunction(5,handler: clos)
```

This code is very easy to read and understand; however, it does take five lines of code. Now, let's look at how to shorten this code by writing the closure inline within the function call:

```
testFunction(5,handler: {print("Hello from Shorthand closure")})
```

In this example, we created the closure inline within the function call using the same syntax that we used with the algorithms for arrays. The closure is placed in between two curly brackets ({ }), which means the code to create our closure is `{print("Hello from Shorthand closure")}`. When this code is executed, it will print out the message, `Hello from Shorthand closure`, five times on the screen.

In *Chapter 3, Using Collections and Cocoa Data Types*, we saw that we were able to pass parameters to the array algorithms using the `$0`, `$1`, `$2`, and so on parameters. Let's look at how to use parameters with this shorthand syntax. We will begin by creating a new function that will accept a closure with a single parameter. We will name this function `testFunction2`. The following example shows what the new `testFunction2` function does:

```
func testFunction2(num: Int, handler:(name: String)->Void) {
  for var i=0; i < num; i++ {
    handler(name: "Me")
  }
}
```

In `testFunction2`, we define our closure like this: `(name: String)->Void`. This definition means that the closure accepts one parameter and does not return any value. Now, let's see how to use the same shorthand syntax to call this function:

```
testFunction2(5,handler: {print("Hello from \($0)")})
```

The difference between this closure definition and the previous one is `$0`. The `$0` parameter is shorthand for the first parameter passed into the function. If we execute this code, it prints out the message, `Hello from Me`, five times.

Using the dollar sign ($) followed by a number with inline closures allows us to define the closure without having to put a parameter list in the definition. The number after the dollar sign defines the position of the parameter in the parameter list. Let's examine this format a bit more because we are not limited to only using the dollar sign ($) and number shorthand format with inline closures. This shorthand syntax can also be used to shorten the closure definition by allowing us to leave the parameter names off. The following example demonstrates this:

```
let clos5: (String, String) ->Void = {
    print("\($0) \($1)")
}
```

In this example, our closure has two string parameters defined; however, we do not give them names. The parameters are defined like this: `(String, String)`. We can then access the parameters within the body of the closure using `$0` and `$1`. Also, note that closure definition is after the colon (`:`), using the same syntax that we use to define a variable type, rather than inside the curly brackets. When we use anonymous arguments, this is how we would define the closure. It will not be valid to define the closure like this:

```
let clos5b = {
    (String, String) -> Void in
    print("\($0) \($1)")
}
```

In this example, we will receive the `Anonymous closure arguments cannot be used inside a closure that has explicit arguments` error.

We will use the `clos5` closure like this:

```
clos5("Hello","Kara")
```

Since `Hello` is the first string in the parameter list, it is accessed with `$0`, and as `Kara` is the second string in the parameter list, it is accessed with `$1`. When we execute this code, we will see the message, `Hello Kara`, printed to the console.

This next example is used when the closure doesn't return any value. Rather than defining the return type as `Void`, we can use parentheses, as the following example shows:

```
let clos6: () -> () = {
    print("Howdy")
}
```

In this example, we define the closure as `() -> ()`. This tells Swift that the closure does not accept any parameters and also does not return a value. We will execute this closure like this:

```
clos6()
```

We have one more shorthand closure example to demonstrate before we begin showing some useful examples of closures. In this last example, we will demonstrate how we can return a value from the closure without the need to include the word, `return`.

If the entire closure body consists of only a single statement, then we can omit the `return` keyword, and the results of the statement will be returned. Let's take a look at an example of this:

```
let clos7 = {
     (first: Int, second: Int) -> Int in
     first + second
}
```

In this example, the closure accepts two parameters of the `Int` type and will return an `Int` type. The only statement within the body of the closure adds the first parameter to the second parameter. However, if you notice, we do not include the `return` keyword before the addition statement. Swift will see that this is a single statement closure and will automatically return the results, just as if we put the `return` keyword before the addition statement. We do need to make sure the result type of our statement matches the return type of the closure.

All of the examples that were shown in the previous two sections were designed to show how to define and use closures. On their own, these examples did not really show off the power of closures and they did not show how incredibly useful closures are. The remainder of this chapter is written to demonstrate the power and usefulness of closures in Swift.

Using closures with Swift's array algorithms

In *Chapter 3, Using Collections and Cocoa Data Types*, we looked at several built-in algorithms that we could use with Swift's arrays. In that chapter, we briefly saw how to add simple rules to each of these algorithms with very basic closures. Now that we have a better understanding of closures, let's see how we can expand on these algorithms using more advanced closures.

In this section, we will primarily be using the map algorithm for consistency purposes; however, we can use the basic ideas demonstrated with any of the algorithms. We will start by defining an array to use:

```
let guests = ["Jon", "Kim", "Kailey", "Kara"]
```

This array contains a list of names and the array is named `guests`. This array will be used for all the examples in this section, except for the very last ones.

Now that we have our `guests` array, let's add a closure that will print a greeting to each of the names in the `guests` array:

```
guests.map({
    (name: String) -> Void in
    print("Hello \(name)")
})
```

Since the map algorithm applies the closure to each item of the array, this example will print out a greeting for each name within the `guests` array. After the first section in this chapter, we should have a pretty good understanding of how this closure works. Using the shorthand syntax that we saw in the last section, we could reduce the preceding example down to the following single line of code:

```
guests.map({print("Hello \($0)")})
```

This is one of the few times, in my opinion, where the shorthand syntax may be easier to read than the standard syntax.

Now, let's say that rather than printing the greeting to the console, we wanted to return a new array that contained the greetings. For this, we would have returned a string type from our closure, as shown in the following example:

```
var messages = guests.map({
    (name:String) -> String in
    return "Welcome \(name)"
})
```

When this code is executed, the `messages` array will contain a greeting to each of the names in the `guests` array while the `guests` array will remain unchanged.

The preceding examples in this section showed how to add a closure to the map algorithm inline. This is good if we only had one closure that we wanted to use with the map algorithm, but what if we had more than one closure that we wanted to use, or if we wanted to use the closure multiple times or reuse them with different arrays. For this, we could assign the closure to a constant or variable and then pass in the closure, using its constant or variable name, as needed. Let's see how to do this. We will begin by defining two closures. One of the closures will print a greeting for each name in the `guests` array, and the other closure will print a goodbye message for each name in the `guests` array:

```
let greetGuest = {
  (name:String) -> Void in
    print("Hello guest named \(name)")
}

let sayGoodbye = {
```

```
    (name:String) -> Void in
      print("Goodbye \(name)")
}
```

Now that we have two closures, we can use them with the map algorithm as needed. The following code shows how to use these closures interchangeably with the `guests` array:

```
guests.map(greetGuest)
guests.map(sayGoodbye)
```

Whenever we use the `greetGuest` closure with the `guests` array, the greetings message is printed to the console, and whenever we use the `sayGoodbye` closure with the `guests` array, the goodbye message is printed to the console. If we had another array named `guests2`, we could use the same closures for that array, as shown in the following example:

```
guests.map(greetGuest)
guests2.map(greetGuest)
guests.map(sayGoodbye)
guests2.map(sayGoodbye)
```

All of the examples, in this section, so far have either printed a message to the console or returned a new array from the closure. We are not limited to such basic functionality in our closures. For example, we can filter the array within our closure, as shown in the following example:

```
let greetGuest2 = {
    (name:String) -> Void in
      if (name.hasPrefix("K")) {
        print("\(name) is on the guest list")
      } else {
      print("\(name) was not invited")
      }
}
```

In this example, we print out a different message depending on whether the name starts with the letter K or not.

As we mentioned earlier in the chapter, closures have the ability to capture and store references to any variable or constant from the context in which they were defined. Let's look at an example of this. Let's say that we have a function that contains the highest temperature for the last seven days at a given location and this function accepts a closure as a parameter. This function will execute the closure on the array of temperature. The function can be written like this:

```
func temperatures(calculate:(Int)->Void) {
```

```
        var tempArray = [72,74,76,68,70,72,66]
        tempArray.map(calculate)

    }
```

This function accepts a closure defined as `(Int)->Void`. We then use the map algorithm to execute this closure for each item of the `tempArray` array. The key to using a closure correctly in this situation is to understand that the `temperatures` function does not know or care what goes on inside the `calculate` closure. Also, be aware that the closure is also unable to update or change the items within the function's context, which means that the closure cannot change any other variable within the temperature's function; however, it can update variables in the context that it was created in.

Let's look at the function that we will create the closure in. We will name this function `testFunction`. Let's take a look at the following code:

```
    func testFunction() {
        var total = 0
        var count = 0
        let addTemps = {
          (num: Int) -> Void in
          total += num
          count++
        }
        temperatures(addTemps)
        print("Total: \(total)")
        print("Count: \(count)")
        print("Average: \(total/count)")
    }
```

In this function, we begin by defining two variables named `total` and `count`, where both variables are of the integer type. We then create a closure named `addTemps` that will be used to add all of the temperatures from the `temperatures` function together. The `addTemps` closure will also count how many temperatures are there in the array. To do this, the `addTemps` closure calculates the sum of each item in the array and keeps the total in the `total` variable that was defined at the beginning of the function. The `addTemps` closure also keeps track of the number of items in the array by incrementing the `count` variable for each item. Notice that neither the `total` nor `count` variables are defined within the closure; however, we are able to use them within the closure because they were defined in the same context as the closure.

We then call the `temperatures` function and pass it the `addTemps` closure. Finally, we print the total, count, and average temperature to the console. When the `testFunction` is executed, we see the following output to the console:

```
Total: 498
Count: 7
Average: 71
```

As we can see from the output, the `addTemps` closure is able to update and use items that are defined within the context that it was created in, even when the closure is used in a different context.

Now that we have looked at using closures with the array map algorithm, let's look at using closures by themselves. We will also look at the ways we can clean up our code to make it easier to read and use.

Standalone closures and good style guidelines

Closures give us the ability to truly separate the data portions of our code from the user interface and business logic portions. This gives us the ability to create reusable classes that focus solely on retrieving our data. This is especially good for developing classes and frameworks that are designed to retrieve data from external services, such as web services, databases, or files. This section will show how to develop a class that will execute a closure once our data is ready to return.

Let's begin by creating a class that will contain the data portion of our code. In this example, the class will be named `Guests` and it will contain an array of `guests` names. Let's take a look at the following code:

```
class Guests {
    var guestNames = ["Jon","Kim","Kailey","Kara","Buddy","Lily","Da
sh"]

    typealias UseArrayClosure = [String] -> Void
    func getGuest(handler:UseArrayClosure) {
        handler(guestNames)
    }

}
```

The first line in the `Guests` class defines an array named `guestNames`. The `guestNames` array contains seven names. After we define the `guestNames` array, we then create a type alias. A type alias defines a named alias for an existing type. Just like a function, closures have types that consist of the parameter types and return types, which can be aliased. This allows us to define the closure once and then use the alias anywhere within our code. Using a type alias can reduce the amount of typing we have to do and also prevent errors. Therefore, it is recommended that we use them rather than trying to retype the closure definition multiple times in our code. It also allows us to change the definition in one location and it will then update throughout the code.

In this example, our type alias is named `UseArrayClosure` and is defined as a closure that accepts an array of strings as the only parameter and does not return a value. We can now use this type alias throughout our code as shorthand for the closure definition.

Finally, we define a `getGuest()` method that accepts a closure named `handler` as its only parameter. Within the `getGuests()` method, the only thing we do is execute the handler. Normally, in this method, we will have the logic to retrieve the data from our external data source; however, in this example, we have an array that is hardcoded with our list of guest names. Therefore, all we need to do is to execute the closure with the `guestsNames` array as the only parameter.

Now, let's say that we want to display this array of names in a `UITableView` view. A `UITableView` is an iOS view that is designed for displaying lists of information. In the view controller, we will need to create an array to hold the data to display in `UITableView` and a variable that will link to `UITableView` in our display. These will both be class variables defined in our view controller class, and they are defined like this:

```
@IBOutlet var tableView:UITableView?
var tableData: [String]?
```

Now, let's create a function called `getData()` that will be used to retrieve the list of guests and update the table view:

```
func getData() {
  let dataClosure: Guests.UseArrayClosure = {
    self.tableData = $0
    if let tView = self.tableView {
      tView.reloadData()
    }
  }

  let guests = Guests()
  guests.getGuest(dataClosure)
}
```

We begin the `getData()` function by defining a closure named `dataClosure`. This closure uses the `UseArrayClosure` type alias that we defined in the `Guests` class for the closure definition. Within the closure definition, we set the `tableData` array, which is defined within the view controller itself (not in the closure), equal to the string array that is passed into the closure. We then verify whether the `tableView` variable contains an instance of the `UITableView` class, and if so, we reload its data. Finally, we create an instance of the `Guests` class and call the `getGuest()` method passing it the `dataClosure` closure.

Keep in mind that the `guestNames` array, which defines the list of names, is defined in the `Guest` class, while the `tableView`, `UITableView`, and `tableData` arrays are defined in the view controller class.

When the `dataClosure` closure is passed to the `getGuests()` method, it will load the array of names, from the `Guests` class, into the `tableData` array. The `tableData` array is then used within the view controller class as the data elements for the `UITableView` array. The key items to note in this example are that we are able to load data from one context (the `Guests` class) into a variable that was defined within the same context as the closure (the view controller), and also have the ability to call methods on instances of classes (`tableView` and `UITableView`) defined within the same context as the closure.

We could have very easily created a method in the `Guest` class that returned the `guestNames` array. With a hardcoded array, such as the one we have in the `Guest` class, this method would have worked very well. However, if we were loading the data from a web service that takes a little time to load; this will not work as well because our UI will freeze while waiting for the data to load. By using a closure, as shown in this example, we can make the web service call asynchronously, and then when the data is returned, the closure will be executed and the UI updates automatically without our UI freezing.

This book is primarily written to teach the Swift language and not specifically iOS development; therefore, we are not covering how the UI elements from the Cocoa Touch framework work in this example. If you want to see the full iOS example, download the code samples for this book.

Changing functionality

Closures also give us the ability to change the functionality of classes on the fly. We saw in *Chapter 11, Working with Generics*, that generics give us the ability to write functions that are valid for multiple types. With closures, we are able to write functions and classes whose functionality can change, based on the closure that is passed into it as a parameter. In this section, we will show how to write a function whose functionality can be changed with a closure.

Let's begin by defining a class that will be used to demonstrate how to swap out functionality. We will name this class `TestClass`:

```
class TestClass {
  typealias getNumClosure = ((Int, Int) -> Int)

  var numOne = 5
  var numTwo = 8

  var results = 0
  func getNum(handler: getNumClosure) -> Int {
    results = handler(numOne,numTwo)
    return results

  }
}
```

We begin this class by defining a type alias for our closure that is named `getNumClosure`. Any closure that is defined as a `getNumClosure` closure will take two integers and return an integer. Within this closure, we assume that it does something with the integers that we pass in to get the value to return, but it really doesn't have to. To be honest, this class doesn't really care what the closure does as long as it conforms to the `getNumClosure` type. Next, we define three integers that are named `numOne`, `NumTwo`, and `results`.

Finally, we define a method named `getNum()`. This method accepts a closure that confirms the `getNumClosure` type as its only parameter. Within the `getNum()` method, we execute the closure by passing in the `numOne` and `numTwo` class variables, and the integer that is returned is put into the `results` class variable.

Now, let's look at several closures that conform to the `getNumClosure` type that we can use with the `getNum()` method:

```
var max: TestClass.getNumClosure = {
  if $0 > $1 {
    return $0
```

```
    } else {
      return $1
    }
  }

  var min: TestClass.getNumClosure = {
    if $0 < $1 {
      return $0
    } else {
      return $1
    }
  }

  var multiply:  TestClass.getNumClosure = {
    return $0 * $1
  }

  var second: TestClass.getNumClosure = {
    return $1
  }

  var answer: TestClass.getNumClosure = {
    var tmp = $0 + $1
    return 42
  }
```

In this code, we define five closures that conform to the `getNumClosure` type:

- `max`: This returns the maximum value of the two integers that are passed in
- `min`: This returns the minimum value of the two integers that are passed in
- `multiply`: This multiplies both the values that are passed in and returns the product
- `second`: This returns the second parameter that was passed in
- `answer`: This returns the answer to life, the universe, and everything

In the `answer` closure, we have an extra line that looks like it does not have a purpose: `var tmp = $0 + $1`. We do this purposely because the following code is not valid:

```
  var answer: TestClass.getNumClosure = {
      return 42
  }
```

This class gives us the `error: tuple types '(Int, Int)' and '()' have a different number of elements (2 vs. 0)` error. As we can see by the error, Swift does not think that our closure accepts any parameters unless we use `$0` and `$1` within the body of the closure. In the closure named `second`, Swifts assumes that there are two parameters because `$1` specifies the second parameter.

We can now pass each one of these closures to the `getNum` method of our `TestClass` to change the functionality of the function to suit our needs. The following code illustrates this:

```
var myClass = TestClass()

myClass.getNum(max)
myClass.getNum(min)
myClass.getNum(multiply)
myClass.getNum(second)
myClass.getNum(answer)
```

When this code is run, we will receive the following results for each of the closures:

- `max`: results = 8
- `min`: results = 5
- `multiply`: results = 40
- `second`: results = 8
- `answer`: results = 42

The last example we are going to show you in this chapter is one that is used a lot in frameworks, especially the ones that have a functionality that is designed to be run asynchronously.

Selecting a closure based on results

In the final example, we will pass two closures to a method, and then depending on some logic, one, or possibly both, of the closures will be executed. Generally, one of the closures is called if the method was successfully executed and the other closure is called if the method failed.

Let's start off by creating a class that will contain a method that will accept two closures and then execute one of the closures based on the defined logic. We will name this class `TestClass`. Here is the code for the `TestClass` class:

```
class TestClass {
  typealias ResultsClosure = ((String) -> Void)
```

```
    func isGreater(numOne: Int, numTwo:Int, successHandler:
      ResultsClosure, failureHandler: ResultsClosure) {
      if numOne > numTwo {
        successHandler("\(numOne) is greater than \(numTwo)")
      }
      else {
        failureHandler("\(numOne) is not greater than \(numTwo)")
      }

    }
  }
```

We begin this class by creating a type alias that defines the closure that we will use for both the successful and failure closures. We will name this type alias `ResultsClosure`. This example will also illustrate why using a type alias, rather than retyping the closure definition, saves us a lot of typing and also prevents us from making mistakes. In this example, if we did not use a type alias, we would need to retype the closure definition four times, and if we needed to change the closure definition, we would need to change it in four spots. With the type alias, we only need to type the closure definition once and then use the alias throughout the remaining code.

We then create a method named `isGreater` that takes two integers as the first two parameters and then two closures as the next two parameters. The first closure is named `successHandler`, and the second closure is named `failureHandler`. Within the `isGreater` method, we check whether the first integer parameter is greater than the second one. If the first integer is greater, the `successHandler` closure is executed; otherwise, the `failureHandler` closure is executed.

Now, let's create two of our closures. The code for these two closures is:

```
var success: TestClass. ResultsClosure = {
    print("Success: \($0)")
}

var failure: TestClass. ResultsClosure = {
    print("Failure: \($0)")
}
```

Note that both closures are defined as the `TestClass.ResultsClosure` type. In each closure, we simply print a message to the console to let us know which closure was executed. Normally, we would put some functionality in the closure.

We will then call the method with both the closures like this:

```
var test = TestClass()
test.isGreater(8, numTwo: 6, successHandler:success,
  failureHandler:failure)
```

Note that in the method call, we are sending both the success closure and the failure closure. In this example, we will see the message, `Success: 8 is greater than 6`. If we reversed the numbers, we would see the message, `Failure: 6 is not greater than 8`. This use case is really good when we call asynchronous methods, such as loading data from a web service. If the web service call was successful, the success closure is called; otherwise, the failure closure is called.

One big advantage of using closures like this is that the UI does not freeze while we wait for the web service call to complete. This also involves a concurrency piece, which we will be covering in *Chapter 14, Concurrency and Parallelism in Swift*, later in this book. As an example, if we tried to retrieve data from a web service like this:

```
var data = myWebClass.myWebServiceCall(someParameter)
```

Our UI would freeze while we wait for the response to come back, or we would have to make the call in a separate thread so that the UI would not hang. With closures, we pass the closures to the networking framework and rely on the framework to execute the appropriate closure when it is done. This does rely on the framework to implement concurrency correctly to make the calls asynchronously, but a decent framework should handle that for us.

Creating strong reference cycles with closures

Earlier in this chapter, we said, "the best thing is, for the most part, Swift will handle the memory management for us". The "for the most part" section of the quote means that if everything is written in a standard way, Swift will handle the memory management of the closures for us. However, just like classes, there are times where the memory management fails us. Memory management will work correctly for all of the examples that we have seen in this chapter so far. It is possible to create a strong reference cycle that would prevent Swift's memory management from working correctly. Let's look at what happens if we create a strong reference cycle with closures.

A strong reference cycle may happen if we assign a closure to a property of a class instance and within that closure, we capture the instance of the class. This capture occurs because we access a property of that particular instance using `self` like `self.someProperty` or we assign self to a variable or constant like `let c = self`. By capturing a property of the instance, we are actually capturing the instance itself, thereby creating a strong reference cycle where the memory manager will not know when to release the instance. As a result, the memory will not be freed correctly.

Let's begin by creating a class that has a closure and an instance of the string type as its two properties. We will also create a type alias for the closure type in this class and define a `deinit()` method that prints a message to the console. The `deinit()` method is called when the class gets released and the memory is freed. We will know when the class gets released when the message from the `deinit()` method is printed to the console. This class will be named `TestClassOne`. Let's take a look at the following code:

```
class TestClassOne {
  typealias nameClosure = (() -> String)

  var name = "Jon"

  lazy var myClosure: nameClosure =  {
    return self.name
  }

  deinit {
    print("TestClassOne deinitialized")
  }
}
```

Now, let's create a second class that will contain a method that accepts a closure that is of the `nameClosure` type that was defined in the `TestClassOne` class. This class will also have a `deinit()` method, so we can also see when it gets released. We will name this class `TestClassTwo`. Let's take a look at the following code:

```
class TestClassTwo {

  func closureExample(handler: TestClassOne.nameClosure) {
    print(handler())
  }

  deinit {
    print("TestClassTwo deinitialized")
  }
}
```

Now, let's see this code in action by creating instances of each class and then trying to manually release the instance by setting them to `nil`:

```
var testClassOne: TestClassOne? = TestClassOne()
var testClassTwo: TestClassTwo? = TestClassTwo()

testClassTwo?.closureExample(testClassOne!.myClosure)

testClassOne = nil
print("testClassOne is gone")

testClassTwo = nil
print("testClassTwo is gone")
```

What we do in this code is create two optionals that may contain an instance of our two test classes or nil. We need to create these variables as optionals because we will be setting them to `nil` later in the code so that we can see whether the instances are released properly.

We then call the `closureExample()` method of the `TestClassTwo` instance and pass it the `myClosure` property from the `TestClassOne` instance. We now try to release the `TestClassOne` and `TestClassTwo` instances by setting them to `nil`. Keep in mind that when an instance of a class is released, it attempts to call the `deinit()` method of the class if it exists. In our case, both classes have a `deinit()` method that prints a message to the console, so we know when the instances are actually released.

If we run this project, we will see the following messages printed to the console:

```
testClassOne is gone
TestClassTwo deinitialized
testClassTwo is gone
```

As we can see, we do attempt to release the `TestClassOne` instances, but the `deinit()` method of the class is never called, indicating that it was not actually released; however, the `TestClassTwo` instance was properly released because the `deinit()` method of that class was called.

To see how this is supposed to work without the strong reference cycle, change the `myClosure` closure to return a string type that is defined within the closure itself, as shown in the following code:

```
lazy var myClosure: nameClosure = {
  return "Just Me"
}
```

Now, if we run the project, we should see the following output:

```
TestClassOne deinitialized
testClassOne is gone
TestClassTwo deinitialized
testClassTwo is gone
```

This shows that the `deinit()` methods from both the `TestClassOne` and `TestClassTwo` instances were properly called, indicating that they were both released properly.

In the first example, we capture an instance of the `TestClassOne` class within the closure because we accessed a property of the `TestClassOne` class using `self.name`. This created a strong reference from the closure to the instance of the `TestClassOne` class, preventing memory management from releasing the instance.

Swift does provide a very easy and elegant way to resolve strong reference cycles in closures. We simply need to tell Swift not to create a strong reference by creating a capture list. A capture list defines the rules to use when capturing reference types within a closure. We can declare each reference to be a weak or unowned reference rather than a strong reference.

A `weak` keyword is used when there is the possibility that the reference will become nil during its lifetime; therefore, the type must be an optional. The `unowned` keyword is used when there is not a possibility of the reference becoming nil.

We define the capture list by pairing the `weak` or `unowned` keywords with a reference to a class instance. These pairings are written within square brackets (`[ ]`). Therefore, if we update the `myClosure` closure and define an `unowned` reference to `self`, we should eliminate the strong reference cycle. The following code shows what the new `myClosure` closure will look similar to:

```
lazy var myClosure: nameClosure =  {
   [unowned self] in
  return self.name
}
```

Notice the new line— `[unowned self] in`. This line says that we do not want to create a strong reference to the instance of `self`. If we run the project now, we should see the following output:

```
TestClassOne deinitialized
testClassOne is gone
TestClassTwo deinitialized
testClassTwo is gone
```

This shows that both the `TestClassOne` and `TestClassTwo` instances were properly released.

Summary

In this chapter, we saw that we can define a closure just like we can define an int or string type. We can assign closures to a variable, pass them as an argument to functions, and also return them from functions.

Closures capture a store references to any constants or variables from the context in which the closure was defined. We do have to be careful with this functionality to make sure that we do not create a strong reference cycle, which would lead to memory leaks in our applications.

Swift closures are very similar to blocks in Objective-C, but they have a much cleaner and eloquent syntax. This makes them a lot easier to use and understand.

Having a good understanding of closures is vital to mastering the Swift programming language and will make it easier to develop great applications that are easy to maintain for OS X and iOS. It is also essential for creating first class frameworks that can be used to create OS X and iOS applications.

The three use cases that we saw in this chapter are by no means the only three *useful* uses for closures. I can promise you that the more you use closures in Swift, the more uses you will find for them. Closures are definitely one of the most powerful and useful features of the Swift language, and Apple did a great job by implementing them in the language.

13
Using Mix and Match

When Apple first introduced Swift at WWDC 2014, my first thought was how much work it would be for developers to rewrite their apps, which were already written in Objective-C, in Swift. I also wondered why a developer would rewrite their apps in Swift. A lot of these applications are pretty complex and would take a pretty large effort to rewrite them. Somewhere in the Swift presentation, Apple spoke about mix and match, which allows Swift and Objective-C to interact within the same project. Mix and match sure sounded like an ideal solution because developers could rewrite sections of their code in Swift as they needed to do updates, instead of having to rewrite their whole application. My big question was how well mix and match would actually work, and I was very surprised; not only does it work well but it is also easy to implement.

In this chapter, we will cover the following topics:

- What is mix and match
- How to use Swift and Objective-C together in the same project
- How to add Swift to an Objective-C project
- How to use Objective-C in a Swift project

What is mix and match

Swift's compatibility with Objective-C allows us to create a project in either language and include files written in the other language. This feature is called **mix and match**. It was arguably one of the most important features that came out with Swift.

The reason why this feature is so important is that there are, well, over a million apps written in Objective-C in Apple's App Store, and it would not be feasible for developers to spend the resources required for converting those apps from Objective-C to Swift. Without mix and match, the adaptation of the Swift language would be very slow. With mix and match, developers can begin to use Swift in their present apps that are written in Objective-C without having to convert the entire code base to Swift.

With mix and match, we can update our current Objective-C project using Swift. We can also use any framework written in Objective-C within our Swift projects and use newer frameworks written in Swift in our Objective-C projects.

For developers that have been using Apple products for a long time, they might find a similarity between mix and match and Rosetta, which Apple started including with OS X 10.4.4 Tiger. OS X 10.4.4 was the first version of Apple's operating system that was released with Apple's first Intel-based machines. Rosetta was written to allow many PowerPC applications to run seamlessly on the new Intel-based machines.

For those developers who are new to Apple products, you might not have heard of Rosetta. This is because Rosetta was not included or supported as of OS X 10.7 Lion. The reason this is mentioned is because if mix and match takes a similar path as Rosetta, it might not be a part of the language forever and from what Apple has said, Swift is the future. It also makes sense from a technological standpoint that as the Swift language evolves and matures, Apple will not want to maintain compatibility with Objective-C.

If you maintain legacy apps written in Objective-C, it might be a good idea to take advantage of mix and match to slowly upgrade your code base to Swift.

Let's look at how Swift and Objective-C can interact together. For this, we will be creating a very basic iOS project whose language will be Objective-C, and then we will add some Swift code for the project to use. In the downloadable code for this book, we have included an Objective-C project that consists of Swift code and a Swift project that includes Objective-C code. One thing to keep in mind is that it does not matter if our project is an Objective-C or a Swift project; interaction between Swift and Objective-C works the same way.

Using Swift and Objective-C together in the same project

In this section, we will be walking through how to add Swift to an Objective-C project. The same steps can also be used to add the Objective-C code to a Swift project. In the downloadable code for this book, you will find both Objective-C and Swift projects. These projects demonstrate how to add the Swift code to an Objective-C project and how to add Objective-C code to a Swift project. In those projects, we can see that mix and match functions exactly the same, no matter what type of project we are using.

Creating the project

Let's begin by creating an iOS project to work with. When we first start Xcode, we should see a screen that looks similar to the following screenshot:

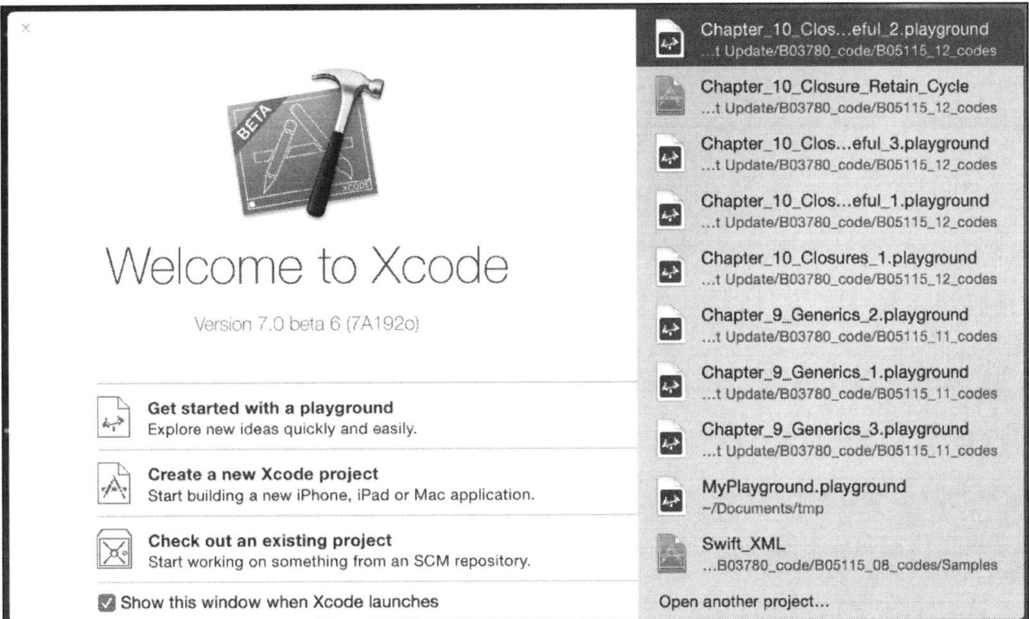

From this menu, we will want to select the **Create a new Xcode project** option. This option will walk us though creating a new Xcode project. Once this option is selected, Xcode will start up and we will see the following menu. As a shortcut, if we do not see this menu, we can also navigate to **File** | **New** | **Project** in the top menu bar, which will display the following screen:

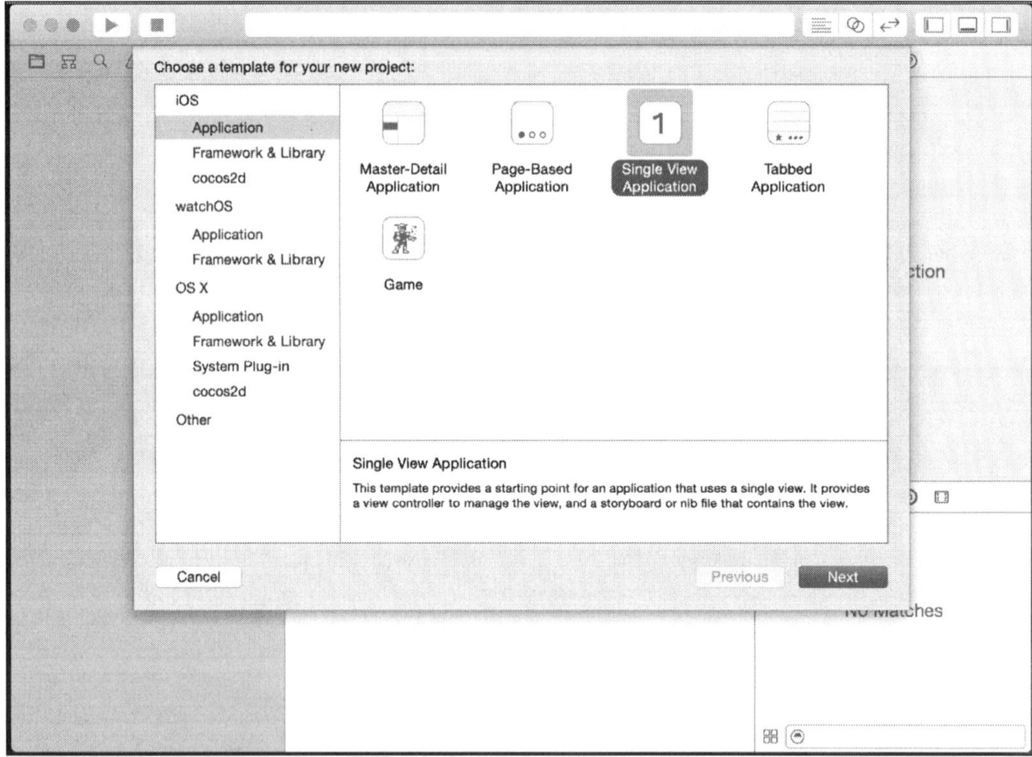

This menu lets us select the type of project we will be creating and also what platform we are targeting (iOS or OS X). For this example, we will be targeting the iOS platform and creating a simple Single View Application. Once we make our selection, we should see the following menu:

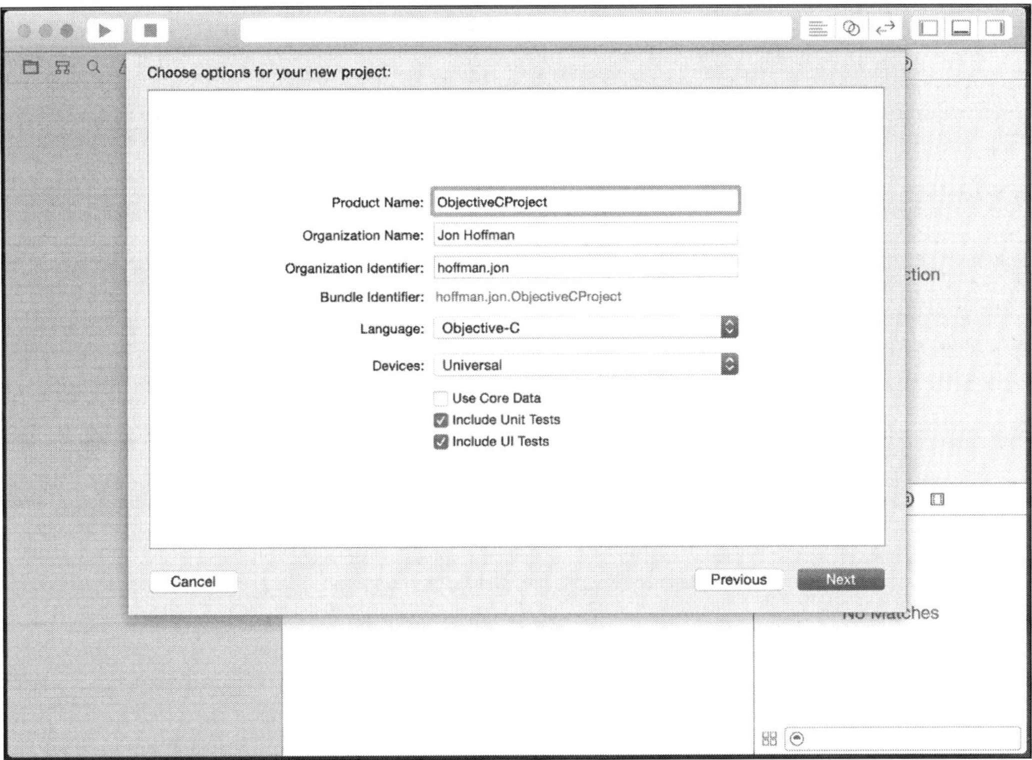

On this menu, we will define several properties about our project. The two properties we need to focus on are the language of the project and product name. For this particular project, we will select Objective-C as the language and name it `ObjectiveCProject`. Once we have all of the properties defined, we can click on the **Next** button. On the last menu, we select where we wish to save the project files, and once we have done that, Xcode creates the project template files for us, and we can begin.

The application that we will be creating will let the user enter a name and will then respond with a personal message to them. The user interface will consist of a `UITextField` field that the user can enter their name into, a `UIButton` that the user will press after they have entered their name, and a `UITextView` that will display the personalized message. Since this book is about Swift programming, we will not go into how the user interface is laid out. Full working applications are available as part of the book's downloadable source code.

Since we are walking through the Objective-C project, the user interface and the `Messages` class, which will generate a message, will be written in Objective-C. The message builder, which will personalize the message, will be written in Swift. This will show us how to access a Swift class from the Objective-C code as well as Objective-C resources from our Swift code within an Objective-C project.

Let's summarize the Objective-C to Swift interaction. The backend for the user interface, which is written in Objective-C, will call the `getPersonalizedMessage()` method of the `MessageBuilder` class written in Swift. The `getPersonalizedMessage()` method of the `MessageBuilder` class will call the `getMessage()` function of the `Messages` class written in Objective-C.

Adding Swift file to the Objective-C project

Let's begin by creating the Swift `MessageBuilder` class. This class will be used to build the personalized message for the user. Within Objective-C projects, I usually create a separate group called `SwiftFiles` to hold the Swift files in. This allows me to very easily see what files are written in Swift and what are written in Objective-C. To add a Swift file to our project, right-click on the group icon that we want to add the file to and we should see the following menu:

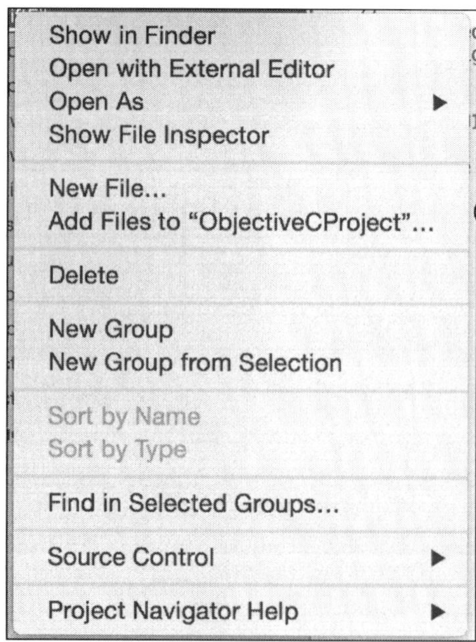

From this menu, select the **New File...** option. This option will walk us through creating a new file for our project. Once you select that option, you should see the following menu:

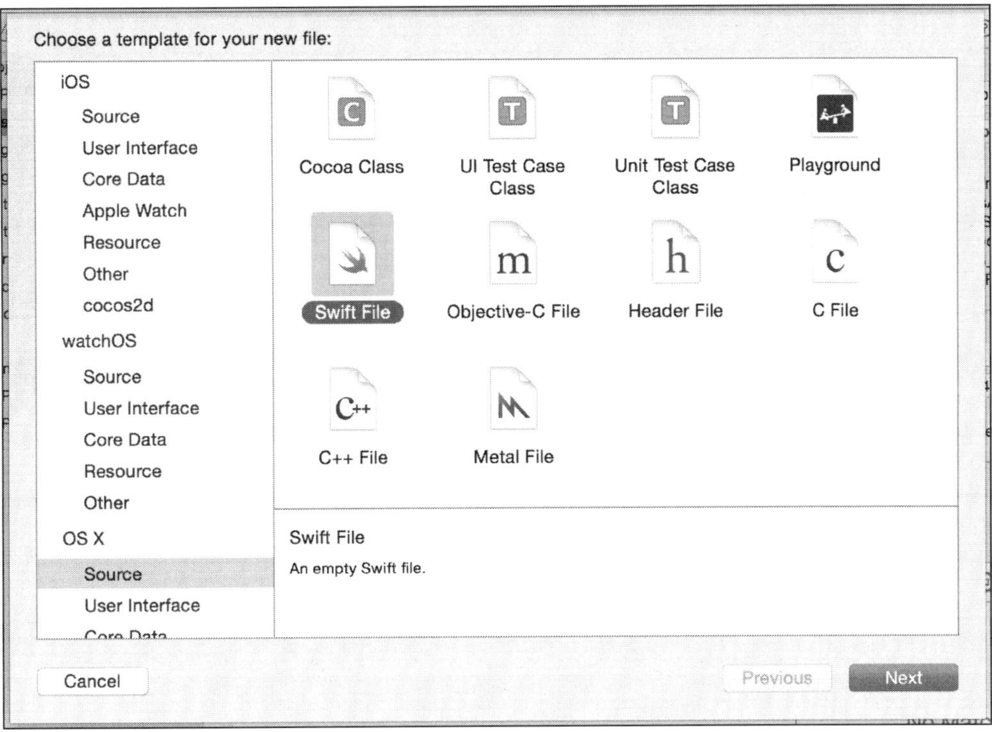

This menu lets us choose what type of file we will be adding to our project. In this case, we will want to add a Swift file to our project; therefore, we will select the **Swift File** option. Once we select this option, we should see the following menu:

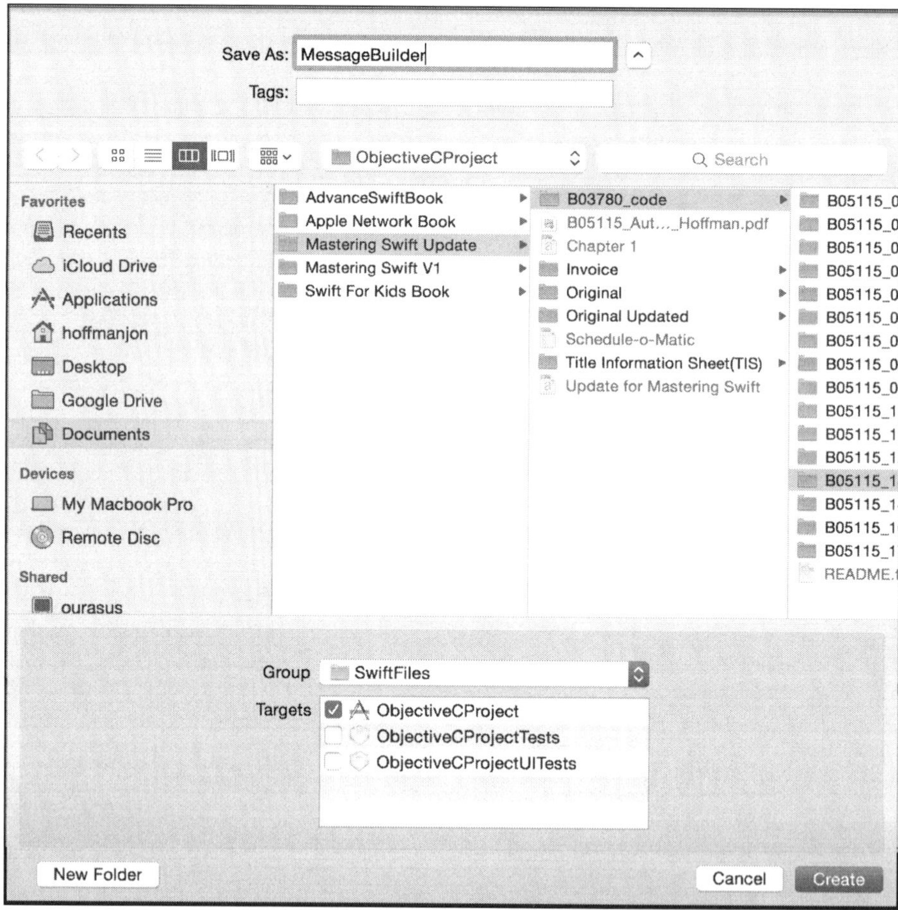

This menu lets us name the file and define some of the properties, such as where we will save the file and what group it will be in. In this case, we name the file `MessageBuilder`. Once we have finished, we will click on the **Create** button. If this is the first Swift file added to an Objective-C project (or the first Objective-C file added to a Swift project), we should see the following menu pop up:

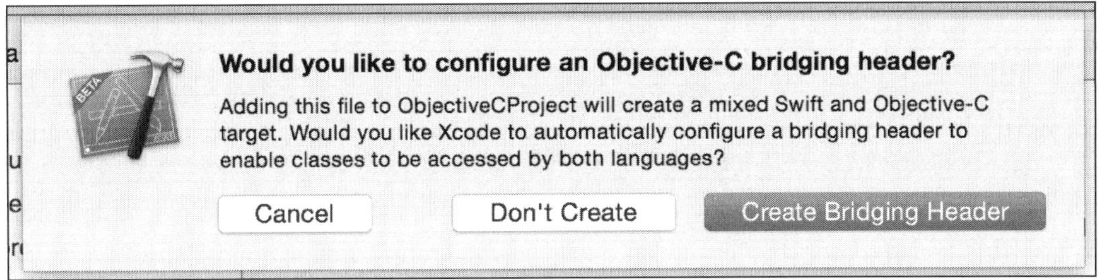

This popup offers to create the bridging header file for use. Select **Create Bridging Header** to create the file.

The Objective-C bridging header file – part 1

In order to expose our Objective-C files to our Swift code, we rely on an Objective-C header file. The first time we add an Objective-C file to a Swift project or a Swift file to an Objective-C project, Xcode offers to create this file for us. It is easier to let Xcode create and configure this file rather than doing it manually, so it is recommended to select **Yes** when Xcode offers to create it.

If for some reason we need to create the Objective-C bridging header file manually, the following steps show how we would do this:

1. Create an Objective-C header file in our project using the **New File...** option we saw earlier. The recommended naming convention for this file is `[MyProjectName]-Bridging-Header.h`, where `[MyProjectName]` is the name of our project. This will be the header file where we import any Objective-C header files for any Objective-C classes that we want our Swift code to access.
2. In the project's **Build Settings**, find the **Swift Compiler - Code Generation** section. In this section, locate the setting, titled **Objective-C Bridging Header**. We will want to set this to the path for the bridging header we created in step 1. The path will be from the project root.

The **Objective-C Bridging Header** setting for the present project that we are working on looks similar to the following screenshot:

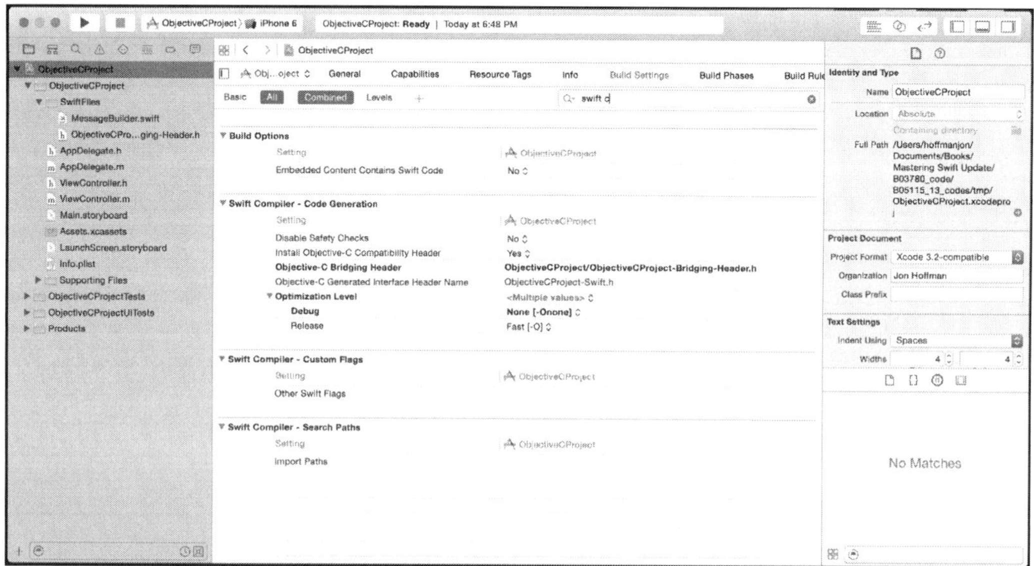

Even though the bridging header is located in the `SwiftFiles` group, we can see in the settings that the file itself is located at the root of the project. If we want to put the header file in another directory within the project, all we would need to do is change the path in this setting.

Adding the Objective-C file to the project

Now that we have our Objective-C bridging header file and the `MessageBuilder` Swift file, let's create the Objective-C class that will generate a generic message to the user. We will name this class `Messages`. To create this file, right-click on the group folder that we want to add the file to, and we should see the following menu:

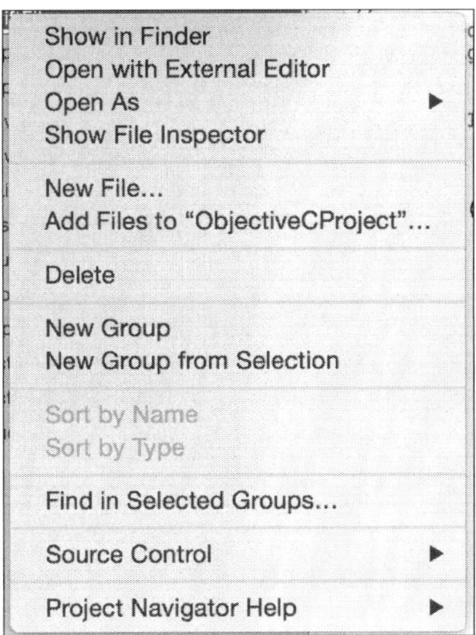

From this menu, select the **New File...** option. This option will walk us through creating a new file for our project. Once you select that option, you should see the following menu:

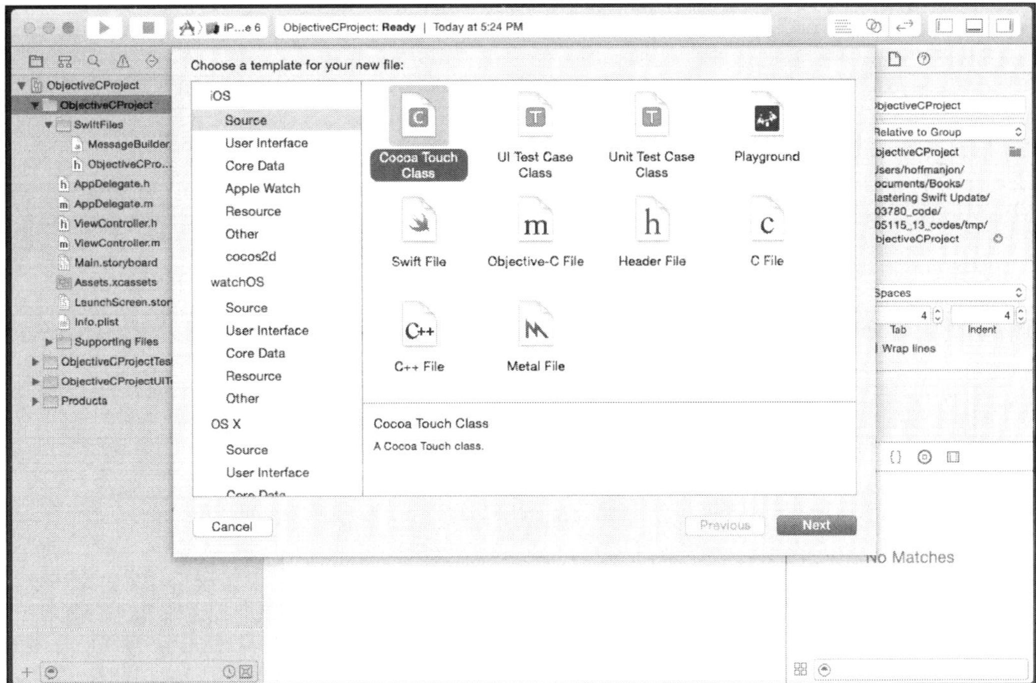

Previously, when we added the `MessageBuilder` Swift file, we selected **Swift File** on this menu. This time, we will be adding an Objective-C file, so we will select the **Cocoa Touch Class** option. Once we select that option, we should see a screen similar to this:

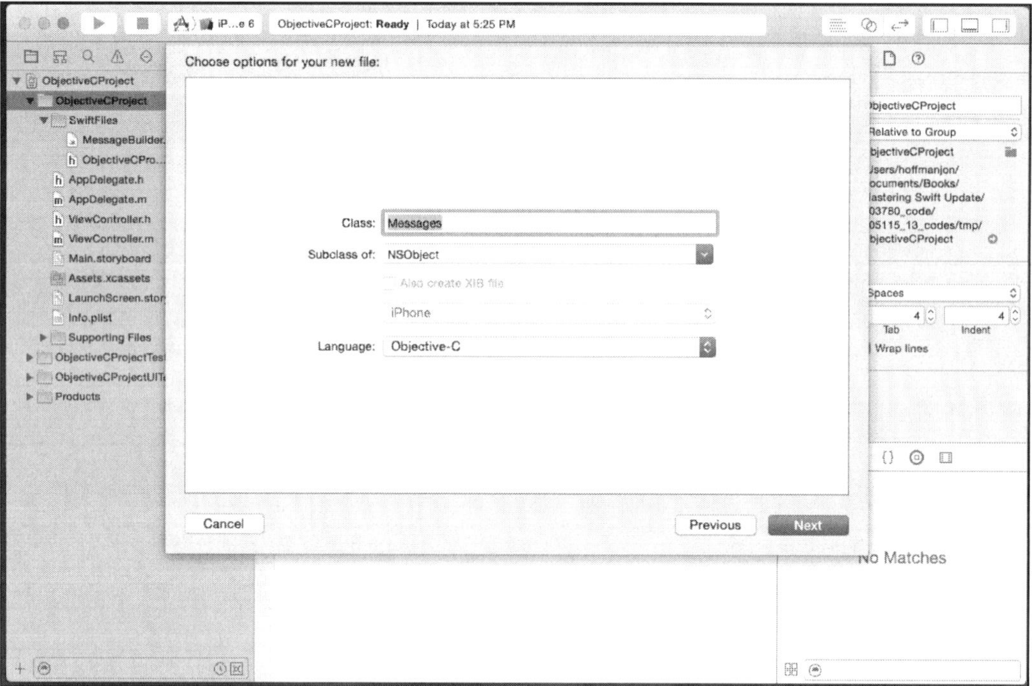

On this menu, we can enter the class name and also the language for the class. Make sure that the language is set to Objective-C. Finally, we click on the **Next** button, which will take us to a menu that will let us select where we want to save our Objective-C files. Once we select the location to save our files, both the header and implementation files will be added to our project.

Now that all of our files have been created, let's begin writing our code and getting Swift and Objective-C to work together. We will begin by adding the code to the Objective-C **Messages** header and implementation files.

The Messages Objective-C class

The `Messages` Objective-C class will contain an array of messages and will expose one method named `getMessage`, which will return one randomly picked message from the array.

The following code shows the Messages header file:

```
#import <Foundation/Foundation.h>

@interface Messages : NSObject

-(NSString *)getMessage;
@end
```

In this header file, we expose one method named getMessage that will return a message when called. The following code shows the implementation file for the Messages class:

```
#import "Messages.h"

@implementation Messages

NSMutableArray *theMessages;

-(id)init {
  if ( self = [super init] ) {
    theMessages = [NSMutableArray new];
    [theMessages addObject:@"You should learn from your
      mistakes"];
    [theMessages addObject:@"It is in the now that we must live"];
    [theMessages addObject:@"The greatest risk is not taking
      one"];
    [theMessages addObject:@"You will be a Swift programmer"];
  }
    return self;
}

-(NSString *)getMessage {
  int num = arc4random() % theMessages.count;

  return theMessages[num];
}
@end
```

In this code, we created the NSArray object that contains a number of messages. We also created the getMessage method that randomly picks one of the messages from the NSArray object and returns it.

The `Messages` class that we just created in Objective-C will need to be accessed by the `MessageBuilder` class that we are going to write in Swift. To access an Objective-C class from the Swift code, we need to edit the `Objective-C Bridging Header` file.

The Objective-C bridging header file – part 2

Now that we have created the `Messages` Objective-C class, we will need to expose it to our Swift code. Those who are familiar with Objective-C (or any C-based language), will know that we need to import the class header using the `#import` or `#include` directive, prior to using it within another class. In that same context, we need to import the header file of any Objective-C class, in the Objective-C header file, prior to using that class in our Swift code. Therefore, to allow our Swift code to access the `Messages` Objective-C class, we need to add the following line to the Objective-C bridging header file that Xcode created for us:

```
#import "Messages.h"
```

Yep, that is it. Pretty simple. Now, let's look at how we would write the `MessageBuilder` Swift class that will use the `Messages` Objective-C class.

The MessageBuilder Swift class – accessing Objective-C code from Swift

The `MessageBuilder` Swift class will contain one method named `getPersonalizedMessage()`. This method will use the `getMessage()` method from the `Messages` Objective-C class to retrieve a message and will then customize that message prior to returning it to the function that called it. Here is the code for the `MessageBuiler` Swift class:

```
import Foundation

class MessageBuilder: NSObject {

  func getPersonalizedMessage(name: String) -> String {
    let messages = Messages()
    let retMessage = "To: " + name + ", " + messages.getMessage()

    return retMessage;
  }
}
```

When we define this class, we create it as a subclass of the `NSObject` class. If a Swift class will be accessed from the Objective-C code, that class needs to be a subclass of the `NSObject` class. If we forget to do this, we will receive the `Use of undeclared identifier'{Class Name}` error when we try to access the class in the Objective-C code.

Now, let's look at how we created an instance of the `Messages` Objective-C class in our Swift code. The following line creates the instances, `let messages = Messages()`. As we can see, we create the instance of the `Messages` Objective-C class, exactly as we would create an instance of any Swift class. We then access the `getMessages()` method of the `Messages` class like we would access a method of any Swift class.

As we can see from this code, Objective-C classes are both initiated and used as if they were written in Swift when we access them from a class written in Swift. This allows us to access our Objective-C and Swift types in a consistent way.

Now that we have created the `MessageBuilder` Swift class, we need a way to call the `getPersonalizedMessage()` method, from the `ViewController` Objective-C class.

The Objective-C class – accessing Swift code from Objective-C

Once the user enters their name and presses the **Get Message** button, we will create an instance of the `MessageBuilder` Swift class, in Objective-C, and call the `getPersonlizedMessage()` method to generate the message to be displayed.

When we access Swift code from Objective-C, we rely on an Xcode-generated header file to expose the Swift classes. This automatically generated header file declares the interface for the Swift classes. The name for this header file is the name of your project, followed by `-Swift.h`. So, the name of the header file for our project is `ObjectiveCProject-Swift.h`. Therefore, the first step to access the Swift code from Objective-C is to import this header file, as shown in the following line of code:

```
#import "ObjectiveCProject-Swift.h"
```

Now that we have imported the header file to expose our Swift classes, we can use the `MessageBuilder` Swift class within the Objective-C code. We create an instance of the `MessageBuilder` Swift class exactly like we would create an instance of any standard Objective-C class. We also call the method and properties of a Swift class exactly like we would call the method and properties from an Objective-C class. The following example shows how we would create an instance of the `MessageBuilder` Swift class, and also how we would call the `getPersonalizedMessage()` method of that class:

```
MessageBuilder *mb = [[MessageBuilder alloc] init];
self.messageView.text = [mb getPersonalizedMessage:@"Jon"];
```

As we can see from this code sample, Swift classes are treated as if they were Objective-C classes when we access them from Objective-C. Once again, this allows us to access both our Objective-C and Swift types in a consistent manner.

Summary

As we saw in this chapter, Apple has made mix and match very easy and convenient to use. In order to access Swift classes from our Objective-C code, all we need to do is import the Xcode-generated header file that exposes the Swift classes. While we do not see this header file as part of our code, Xcode automatically creates it for mixed language projects. The name of this header file takes the format of `{Project Name}-Swift.h`, where `{Project Name}` is the name of our project.

It is also very easy to use Objective-C classes within our Swift code. To expose Objective-C classes to our Swift code, all we need to do is add the Objective-C header file to the Objective-C bridging header file. Xcode can create this bridging header file for us the first time we add an Objective-C file to a Swift project, or the first time we add a Swift file to an Objective-C project.

While Apple has said that the future of application development for iOS and OS X platforms is in Swift, mix and match can be used to slowly migrate our current Objective-C code base to Swift. Mix and match also lets us use Objective-C frameworks in our Swift projects or Swift frameworks in our Objective-C projects.

14
Concurrency and Parallelism in Swift

When I first started learning Objective-C, I already had a good understanding of concurrency and multitasking with my background in other languages such as C and Java. This background made it very easy for me to create multithreaded applications using threads in Objective-C. Then, Apple changed everything for me when they released **Grand Central Dispatch** (**GCD**) with OS X 10.6 and iOS 4. At first, I went into denial; there was no way GCD could manage my application's threads better than I could. Then I entered the anger phase, GCD was hard to use and understand. Next was the bargaining phase, maybe I can use GCD with my threading code, so I could still control how the threading worked. Then there was the depression phase, maybe GCD does handle the threading better than I can. Finally, I entered the wow phase; this GCD thing is really easy to use and works amazingly well. After using Grand Central Dispatch and Operation Queues with Objective-C, I do not see a reason for using manual threads with Swift.

In this chapter, we will learn the following topics:

- Basics of concurrency and parallelism
- How to use GCD to create and manage concurrent dispatch queues
- How to use GCD to create and manage serial dispatch queues
- How to use various GCD functions to add tasks to the dispatch queues
- How to use `NSOperation` and `NSOperationQueues` to add concurrency to our applications

Concurrency and parallelism

Concurrency is the concept of multiple tasks starting, running, and completing within the same time period. This does not necessarily mean that the tasks are executing simultaneously. In order for tasks to be run simultaneously, our application needs to be running on a multicore or multiprocessor system. Concurrency allows us to share the processor or cores with multiple tasks; however, a single core can only execute one task at a given time.

Parallelism is the concept of two or more tasks running simultaneously. Since each core of our processor can only execute one task at a time, the number of tasks executing simultaneously is limited to the number of cores within our processors. Therefore, if we have, for example, a four-core processor, then we are limited to only four tasks running simultaneously. Today's processors can execute tasks so quickly that it may appear that larger tasks are executing simultaneously. However, within the system, the larger tasks are actually taking turns executing subtasks on the cores.

In order to understand the difference between concurrency and parallelism, let's look at how a juggler juggles balls. If you watch a juggler, it seems they are catching and throwing multiple balls at any given time; however, a closer look reveals that they are, in fact, only catching and throwing one ball at a time. The other balls are in the air waiting to be caught and thrown. If we want to be able to catch and throw multiple balls simultaneously, we need to add multiple jugglers.

This example is really good because we can think of jugglers as the cores of a processer. A system with a single core processor (one juggler), regardless of how it seems, can only execute one task (catch and throw one ball) at a time. If we want to execute more than one task at a time, we need to use a multicore processor (more than one juggler).

Back in the old days when all the processors were single core, the only way to have a system that executed tasks simultaneously was to have multiple processors in the system. This also required specialized software to take advantage of the multiple processors. In today's world, just about every device has a processor that has multiple cores, and both the iOS and OS X operating systems are designed to take advantage of the multiple cores to run tasks simultaneously.

Traditionally, the way applications added concurrency was to create multiple threads; however, this model does not scale well to an arbitrary number of cores. The biggest problem with using threads was that our applications ran on a variety of systems (and processors), and in order to optimize our code, we needed to know how many cores/processors could be efficiently used at a given time, which is sometimes not known at the time of development.

In order to solve this problem, many operating systems, including iOS and OS X, started relying on asynchronous functions. These functions are often used to initiate tasks that could possibly take a long time to complete, such as making an HTTP request or writing data to disk. An asynchronous function typically starts the long running task and then returns prior to the task completion. Usually, this task runs in the background and uses a callback function (such as closure in Swift) when the task completes.

These asynchronous functions work great for the tasks that the OS provides them for, but what if we needed to create our own asynchronous functions and do not want to manage the threads ourselves? For this, Apple provides a couple of technologies. In this chapter, we will be covering two of these technologies. These are GCD and operation queues.

GCD is a low-level C-based API that allows specific tasks to be queued up for execution and schedules the execution on any of the available processor cores. Operation queues are similar to GCD; however, they are Cocoa objects and are internally implemented using GCD.

Let's begin by looking at GCD.

Grand Central Dispatch

Grand Central Dispatch provides what is known as dispatch queues to manage submitted tasks. The queues manage these submitted tasks and execute them in a **first-in, first-out** (**FIFO**) order. This ensures that the tasks are started in the order they were submitted.

A task is simply some work that our application needs to perform. As examples, we can create tasks that perform simple calculations, read/write data to disk, make an HTTP request, or anything else that our application needs to do. We define these tasks by placing the code inside either a function or a closure and adding it to a dispatch queue.

GCD provides three types of queues:

- **Serial queues**: Tasks in a serial queue (also known as a **private queue**) are executed one at a time in the order they were submitted. Each task is started only after the preceding task is completed. Serial queues are often used to synchronize access to specific resources because we are guaranteed that no two tasks in a serial queue will ever run simultaneously. Therefore, if the only way to access the specific resource is through the tasks in the serial queue, then no two tasks will attempt to access the resource at the same time or be out of order.

- **Concurrent queues**: Tasks in a concurrent queue (also known as a **global dispatch queue**) execute concurrently; however, the tasks are still started in the order that they were added to the queue. The exact number of tasks that can be executing at any given instance is variable and is dependent on the system's current conditions and resources. The decision on when to start a task is up to GCD and is not something that we can control within our application.
- **Main dispatch queue**: The main dispatch queue is a globally available serial queue that executes tasks on the application's main thread. Since tasks put into the main dispatch queue run on the main thread, it is usually called from a background queue when some background processing has finished and the user interface needs to be updated.

Dispatch queues offer a number of advantages over traditional threads. The first and foremost advantage is, with dispatch queues, the system handles the creation and management of threads rather than the application itself. The system can scale the number of threads, dynamically based on the overall available resources of the system and the current system conditions. This means that dispatch queues can manage the threads with greater efficiency than we could.

Another advantage of dispatch queues is we are able to control the order that our tasks are started. With serial queues, not only do we control the order in which tasks are started, but also ensure that one task does not start before the preceding one is complete. With traditional threads, this can be very cumbersome and brittle to implement, but with dispatch queues, as we will see later in this chapter, it is quite easy.

Creating and managing dispatch queues

Let's look at how to create and use a dispatch queue. The following three functions are used to create or retrieve queues. These functions are as follows:

- `dispatch_queue_create`: This creates a dispatch queue of either the concurrent or serial type
- `dispatch_get_global_queue`: This returns a system-defined global concurrent queue with a specified quality of service
- `dispatch_get_main_queue`: This returns the serial dispatch queue associated with the application's main thread

We will also be looking at several functions that submit tasks to a queue for execution. These functions are as follows:

- `dispatch_async`: This submits a task for asynchronous execution and returns immediately.
- `dispatch_sync`: This submits a task for synchronous execution and waits until it is complete before it returns.
- `dispatch_after`: This submits a task for execution at a specified time.
- `dispatch_once`: This submits a task to be executed once and only once while this application is running. It will execute the task again if the application restarts.

Before we look at how to use the dispatch queues, we need to create a class that will help us demonstrate how the various types of queues work. This class will contain two basic functions. The first function will simply perform some basic calculations and then return a value. Here is the code for this function, which is named `doCalc()`:

```
func doCalc() {
  var x=100
  var y = x*x
  _ = y/x
}
```

The other function, which is named `performCalculation()`, accepts two parameters. One is an integer named `iterations`, and the other is a string named `tag`. The `performCalculation()` function calls the `doCalc()` function repeatedly until it calls the function the same number of times as defined by the iterations parameter. We also use the `CFAbsoluteTimeGetCurrent()` function to calculate the elapsed time it took to perform all of the iterations and then print the elapse time with the `tag` string to the console. This will let us know when the function completes and how long it took to complete it. The code for this function looks similar to this:

```
func performCalculation(iterations: Int, tag: String) {
  let start = CFAbsoluteTimeGetCurrent()
  for var i=0; i<iterations; i++ {
    self.doCalc()
  }
  let end = CFAbsoluteTimeGetCurrent()
  print("time for \(tag):  \(end-start)")
}
```

These functions will be used together to keep our queues busy, so we can see how they work. Let's begin by looking at the GCD functions by using the `dispatch_queue_create()` function to create both concurrent and serial queues.

Creating queues with the dispatch_queue_create() function

The `dispatch_queue_create()` function is used to create both concurrent and serial queues. The syntax of the `dispatch_queue_create()` function looks similar to this:

```
func dispatch_queue_t dispatch_queue_create(label:
  UnsafePointer<Int8>, attr: dispatch_queue_attr_t!) ->
    dispatch_queue_t!
```

It takes the following parameters:

- `label`: This is a string label that is attached to the queue to uniquely identify it in debugging tools, such as Instruments and crash reports. It is recommended that we use a reverse DNS naming convention. This parameter is optional and can be nil.
- `attr`: This specifies the type of queue to make. This can be `DISPATCH_QUEUE_SERIAL`, `DISPATCH_QUEUE_CONCURRENT` or nil. If this parameter is nil, a serial queue is created.

The return value for this function is the newly created dispatch queue. Let's see how to use the `dispatch_queue_create()` function by creating a concurrent queue and seeing how it works.

Some programming languages use the reverse DNS naming convention to name certain components. This convention is based on a registered domain name that is reversed. As an example, if we worked for company that had a domain name `mycompany.com` with a product called `widget`, the reverse DNS name will be `com.mycompany.widget`.

Creating concurrent dispatch queues with the dispatch_queue_create() function

The following line creates a concurrent dispatch queue with the label of `cqueue.hoffman.jon`:

```
let queue = dispatch_queue_create("cqueue.hoffman.jon",
  DISPATCH_QUEUE_CONCURRENT)
```

As we saw in the beginning of this section, there are several functions that we can use to submit tasks to a dispatch queue. When we work with queues, we generally want to use the `dispatch_async()` function to submit tasks because when we submit a task to a queue, we usually do not want to wait for a response. The `dispatch_async()` function has the following signature:

```
func dispatch_async(queue: dispatch_queue_t!, block: dispatch_queue_
block!)
```

The following example shows how to use the `dispatch_async()` function with the concurrent queue we just created:

```
let c = { performCalculation(1000, tag: "async0") }
dispatch_async(queue, c)
```

In the preceding code, we created a closure, which represents our task, that simply calls the `performCalculation()` function of the `DoCalculation` instance requesting that it runs through 1000 iterations of the `doCalc()` function. Finally, we use the `dispatch_async()` function to submit the task to the concurrent dispatch queue. This code will execute the task in a concurrent dispatch queue, which is separate from the main thread.

While the preceding example works perfectly, we can actually shorten the code a little bit. The next example shows that we do not need to create a separate closure as we did in the preceding example; we can also submit the task to execute like this:

```
dispatch_async(queue) {
  calculation.performCalculation(10000000, tag: "async1")
}
```

This shorthand version is how we usually submit small code blocks to our queues. If we have larger tasks, or tasks that we need to submit multiple times, we will generally want to create a closure and submit the closure to the queue as we showed originally.

Let's see how the concurrent queue actually works by adding several items to the queue and looking at the order and time that they return. The following code will add three tasks to the queue. Each task will call the `performCalculation()` function with various iteration counts. Remember that the `performCalculation()` function will execute the calculation routine continuously until it is executed the number of times as defined by the iteration count passed in. Therefore, the larger the iteration count we pass into the `performCalculation()` function, the longer it should take to execute. Let's take a look at the following code:

```
dispatch_async(queue) {
  calculation.performCalculation(10000000, tag: "async1")
```

```
}

dispatch_async(queue) {
  calculation.performCalculation(1000, tag: "async2")
}

dispatch_async(queue) {
  calculation.performCalculation(100000, tag: "async3")
}
```

Notice that each of the functions is called with a different value in the `tag` parameter. Since the `performCalculation()` function prints out the `tag` variable with the elapsed time, we can see the order in which the tasks complete and the time it took to execute. If we execute the preceding code, we should see the following results:

```
time for async2:  0.000200986862182617
time for async3:  0.00800204277038574
time for async1:  0.461670994758606
```

The elapse time will vary from one run to the next and from system to system.

Since the queues function in a FIFO order, the task that had the tag of `async1` was executed first. However, as we can see from the results, it was the last task to finish. Since this is a concurrent queue, if it is possible (if the system has available resources), the blocks of code will execute concurrently. This is why the tasks with the tags of `async2` and `async3` completed prior to the task that had the `async1` tag, even though the execution of the `async1` task began before the other two.

Now, let's see how a serial queue executes tasks.

Creating a serial dispatch queue with the dispatch_queue_create() function

A serial queue functions is a little different than a concurrent queue. A serial queue will only execute one task at a time and will wait for one task to complete before starting the next task. This queue, like the concurrent dispatch queue, follows a first-in first-out order. The following line of code will create a serial queue with the label of `squeue.hoffman.jon`:

```
let queue2 = dispatch_queue_create("squeue.hoffman.jon",
  DISPATCH_QUEUE_SERIAL)
```

Notice that we create the serial queue with the `DISPATCH_QUEUE_SERIAL` attribute. If you recall, when we created the concurrent queue, we created it with the `DISPATCH_QUEUE_CONCURRENT` attribute. We can also set this attribute to `nil`, which will create a serial queue by default. However, it is recommended to always set the attribute to either `DISPATCH_QUEUE_SERIAL` or `DISPATCH_QUEUE_CONCURRENT` to make it easier to identify which type of queue we are creating.

As we saw with the concurrent dispatch queues, we generally want to use the `dispatch_async()` function to submit tasks because when we submit a task to a queue, we usually do not want to wait for a response. If, however, we did want to wait for a response, we would use the `dispatch_synch()` function.

```
var calculation = DoCalculations()
let c = { calculation.performCalculation(1000, tag: "sync0") }
dispatch_async(queue2, c)
```

Just like with the concurrent queues, we do not need to create a closure to submit a task to the queue. We can also submit the task like this:

```
dispatch_async(queue2) {
    calculation.performCalculation(100000, tag: "sync1")
}
```

Let's see how the serial queues works by adding several items to the queue and looking at the order and time that they complete. The following code will add three tasks, which will call the `performCalculation()` function with various iteration counts, to the queue:

```
dispatch_async(queue2) {
    calculation.performCalculation(100000, tag: "sync1")
}

dispatch_async(queue2) {
    calculation.performCalculation(1000, tag: "sync2")
}

dispatch_async(queue2) {
    calculation.performCalculation(100000, tag: "sync3")
}
```

Just like with the concurrent queue example, we call the `performCalculation()` function with various iteration counts and different values in the `tag` parameter. Since the `performCalculation()` function prints out the `tag` string with the elapsed time, we can see the order that the tasks complete in and the time it takes to execute. If we execute this code, we should see the following results:

```
time for sync1:  0.00648999214172363
time for sync2:  0.0000960230827331 5
time for sync3:  0.00515800714492798
```

The elapse time will vary from one run to the next and from system to system.

Unlike the concurrent queues, we can see that the tasks completed in the same order that they were submitted, even though the `sync2` and `sync3` tasks took considerably less time to complete. This demonstrates that a serial queue only executes one task at a time and that the queue waits for each task to complete before starting the next one.

Now that we have seen how to use the `dispatch_queue_create()` function to create both concurrent and serial queues, let's look at how we can get one of the four system-defined, global concurrent queues using the `dispatch_get_global_queue()` function.

Requesting concurrent queues with the dispatch_get_global_queue() function

The system provides each application with four concurrent global dispatch queues of different priority levels. The different priority levels are what distinguish these queues. The four priorities are:

- `DISPATCH_QUEUE_PRIORITY_HIGH`: The items in this queue run with the highest priority and are scheduled before items in the default and low priority queues
- `DISPATCH_QUEUE_PRIORITY_DEFAULT`: The items in this queue run at the default priority and are scheduled before items in the low priority queue but after items in the high priority queue
- `DISPATCH_QUEUE_PRIORITY_LOW`: The items in this queue run with a low priority and are schedule only after items in the high and default queues
- `DISPATCH_QUEUE_PRIORITY_BACKGROUND`: The items in this queue run with a background priority, which has the lowest priority

Since these are global queues, we do not need to actually create them; instead, we ask for a reference to the queue with the priority level needed. To request a global queue, we use the `dispatch_get_global_queue()` function. This function has the following syntax:

```
func dispatch_get_global_queue(identifier: Int, flags: UInt) ->
dispatch_queue_t!
```

Here, the following parameters are defined:

- `identifier`: This is the priority of the queue we are requesting
- `flags`: This is reserved for future expansion and should be set to zero at this time

We request a queue using the `dispatch_get_global_queue()` function, as shown in the following example:

```
let queue =
  dispatch_get_global_queue(DISPATCH_QUEUE_PRIORITY_DEFAULT, 0)
```

In this example, we are requesting the global queue with the default priority. We can then use this queue exactly as we used the concurrent queues that we created with the `dispatch_queue_create()` function. The difference between the queues returned with the `dispatch_get_global_queue()` function and the ones created with the `dispatch_create_queue()` function is that with the `dispatch_create_queue()` function, we are actually creating a new queue. The queues that are returned with the `dispatch_get_global_queue()` function are global queues that are created when our application first starts; therefore, we are requesting a queue rather than creating a new one.

When we use the `dispatch_get_global_queue()` function, we avoid the overhead of creating the queue; therefore, I recommend using the `dispatch_get_global_queue()` function unless you have a specific reason to create a queue.

Requesting the main queue with the dispatch_get_main_queue() function

The `dispatch_get_main_queue()` function returns the main queue for our application. The main queue is automatically created for the main thread when the application starts. This main queue is a serial queue; therefore, items in this queue are executed one at a time, in the order that they were submitted. We will generally want to avoid using this queue unless we have a need to update the user interface from a background thread.

The `dispatch_get_main_queue()` function has the following syntax:

```
func dispatch_get_main_queue() -> dispatch_queue_t!
```

The following code example shows how to request the main queue:

```
let mainQueue = dispatch_get_main_queue();
```

We will then submit tasks to the main queue exactly as we would any other serial queue. Just remember that anything submitted to this queue will run on the main thread, which is the thread that all the user interface updates run on; therefore, if we submitted a long running task, the user interface will freeze until that task is completed.

In the previous sections, we saw how the `dispatch_async()` functions submit tasks to concurrent and serial queues. Now, let's look at two additional functions that we can use to submit tasks to our queues. The first function we will look at is the `dispatch_after()` function.

Using the dispatch_after() function

There will be times that we need to execute tasks after a delay. If we were using a threading model, we would need to create a new thread, perform some sort of delay or sleep function, and execute our task. With GCD, we can use the `dispatch_after()` function. The `dispatch_after()` function takes the following syntax:

```
func dispatch_after(when: dispatch_time_t, queue:
  dispatch_queue_t, block: dispatch_block_t)
```

Here, the `dispatch_after()` function takes the following parameters:

- `when`: This is the time that we wish the queue to execute our task in
- `queue`: This is the queue that we want to execute our task in
- `block`: This is the task to execute

As with the `dispatch_async()` and `dispatch_synch()` functions, we do not need to include our task as a parameter. We can include our task to execute between two curly brackets exactly as we did previously with the `dispatch_async()` and `dispatch_synch()` functions.

As we can see from the `dispatch_after()` function, we use the `dispatch_time_t` type to define the time to execute the task. We use the `dispatch_time()` function to create the `dispatch_time_t` type. The `dispatch_time()` function has the following syntax:

```
func dispatch_time(when: dispatch_time_t, delta:Int64) ->
  dispatch_time_t
```

Here, the `dispatch_time()` function takes the following parameter:

- `when`: This value is used as the basis for the time to execute the task. We generally pass the `DISPATCH_TIME_NOW` value to create the time, based on the current time.
- `delta`: This is the number of nanoseconds to add to the `when` parameter to get our time.

We will use the `dispatch_time()` and `dispatch_after()` functions like this:

```
var delayInSeconds = 2.0
let eTime = dispatch_time(DISPATCH_TIME_NOW, Int64(delayInSeconds
  * Double(NSEC_PER_SEC)))
dispatch_after(eTime, queue2) {
  print("Times Up")
}
```

The preceding code will execute the task after a two-second delay. In the `dispatch_ time()` function, we create a `dispatch_time_t` type that is two seconds in the future. The `NSEC_PER_SEC` constant is use to calculate the nanoseconds from seconds. After the two-second delay, we print the message, `Times Up`, to the console.

There is one thing to watch out for with the `dispatch_after()` function. Let's take a look at the following code:

```
let queue2 = dispatch_queue_create("squeue.hoffman.jon",
  DISPATCH_QUEUE_SERIAL)

var delayInSeconds = 2.0
let pTime = dispatch_time(DISPATCH_TIME_NOW,Int64(delayInSeconds *
  Double(NSEC_PER_SEC)))
dispatch_after(pTime, queue2) {
  print("Times Up")
}

dispatch_sync(queue2) {
  calculation.performCalculation(100000, tag: "sync1")
}
```

In this code, we begin by creating a serial queue and then adding two tasks to the queue. The first task uses the `dispatch_after()` function, and the second task uses the `dispatch_sync()` function. Our initial thought would be that when we executed this code within the serial queue, the first task would execute after a two-second delay and then the second task would execute; however, this would not be correct. The first task is submitted to the queue and executed immediately. It also returns immediately, which lets the queue execute the next task while it waits for the correct time to execute the first task. Therefore, even though we are running the tasks in a serial queue, the second task completes before the first task. The following is an example of the output if we run the preceding code:

```
time for sync1:  0.00407701730728149
Times Up
```

The final GCD function that we are going to look at is `dispatch_once()`.

Using the dispatch_once() function

The `dispatch_once()` function will execute a task once, and only once, for the lifetime of the application. What this means is that the task will be executed and marked as executed, then that task will not be executed again unless the application restarts. While the `dispatch_once()` function can be and has been used to implement the singleton pattern, there are other easier ways to do this. Refer to *Chapter 17, Adopting Design Patterns in Swift*, for examples on how to implement the singleton design pattern.

The `dispatch_once()` function is great for executing initialization tasks that need to run when our application initially starts. These initialization tasks can consist of initializing our data store or variables and objects. The following code shows the syntax for the `dispatch_once()` function:

```
func dispatch_once(predicate:
  UnsafeMutablePointer<dispatch_once_t>,block: dispatch_block_t!)
```

Let's look at how to use the `dispatch_once()` function:

```
var token: dispatch_once_t = 0
func example() {
    dispatch_once(&token) {
        print("Printed only on the first call")
    }
    print("Printed for each call")
}
```

In this example, the line that prints the message, `Printed only on the first call`, will be executed only once, no matter how many times the function is called. However, the line that prints the `Printed for each call` message will be executed each time the function is called. Let's see this in action by calling this function four times, like this:

```
for i in 0..<4 {
   example()
}
```

If we execute this example, we should see the following output:

```
Printed only on the first call
Printed for each call
Printed for each call
Printed for each call
Printed for each call
```

Notice, in this example, that we only see the `Printed only on the first call` message once whereas we see the `Printed for each call` message all the four times that we call the function.

Now that we have looked at GCD, let's take a look at operation queues.

Using NSOperation and NSOperationQueue types

The `NSOperation` and `NSOperationQueues` types, working together, provide us with an alternative to GCD for adding concurrency to our applications. Operation queues are Cocoa objects that function like dispatch queues and internally, operation queues are implemented using GCD. We define the tasks (`NSOperations`) that we wish to execute and then add the task to the operation queue (`NSOperationQueue`). The operation queue will then handle the scheduling and execution of tasks. Operation queues are instances of the `NSOperationQueue` class and operations are instances of the `NSOperation` class.

The operation represents a single unit of work or task. The `NSOperation` type is an abstract class that provides a thread-safe structure for modeling the state, priority, and dependencies. This class must be subclassed in order to perform any useful work.

Apple does provide two concrete implementations of the `NSOperation` type that we can use as-is for situations where it does not make sense to build a custom subclass. These subclasses are `NSBlockOperation` and `NSInvocationOperation`.

More than one operation queue can exist at the same time, and actually, there is always at least one operation queue running. This operation queue is known as the **main queue**. The main queue is automatically created for the main thread when the application starts and is where all the UI operations are performed.

There are several ways that we can use the `NSOperation` and `NSOperationQueues` classes to add concurrency to our application. In this chapter, we will look at three different ways. The first one we will look at is using the `NSBlockOperation` implementation of the `NSOperation` abstract class.

Using the NSBlockOperation implementation of NSOperation

In this section, we will be using the same `DoCalculation` class that we used in the *Grand Central Dispatch* section to keep our queues busy with work so that we can see how the `NSOpererationQueues` class work.

The `NSBlockOperation` class is a concrete implementation of the `NSOperation` type that can manage the execution of one or more blocks. This class can be used to execute several tasks at once without the need to create separate operations for each task.

Let's see how to use the `NSBlockOperation` class to add concurrency to our application. The following code shows how to add three tasks to an operation queue using a single `NSBlockOperation` instance:

```
let calculation = DoCalculations()
let operationQueue = NSOperationQueue()

let blockOperation1: NSBlockOperation =
  NSBlockOperation.init(block: {
  calculation.performCalculation(10000000, tag: "Operation 1")
})

blockOperation1.addExecutionBlock(
  {
    calculation.performCalculation(10000, tag: "Operation 2")
  }
)

blockOperation1.addExecutionBlock(
  {
    calculation.performCalculation(1000000, tag: "Operation 3")
```

```
    }
)

operationQueue.addOperation(blockOperation1)
```

In this code, we begin by creating an instance of the `DoCalculation` class and an instance of the `NSOperationQueue` class. Next, we created an instance of the `NSBlockOperation` class using the `init` constructor. This constructor takes a single parameter, which is a block of code that represents one of the tasks we want to execute in the queue. Next, we add two additional tasks to the `NSBlockOperation` instance using the `addExecutionBlock()` method.

This is one of the differences between dispatch queues and operations. With dispatch queues, if resources are available, the tasks are executed as they are added to the queue. With operations, the individual tasks are not executed until the operation itself is submitted to an operation queue.

Once we add all of the tasks to the `NSBlockOperation` instance, we then add the operation to the `NSOperationQueue` instance that we created at the beginning of the code. At this point, the individual tasks within the operation start to execute.

This example shows how to use `NSBlockOperation` to queue up multiple tasks and then pass the tasks to the operation queue. The tasks are executed in a FIFO order; therefore, the first task that is added to the `NSBlockOperation` instance will be the first task executed. However, since the tasks can be executed concurrently if we have the available resources, the output from this code should look similar to this:

```
time for Operation 2:  0.00546294450759888
time for Operation 3:  0.0800899863243103
time for Operation 1:  0.484337985515594
```

What if we do not want our tasks to run concurrently? What if we wanted them to run serially like the serial dispatch queue? We can set a property in our operation queue that defines the number of tasks that can be run concurrently in the queue. The property is called `maxConcurrentOperationCount` and is used like this:

```
operationQueue.maxConcurrentOperationCount = 1
```

However, if we added this line to our previous example, it will not work as expected. To see why this is, we need to understand what the property actually defines. If we look at Apple's `NSOperationQueue` class reference, the definition of the property says, "The maximum number of queued operations that can execute at the same time."

What this tells us is that the `maxConcurrentOperationCount` property defines the number of operations (this is the key word) that can be executed at the same time. The `NSBlockOperation` instance, which we added all of our tasks to, represents a single operation; therefore, no other `NSBlockOperation` added to the queue will execute until the first one is complete, but the individual tasks within the operation will execute concurrently. To run the tasks serially, we would need to create a separate instance of the `NSBlockOperations` for each task.

Using an instance of the `NSBlockOperation` class good if we have a number of tasks that we want to execute concurrently, but they will not start executing until we add the operation to an operation queue. Let's look at a simpler way of adding tasks to an operation queue using the queues `addOperationWithBlock()` methods.

Using the addOperationWithBlock() method of the operation queue

The `NSOperationQueue` class has a method named `addOperationWithBlock()` that makes it easy to add a block of code to the queue. This method automatically wraps the block of code in an operation object and then passes that operation to the queue itself. Let's see how to use this method to add tasks to a queue:

```
let operationQueue = NSOperationQueue()
let calculation = DoCalculations()

operationQueue.addOperationWithBlock() {
  calculation.performCalculation(10000000, tag: "Operation1")
}

operationQueue.addOperationWithBlock() {
  calculation.performCalculation(10000, tag: "Operation2")
}

operationQueue.addOperationWithBlock() {
  calculation.performCalculation(1000000, tag: "Operation3")
}
```

In the `NSBlockOperation` example, earlier in this chapter, we added the tasks that we wished to execute into an `NSBlockOperation` instance. In this example, we are adding the tasks directly to the operation queue, and each task represents one complete operation. Once we create the instance of the operation queue, we then use the `addOperationWithBlock()` method to add the tasks to the queue.

Also, in the `NSBlockOperation` example, the individual tasks did not execute until all of the tasks were added to the `NSBlockOperation` object and then that operation was added to the queue. This `addOperationWithBlock()` example is similar to the GCD example where the tasks begin executing as soon as they are added to the operation queue.

If we run the preceding code, the output should be similar to this:

```
time for Operation2:  0.0115870237350464
time for Operation3:  0.0790849924087524
time for Operation1:  0.520610988140106
```

You will notice that the operations are executed concurrently. With this example, we can execute the tasks serially by using the `maxConcurrentOperationCount` property that we mentioned earlier. Let's try this by initializing the `NSOperationQueue` instance like this:

```
var operationQueue = NSOperationQueue()
operationQueue.maxConcurrentOperationCount = 1
```

Now, if we run the example, the output should be similar to this:

```
time for Operation1:  0.418763995170593
time for Operation2:  0.000427007675170898
time for Operation3:  0.0441589951515198
```

In this example, we can see that each task waited for the previous task to complete prior to starting.

Using the `addOperationWithBlock()` method to add tasks, the operation queue is generally easier than using the `NSBlockOperation` method; however, the tasks will begin as soon as they are added to the queue, which is usually the desired behavior.

Now, let's look at how we can subclass the `NSOperation` class to create an operation that we can add directly to an operation queue.

Subclassing the NSOperation class

The previous two examples showed how to add small blocks of code to our operation queues. In these examples, we called the `performCalculations` method in the `DoCalculation` class to perform our tasks. These examples illustrate two really good ways to add concurrency for functionally that is already written, but what if, at design time, we want to design our `DoCalculation` class for concurrency? For this, we can subclass the `NSOperation` class.

The `NSOperation` abstract class provides a significant amount of infrastructure. This allows us to very easily create a subclass without a lot of work. We should at least provide an `initialization` method and a `main` method. The `main` method will be called when the queue begins executing the operation:

Let's see how to implement the `DoCalculation` class as a subclass of the `NSOperation` class; we will call this new class `MyOperation`:

```
class MyOperation: NSOperation {
  let iterations: Int
  let tag: String

  init(iterations: Int, tag: String) {
    self.iterations = iterations
    self.tag = tag
  }

  override func main() {
    performCalculation()
  }

  func performCalculation() {
    let start = CFAbsoluteTimeGetCurrent()
    for var i=0; i<iterations; i++ {
      self.doCalc()
    }
    let end = CFAbsoluteTimeGetCurrent()
    print("time for \(tag):  \(end-start)")
  }

  func doCalc() {
    let x=100
    let y = x*x
    _ = y/x
  }
}
```

We begin by defining that the `MyOperation` class is a subclass of the `NSOperation` class. Within the implementation of the class, we define two class constants, which represent the iteration count and the tag that the `performCalculations()` method uses. Keep in mind that when the operation queue begins executing the operation, it will call the `main()` method with no parameters; therefore, any parameters that we need to pass in must be passed in through the initializer.

In this example, our initializer takes two parameters that are used to set the `iterations` and `tag` classes constants. Then the `main()` method, that the operation queue is going to call to begin execution of the operation, simply calls the `performCalculation()` method.

We can now very easily add instances of our `MyOperation` class to an operation queue, like this:

```
var operationQueue = NSOperationQueue()
operationQueue.addOperation(MyOperation(iterations: 10000000, tag:
  "Operation 1"))
operationQueue.addOperation(MyOperation(iterations: 10000, tag:
  "Operation 2"))
operationQueue.addOperation(MyOperation(iterations: 1000000, tag:
  "Operation 3"))
```

If we run this code, we will see the following results:

```
time for Operation 2:  0.00187397003173828
time for Operation 3:  0.104826986789703
time for Operation 1:  0.866684019565582
```

As we saw earlier, we can also execute the tasks serially by adding the following line, which sets the `maxConcurrentOperationCount` property of the operation queue:

```
operationQueue.maxConcurrentOperationCount = 1
```

If we know that we need to execute some functionality concurrently prior to writing the code, I will recommend subclassing the `NSOperation` class, as shown in this example, rather than using the previous examples. This gives us the cleanest implementation; however, there is nothing wrong with using the `NSBlockOperation` class or the `addOperationWithBlock()` methods described earlier in this section.

Summary

Before we consider adding concurrency to our application, we should make sure that we understand why we are adding it and ask ourselves whether it is necessary. While concurrency can make our application more responsive by offloading work from our main application thread to a background thread, it also adds extra complexity to our code and overhead to our application. I have even seen numerous applications, in various languages, which actually run better after we pulled out some of the concurrency code. This is because the concurrency was not well thought out or planned. With this in mind, it is always a good idea to think and talk about concurrency while we are discussing the application's expected behavior.

At the start of this chapter, we had a discussion about running tasks concurrently compared to running tasks in parallel. We also discussed the hardware limitation that limits how many tasks can run in parallel on a given device. Having a good understanding of those concepts is very important to understanding how and when to add concurrency to our projects.

While GCD is not limited to system-level applications, before we use it in our application, we should consider whether operation queues would be easier and more appropriate for our needs. In general, we should use the highest level of abstraction that meets our needs. This will usually point us to using operation queues; however, there really is nothing preventing us from using GCD, and it may be more appropriate for our needs.

One thing to keep in mind with operation queues is that they do add additional overhead because they are Cocoa objects. For the large majority of applications, this little extra overhead should not be an issue or even noticed; however, for some projects, such as games that need every last resource that they can get, this extra overhead might very well be an issue.

15
Swift Formatting and Style Guide

Throughout my development experience, every time I learned a new programming language, there was usually some mention of how code for that language should be written and formatted. Early in my development career (which was a long time ago), these recommendations were very basic formatting recommendations, such as how to indent your code, or just having one statement per line. It really wasn't until the last 10 to 12 years that I started to see complex and detailed formatting and style guides for different programming languages. Today, you will be hard pressed to find a development shop with more than two or three developers who did not have style/formatting guides for each language that they use. Even companies that do not create their own style guides generally refer back to some standard guide published by other companies, such as Google, Oracle, or Microsoft. These style guides help teams to write consistent and easy-to-maintain code.

What is a programming style guide?

Coding styles are very personal and every developer has his or her own preferred style. These styles can vary from language to language, person to person, and also change over time. The personal nature of coding styles can make it difficult to have a consistent and readable code base when numerous individuals are contributing to the code.

While most developers might have their own preferred styles, the recommended or preferred style between languages can vary. As an example, in C#, when we name a method or function, it is preferred to use camel case with the first letter being capitalized. While in most languages, such as C, Objective-C, and Java, it is also recommended that we use camel case, but we should make the first letter lower case.

The best applications are coded properly, and by properly, we do not just mean that they function correctly but also that they are easy to maintain and the code is easy to read. It is hard for large projects and companies with a large number of developers to have code that is easy to maintain and read if every developer uses their own coding style. This is why companies and projects with multiple developers usually adopt programming style guides for each language that they use.

A programming style guide defines a set of rules and guidelines that a developer should follow while writing applications with a specific language within a project or company. These style guides can differ greatly between companies or projects and reflect how that company or project expects code to be written. These guides can also change over time. It is important to follow these style guides to maintain a consistent code base.

A lot of developers do not like the idea of being told how they should write code, and claim that as long as their code functions correctly, why should it matter how they format their code. I link this to a basketball team. If all of the players come in believing that how they want to play is correct and believe that the team is better when they are doing their own thing, then that team is probably going to lose the majority of their games. It is impossible for a basketball team (or any sports team, for that matter) to win the majority of their games unless they are working together. It is up to the coach to make sure that everyone is working together and executing the same game plan, just like it is up to the team leader of the development project to make sure all the developers are writing code according to the adopted style guide.

Your style guide

The style guide that we define in this book is just a guide. It reflects the author's opinion on how Swift code should be written and is meant to be a good starting point for creating your own style guide. If you really like this guide and adopt it as it is, great. If there are parts that you do not agree with and you change them within your guide, that is great as well. The appropriate style for you and your team is the one that you and your team feel comfortable with, and it may or may not be different from the guide in this book. We should also point out that Swift is a very young language and people are still trying to figure out the appropriate style to use with Swift; therefore, what is recommended today maybe frowned upon tomorrow. Don't be afraid to adjust your style guide as needed.

One thing that is noticeable in the style guide within this chapter, and most good style guides, is that there is very little explanation about why each item is preferred or not preferred. Style guides should give enough details so that the reader understands the preferred and non-preferred methods for each item, but should also be small and compact to make it easy and quick to read.

If a developer has questions about why a particular method is preferred, he or she should bring that concern up to the development group.

With that in mind, let's get started with the guide.

Do not use semicolons at the end of statements

Unlike a lot of languages, Swift does not require semicolons at the end of statements. Therefore, we should not use them. Let's take a look at the following code:

```
//Preferred Method
var name = "Jon"
print(name)

//Non-preferred Method
var name = "Jon";
print(name);
```

Do not use parentheses for conditional statements

Unlike a lot of languages, the parentheses are not required around conditional statements; therefore, we should avoid using them unless they are needed for clarification. Let's take a look at the following code:

```
//Preferred Method
if speed == 300000000 {
    print("Speed of light")
}

//Non-Preferred Method
if (speed == 300000000) {
    print("Speed of light")
}
```

Naming

We should always use descriptive names with camel case for classes, methods, variables, constants, and so on. Let's look at some general naming rules.

Classes

Class names should have a descriptive name that describes what the class is for. The name should begin with a capital letter and be in camel case. Here are examples of proper names and non-proper names based on our style guide:

```
// Proper Naming Convention
BaseballTeam
LaptopComputer
//Non-Proper Naming Convention
baseballTeam            //Starts with a lowercase letter
Laptop_Computer         //Uses an underscore
```

Functions and methods

Function names should be descriptive, describing the function or method. They should begin with a lowercase letter and be in camel case. Here are some examples of proper and non-proper names:

```
//Proper Naming Convention
getCityName
playSound

//
//Non-Proper Naming Convention
get_city_name          //All lowercase and has an underscore
PlaySound              //Begins with an upper case letter
```

Constants and variables

Constants and variables should have a descriptive name. Generally, they begin with a lowercase letter and are in camel case. The only exception is when the constant is global; in that case, the name of the constant should contain all the uppercase characters with the words separated by underscores. I have seen numerous guides that frown on having all uppercase names, but I personally like them for constants in the global scope because it stands out that they are globally, not locally, scoped. Here are some examples of proper and non-proper names:

```
//Proper Names
playerName
```

```
driveSize
PLAYERS_ON_A_TEAM      //Only for globally scoped constants

//Non-Proper Names
PlayerName             //Starts with uppercase letter
drive_size             //Has underscore in name
```

Indenting

The indenting width in Xcode, by default, is defined as four spaces, and the tab width is also defined as four spaces. We should leave this as the default. The following screenshot shows the indentation setting in Xcode:

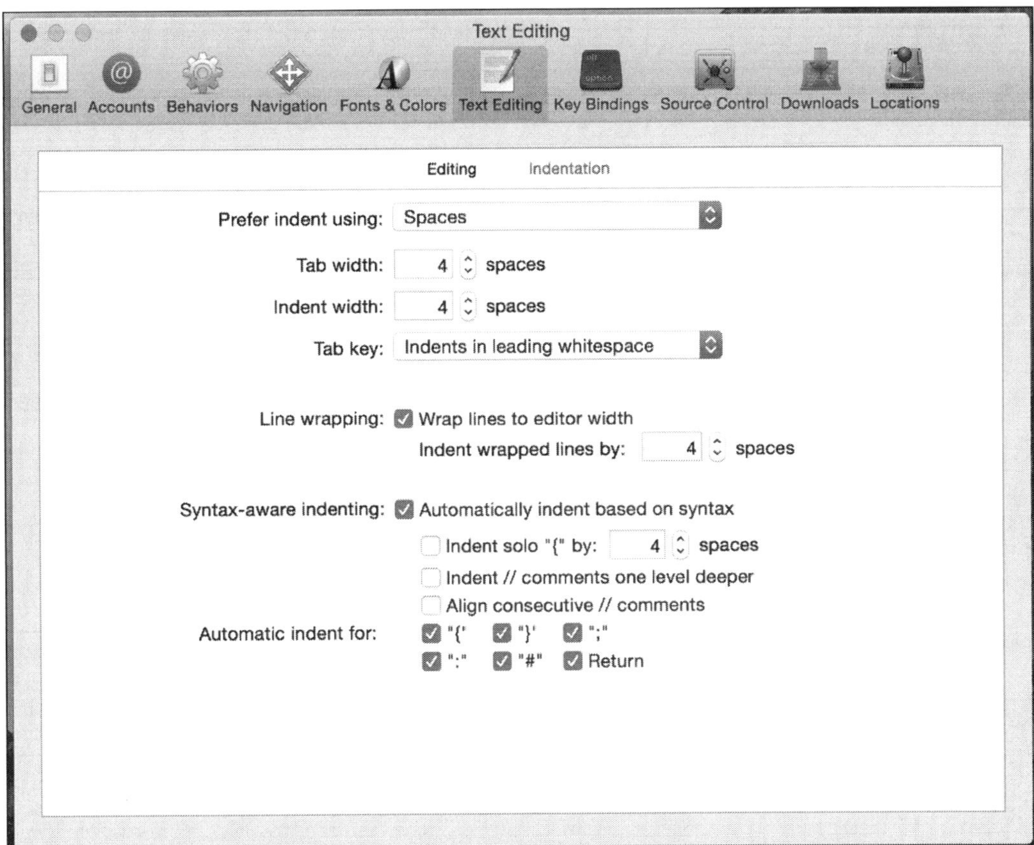

We should also add an extra blank line between functions/methods. We should also use a blank line to separate the functionality within a function or method. That being said, using many blank lines within a function or method might signify that we should break the function into multiple functions.

Comments

We should use comments as needed to explain how and why our code is written. We should use block comments before classes and functions, while we should use the double slashes to comment code in line. Here is an example of how to write comments:

```
/**
* This is a block comment that should be used
* to explain a class or function
*/
public class EmployeeClass {
  // This is an inline comment with double slashes
  var firstName = ""
  var lastName = ""

  /**
Use Block comments for functions

  :parm: paramName  use this tag for parameters
  :returns:  explain what is returned
  */
  func getFullName() -> String {
    return firstName + " " + lastName
  }
}
```

When we are commenting methods, we should also use the documentation tags that will generate documentation in Xcode, as shown in the preceding example. At a minimum, we should use the following tags if they apply to our method:

- `:param`: This is used for parameters
- `:return`: This is used for what is returned

Using the self keyword

Since Swift does not require us to use the `self` keyword when accessing properties or invoking methods of an object, we should avoid using it unless we need to distinguish between an object's property and local variables. Here is an example of when you should use the `self` keyword:

```
public class EmployeeClass {
  var firstName = ""
  var lastName = ""
```

```
    func setName(firstName: String, lastName: String) {
      self.firstName = firstName
      self.lastName = lastName
    }
  }
```

Here is an example of when not to use the `self` keyword:

```
  public class EmployeeClass {
      var firstName = ""
      var lastName = ""
      func getFullName() -> String {
          return self.firstName + " " + self.lastName
      }
  }
```

Types

We should always use Swift native types when possible. If we remember, Swift offers bridging to Objective-C types, so even if we are using a Swift native type, we still have access to the full set of methods offered by Objective-C types. The following code shows the preferred and non-preferred ways to use native types:

```
//Preferred way
let amount = 25.34
let amountStr = (amount as NSNumber).stringValue

//Non-preferred way
let amount: NSNumber = 25.34
let amountStr = amount.stringValue
```

Constants and variables

The difference between constants and variables is that the value of a constant never changes, whereas the value of a variable may change. Wherever possible, we should define constants rather than variables.

One of the easiest ways of doing this is to define everything as a constant, by default, and then change the definition to a variable only after you reach a point in your code that requires you to change it. With Swift 2, you will get a warning if you define a variable and then never change the value within your code.

Optional types

Only use optional types when absolutely necessary. If there is no absolute need for a nil value to be assigned to a variable, we should not define it as an optional.

Use optional binding

We should avoid forced unwrapping of optionals as there is rarely any need to do this. We should prefer optional binding or optional chaining for force unwrapping.

The following examples show the preferred and non-preferred methods where the `myOptional` variable is defined as an optional:

```
//Preferred Method Optional Binding
if let value = myOptional {
  // code if myOptional is not nil
} else {
  // code if myOptional is nil
}

//Non-Preferred Method
if myOptional != nil {
  // code if myOptional is not nil
} else {
  //  code if myOptional is nil
}
```

If there is more than one optional that we need to unwrap, we should include them on the same line rather than unwrapping them on separate lines if our business logic does not require separate paths if the unwrapping fails. The following examples show the preferred and non-preferred methods:

```
//Preferred Method Optional Binding
if let value1 = myOptional1, value2 = myOptional2 {
  // code if myOptional1 and myOptional2 is not nil
} else {
  // code if myOptional1 and myOptional2 is nil
}

//Non-Preferred Method Optional Binding
if let value1 = myOptional1 {
    if let value2 = myOptional2 {
        // code if myOptional is not nil
    } else {
```

```
        // code if myOptional2 is nil
      }
  } else {
    // code if myOptional1 is nil
  }
```

Use optional chaining over optional binding for multiple unwrapping

When we need to unwrap multiple layers, we should use optional chaining over multiple optional binding statements. The following example shows the preferred and non-preferred methods:

```
//Preferred Method
if let color = jon.pet?.collar?.color {
    print("The color of the collar is \(color)")
} else {
    print("Cannot retrieve color")
}

//Non-Preferred Method
if let tmpPet = jon.pet, tmpCollar = tmpPet.collar  {
    print("The color of the collar is \(tmpCollar.color)")
} else {
    print("Cannot retrieve color")
}
```

Use type inference

Rather than defining the variable types, we should let Swift infer the type. The only time we should define the variable or constant type is when we are not giving it a value while defining it. Let's take a look at the following code:

```
//Preferred method
var myVar = "String Type"  //Infers a String type
var myNum = 2.25           //Infers a Double type

//Non-Preferred method
var myVar: String = "String Type"
var myNum: Double = 2.25
```

Use shorthand declaration for collections

When declaring native Swift collection types, we should use the shorthand syntax, and unless absolutely necessary, we should initialize the collection. The following example shows the preferred and non-preferred methods:

```
//Preferred Method
var myDictionary: [String: String] = [:]
var strArray: [String] = []
var strOptional: String?

//
//Non-Preferred Method
var myDictionary: Dictionary<String,String>
var strArray: Array<String>
var strOptional: Optional<String>
```

Use for-in loops over for loops

We should use `for-in` loops over `for` loops, especially when looping through collections. The following examples show the preferred and non-preferred methods:

```
//Preferred Method
for str in strArray {
    print(str)
}
for num in 0...3 {
    print(num)
}

//
//Non-Preferred Method
for var i = 0; i < strArray.count; i++ {
    print(strArray[i])
}

for var num = 0; num <= 3; num++ {
    print(num)
}
```

Use switch rather than multiple if statements

Wherever possible, we should prefer to use a single `switch` statement over multiple `if` statements. The following example shows the preferred and non-preferred methods:

```
//Preferred Method
let speed = 300000000
switch speed {
case 300000000:
    print("Speed of light")
case 340:
    print("Speed of sound")
default:
    print("Unknown speed")
}

//Non-preferred Method
let speed = 300000000
if speed == 300000000 {
    print("Speed of light")
} else if speed == 340 {
    print("Speed of sound")
} else {
    print("Unknown speed")
}
```

Don't leave commented-out code in your application

If we comment out a block of code while we attempt to replace it, once we are comfortable with the changes, we should remove the code that we commented out. Having large blocks of code commented out can make the code base look messy and harder to follow.

Grand Central Dispatch

Grand Central Dispatch, which was discussed in *Chapter 14, Concurrency and Parallelism in Swift*, is a low-level C-based API that allows specific tasks to be queued up for execution and schedules the execution on any of the available processor cores.

Set the attribute in the dispatch_queue_create() function

When using the `dispath_queue_create()` function to create a serial queue, we are able to set the `attribute` parameter to `nil` (which defines a serial queue); however, we should always set the attribute to `DISPATCH_QUEUE_SERIAL` or `DISPATCH_QUEUE_CONCURRENT` to explicitly define what type of queue we are creating. The following example shows the preferred and non-preferred methods:

```
//Preferred method
let queue2 = dispatch_queue_create("squeue.hoffman.jon", DISPATCH_
QUEUE_SERIAL)

//Non-Preferred method
let queue2 = dispatch_queue_create("squeue.hoffman.jon", nil)
```

Use a reverse DNS name for the tag parameter of the dispatch_queue_create() function

We are able to set the `tag` parameter of the `dispatch_queue_create` function to any valid string; however, for consistency and easy troubleshooting, we should always use a reverse DNS naming scheme. The following code shows the preferred and non-preferred methods:

```
//Preferred method
let queue2 = dispatch_queue_create("squeue.hoffman.jon",
  DISPATCH_QUEUE_SERIAL)

let queue = dispatch_queue_create("cqueue.hoffman.jon",
  DISPATCH_QUEUE_CONCURRENT)

//Non-Preferred method
let queue2 = dispatch_queue_create("Serial_Queue",
  DISPATCH_QUEUE_SERIAL)

let queue = dispatch_queue_create("Concurrent_Queue",
  DISPATCH_QUEUE_CONCURRENT)
```

Use dispatch_get_global_queue() over dispatch_queue_create()

While it is perfectly acceptable to use the `dispatch_queue_create()` function to create a new concurrent queue, we should prefer to use the `dispatch_get_global_queue()` function to retrieve a concurrent queue that is already created for use. The following examples show the preferred and non-preferred methods:

```
//Preferred Method
let queue =
  dispatch_get_global_queue(DISPATCH_QUEUE_PRIORITY_DEFAULT, 0)

//Non-preferred Method
let queue = dispatch_queue_create("cqueue.hoffman.jon",
  DISPATCH_QUEUE_CONCURRENT)
```

Summary

When we are developing an application in a team environment, it is important to have a well-defined coding style that everyone on the team adheres to. This allows us to have a code base that is easy to read and maintain.

If a style guide remains static for too long, it means that it is probably not keeping up with the latest changes within the language. What is too long is different for each language. For example, with the C language, too long will be defined in years, since the language is very stable; however, with Swift, the language is so new and changes are coming pretty often, so too long can probably be defined as a couple of months.

It is recommended that we keep our style guides in a versioning control system so that we can refer to the older versions if need be. This allows us to pull the older versions of the style guide and refer back to them when we are looking at older code.

16
Network Development with Swift

I took several networking courses when I was in college, and I still recall setting up my first Novell NetWare network in one of those courses. I was absolutely fascinated to see and learn how computers communicated over the network. Then, in the early 90s, I bought my first modem and started dialing into bulletin board services that were local to me. This was really exciting because now I could connect to bulletin board services that were located in the city that I lived in. This allowed me to download and upload files from these bulletin board services, and I started downloading everything I could find that talked about how computers communicated. This led to my early career in network security and administration. Then, when my first daughter was born, I decided that I did not want to be on call all the time, so I went back to what got me into computers in the first place, which was programming. However, I still really enjoyed the field of networking and network security. My background in both networking and programming has given me a unique understanding of both. What constitutes networking today (the Internet and TCP/IP networks) is completely different to what constituted networking back when I was in college, but the good thing is how our applications communicate over the network has become much more standardized, which makes it easier to write applications that communicate over a network.

In this chapter, you will learn the following topics:

- How to make an HTTP GET request using the `NSURLSession` API
- How to make an HTTP POST request using the `NSURLSession` API
- How to use the System Configuration API to check our network connection
- How to use the `RSNetworking2` library to easily add network functionality to your applications

What is network development?

Network development is writing code that will allow our application to send and receive data from remote services or devices. In the introduction of this chapter, I mentioned buying my first modem and connecting with bulletin board services across the city that I lived in. The large majority of these bulletin board services used a single modem, which meant that only one user could connect to them at any one time. These bulletin boards would seem very strange and archaic for those that grew up with the Internet; however, back then, they were how computers shared information. At that time, being able to connect to a computer across town and upload/download files was amazing. Today, however, we communicate with services and devices all over the world without thinking twice about it.

Back then when I first started writing applications, it was rare to develop an application that communicated over a networked connection, and it was also hard to find developers with experience in network development. In today's world, just about every application has a requirement for some sort of network communication.

In this chapter, we will show you how to connect to **Representational State Transfer** (**REST**)-based web services. Representational State Transfer is the software architectural style of the World Wide Web. Typically, these services communicate over HTTP using the same HTTP verbs (get, put, delete, and post) which web browsers use.

In this chapter, we will use the REST-based service that Apple supplies, which lets developers search the iTunes Store. We will be using Apple's service for several examples in this chapter. Apple has documented this service very well. The documentation can be found at `https://www.apple.com/itunes/affiliates/resources/documentation/itunes-store-web-service-search-api.html`.

If you would like a more detailed discussion on network development, I would recommend you to read my first book, titled *iOS and OS X Network Programming Cookbook*, by *Packt Publishing*. In this chapter, we will be focusing on how to connect to the standard REST-based services.

Before we look at how to connect to REST services, let's look at the classes in Apple's networking API that we will be using. These classes are part of Apple's powerful URL loading system.

An overview of the URL session classes

Apple's URL loading system is a framework of classes available to interact with URLs. Using these classes together lets us communicate with services that use standard Internet protocols. The classes that we will be using in this chapter to connect to and retrieve information from REST services are as follows:

- `NSURLSession`: This is the main session object. It was written as a replacement for the older `NSURLConnection` API.
- `NSURLSessionConfiguration`: This is used to configure the behavior of the `NSURLSession` object.
- `NSURLSessionTask`: This is a base class to handle the data being retrieved from the URL. Apple provides three concrete subclasses of the `NSURLSessionTask` class.
- `NSURL`: This is an object that represents the URL to connect to.
- `NSMutableURLRequest`: This class contains information about the request that we are making and is used by the `NSURLSessionTask` service to make the request.
- `NSHTTPURLResponse`: This class contains the response to our request.

Now, let's look at each of these classes a little more in depth so that we have a basic understanding of what each does.

NSURLSession

Prior to iOS 7 and OS X 10.9, when a developer wanted to retrieve contents from a URL, he/she used the `NSURLConnection` API. Starting with iOS 7 and OS X 10.9, `NSURLSession` became the preferred API. The `NSURLSession` API can be thought of as an improvement to the older `NSURLConnection` API.

An `NSURLSession` object provides an API for interacting with various protocols such as HTTP and HTTPS. The session object, which is an instance of the `NSURLSession`, manages this interaction. These session objects are highly configurable, which allows us to control how our requests are made and how we handle the data that is returned.

Like most networking API, `NSURLSession` is asynchronous. This means that we have to provide a way to return the response from the service back to the code that needs it. The most popular way to return the results from a session is to pass a completion handler block (closure) to the session. This completion handler is then called when the service successfully responds or we receive an error. All of the examples in this chapter use completion handlers to process the data that is returned from the services.

NSURLSessionConfiguration

The `NSURLSessionConfiguration` class defines the behavior and policies to use when using the `NSURLSession` object to connect to a URL. When using the `NSURLSession` object, we usually create an `NSURLSessionConfiguration` instance first because an instance of this class is required when we create an instance of the `NSURLSession` class.

The `NSURLSessionConfiguration` class defines three session types:

- **Default session configuration**: This configuration behaves similar to the `NSURLConnection` API
- **Ephemeral session configuration**: This configuration behaves similar to the default session configuration, except that it does not cache anything to disk
- **Background session configuration**: This session allows for uploads and downloads to be performed, even when the app is running in the background

It is important to note that we should make sure that we configure the `NSURLSessionConfiguration` object appropriately before we use it to create an instance of the `NSURLSession` class. When the session object is created, it creates a copy of the configuration object that we provided it. Any changes made to the configuration object once the session object is created are ignored by the session. If we need to make changes to the configuration, we must create another instance of the `NSURLSession` class.

NSURLSessionTask

The `NSURLSession` service uses an instance of the `NSURLSessionTask` classes to make the call to the service that we are connecting to. The `NSURLSessionTask` class is a base class, and Apple has provided three concrete subclasses that we can use:

- `NSURLSessionDataTask`: This returns the response, in memory, directly to the application as one or more `NSData` objects. This is the task that we generally use most often.
- `NSURLSessionDownloadTask`: This writes the response directly to a temporary file.
- `NSURLSessionUploadTask`: This is used for making requests that require a request body such as a POST or PUT request.

It is important to note that a task will not send the request to the service until we call the `resume()` method.

Using the NSURL class

The `NSURL` object represents the URL that we are going to connect to. The `NSURL` class is not limited to URLs that represent remote servers, but it can also be used to represent a local file on disk. In this chapter, we will be using the `NSURL` class exclusively to represent the URL of the remote service that we are connecting to.

NSMutableURLRequest

The `NSMutableURLRequest` class is a mutable subclass of the `NSURLRequest` class, which represents a URL load request. We use the `NSMutableRequest` class to encapsulate our URL and the request properties.

It is important to understand that the `NSMutableURLRequest` class is used to encapsulate the necessary information to make our request, but it does not make the actual request. To make the request, we use instances of the `NSURLSession` and `NSURLSessionTask` classes.

NSURLHTTPResponse

The `NSURLHTTPResponse` class is a subclass of the `NSURLResponse` class that encapsulates the metadata associated with the response to a URL request. The `NSURLHTTPResponse` class provides methods for accessing specific information associated with an HTTP response. Specifically, this class allows us to access the HTTP header fields and the response status codes.

We briefly covered a number of classes in this section and it may not be clear how they all actually fit together; however, once you see the examples a little further in this chapter, it will become much clearer. Before we go into our examples, let's take a quick look at the type of service that we will be connecting to.

REST web services

REST has become one of the most important technologies for stateless communications between devices. Due to the lightweight and stateless nature of the REST-based services, its importance is likely to continue to grow as more devices are connected to the Internet.

REST is an architecture style for designing networked applications. The idea behind REST is that instead of using complex mechanisms, such as SOAP or CORBA to communicate between devices, we use simple HTTP requests for the communication. While, in theory, REST is not dependent on the Internet protocols, it is almost always implemented using them. Therefore, when we are accessing REST services, we are almost always interacting with web servers in the same way that our web browsers interact with these servers.

REST web services use the HTTP POST, GET, PUT, or DELETE methods. If we think about a standard CRUD (create/read/update/delete) application, we would use a POST request to create or update data, a GET request to read data, and a DELETE request to delete data.

When we type a URL into our browser's address bar and hit *Enter*, we are generally making a GET request to the server and asking it to send us the web page associated with that URL. When we fill out a web form and click the submit button, we are generally making a POST request to the server. We then include the parameters from the web form in the body of our POST request.

Now, let's look at how to make an HTTP GET request using Apple's networking API.

Making an HTTP GET request

In this example, we will make a GET request to Apple's iTunes search API to get a list of items related to the search term Jimmy Buffett. Since we are retrieving data from the service, by REST standards, we should use a GET request to retrieve the data.

While the REST standard is to use GET requests to retrieve data from a service, there is nothing stopping a developer of a web service from using a GET request to create or update a data object. It is not recommended to use a GET request in this manner, but just be aware that there are services out there that do not adhere to the REST standards.

The following code makes a request to Apple's iTunes search API and then prints the results to the console:

```
public typealias dataFromURLCompletionClosure = (NSURLResponse!,
NSData!) -> Void

public func sendGetRequest(handler: public func getConnect(
        handler: dataFromURLCompletionClosure) {

        let sessionConfiguration =
          NSURLSessionConfiguration.defaultSessionConfiguration();

        let urlString =
```

```
            "https://itunes.apple.com/search?term=jimmy+buffett"

        if let encodeString =
    urlString.stringByAddingPercentEncodingWithAllowedCharacters(
                NSCharacterSet.URLQueryAllowedCharacterSet()),
            url = NSURL(string: encodeString) {

            let request = NSMutableURLRequest(URL:url)
            request.HTTPMethod = "GET"
            let urlSession = NSURLSession(
                configuration:sessionConfiguration, delegate: nil,
 delegateQueue: nil)

            let sessionTask =
 urlSession.dataTaskWithRequest(request) {
                (data, response, error) in

                handler(response, data)
            }
            sessionTask.resume()
        }
    }
```

We start off by creating a type alias named `DataFromURLCompletionClosure`. The `DataFromURLCompletionClosure` type will be used for both the GET and POST examples of this chapter. If you are not familiar with using a `typealias` object to define a closure type, please refer to *Chapter 12, Working with Closures*, for more information.

We then create a function named `sendGetRequest()` that will be used to make the GET request to Apple's iTunes API. This function accepts one argument named handler, which is a closure that conforms to the `DataFromURLCompletionClosure` type. The handler closure will be used to return the results from the request.

Within our `sendGetRequest()` method, we begin by creating an instance of the `NSURLSessionConfiguration` class using the `defaultSessionConfiguration()` method, which creates a default session configuration instance. If we need to, we can modify the session configuration properties after we create it, but in this example, the default configuration is what we want.

After we create our session configuration, we create the URL string. This is the URL of the service we are connecting to. With a GET request, we put our parameters in the URL itself. In this specific example, `https://itunes.apple.com/search` is the URL of the web service. We then follow the web service URL with a question mark (`?`), which indicates that the rest of the URL string consists of parameters for the web service.

The parameters take the form of key/value pairs, which means that each parameter has a key and a value. The key and value of a parameter, in a URL, are separated by an equals sign (=). In our example, the key is `term` and the value is `jimmy+buffett`. Next, we run the URL string that we just created through the `stringByAddingPercentEncodingWithAllowedCharacters()` method to make sure our URL string is encoded properly. We use the `URLQueryAllowedCharacterSet` character set with this method to ensure we have a valid URL string.

Next, we use the URL string that we just built to create an `NSURL` instance named `url`. Since we are making a GET request, this `NSURL` instance will represent both the location of the web service and the parameters that we are sending to it.

We create an instance of the `NSMutableURLRequest` class using the `NSURL` instance that we just created. We use the `NSMutableURLRequest` class, instead of the `NSURLRequest` class so that we can set the properties needed for our request. In this example, we set the `HTTPMethod` property; however, we can also set other properties such as the timeout interval or add items to our HTTP header.

Now, we use the `sessionConfiguration` variable (instance of the `NSURLSessionConfiguration class`) that we created at the beginning of the `sendGetRequest()` function to create an instance of the `NSURLSession` class. The `NSURLSession` class provides the API that we will use to connect to Apple's iTunes search API. In this example, we use the `dataTaskWithRequest()` method of the `NSURLSession` instance to return an instance of the `NSURLSessionDataTask` instance named `sessionTask`.

The `sessionTask` instance is what makes the request to the iTunes search API. When we receive the response from the service, we use the handler callback to return both the `NSURLResponse` object and the `NSData` object. The `NSURLResponse` contains information about the response, and the `NSData` instance contains the body of the response.

Finally, we call the `resume()` method of the `NSURLSessionDataTask` instance to make the request to the web service. Remember, as we mentioned earlier, an `NSURLSessionTask` instance will not send the request to the service until we call the `resume()` method.

Now, let's look at how we would call the `sendGetRequest()` function. The first thing we need to do is to create a closure that will be passed to the `sendGetRequest()` function and called when the response from the web service is received. In this example, we will simply print the response to the console. Since the response is in the JSON format, we could use the `NSJSONSerialization` class, as describe in *Chapter 8, Working with XML and JSON Data*, to parse the response; however, since this chapter is on networking, we will simply print the response to the console. Here is the code:

```
var printResultsClosure: HttpConnect.DataFromURLCompletionClosure
  = {

  if let data = $1 {
    let sString = NSString(data: data, encoding:
      NSUTF8StringEncoding)
    print(sString)
  }
}
```

We define this closure, named `printResultsClosure`, to be an instance of the `DataFromURLCompletionClosure` type. Within the closure, we unwrap the first parameter and set the value to a constant named `data`. If the first parameter is not nil, we convert the data constant to an instance of the `NSString` class, which is then printed to the console.

Now, let's call the `sendGetRequest()` method with the following code:

```
let aConnect = HttpConnect()
aConnect.sendGetRequest(printResultsClosure)
```

This code creates an instance of the `HttpConnect` class and then calls the `sendGetRequest()` method, passing the `printResultsClosure` closure as the only parameter. If we run this code while we are connected to the Internet, we will receive a JSON response that contains a list of items related to Jimmy Buffett on iTunes.

Now that we have seen how to make a simple HTTP GET request, let's look at how we would make an HTTP POST request to a web service.

Making an HTTP POST request

Since Apple's iTunes, APIs use GET requests to retrieve data. In this section, we will use the free `http://httpbin.org` service to show you how to make a POST request. The POST service that `http://httpbin.org` provides can be found at `http://httpbin.org/post`. This service will echo back the parameters that it receives so that we can verify that our request was made properly.

When we make a POST request, we generally have some data that we want to send or post to the server. This data takes the form of key/value pairs. These pairs are separated by an ampersand (&) symbol, and each key is separated from its value by an equals sign (=). As an example, let's say that we want to submit the following data to our service:

```
firstname: Jon
lastname: Hoffman
age: 47 years
```

The body of the POST request would take the following format:

```
firstname=Jon&lastname=Hoffman&age=47
```

Once we have the data in the proper format, we will then use the `dataUsingEncoding()` method, as we did with the GET request to properly encode the POST data.

Since the data going to the server is in the key/value format, the most appropriate way to store this data, prior to sending it to the service, is with a `Dictionary` object. With this in mind, we will need to create a method that will take a `Dictionary` object and return a string object that can be used for the POST request. The following code will do that:

```
func dictionaryToQueryString(dict: [String : String]) -> String {
  var parts = [String]()
  for (key, value) in dict {
    let part: String = key + "=" + value
    parts.append(part);
  }
  return parts.joinWithSeparator("&")
}
```

This function loops through each key/value pair of the `Dictionary` object and creates a `String` object that contains the key and the value separated by the equals sign (=). We then use the `joinWithSeperator()` function to join each item in the array, separated by the specified sting. In our case, we want to separate each string with the ampersand symbol (&). We then return this newly created string to the code that called it.

Now, let's create our `sendPostRequest()` function that will send the POST request to the `http://httpbin.org` post service. We will see a lot of similarities between this `sendPostRequest()` function and the `sendGetRequest()` function, which we showed you in the *Making an HTTP GET request* section of this chapter. Let's take a look at the following code:

```
public func sendPostRequest(handler: dataFromURLCompletionClosure)
{

        let sessionConfiguration =
        NSURLSessionConfiguration.defaultSessionConfiguration()

        let urlString = "http://httpbin.org/post"
        if let encodeString =
            urlString.
stringByAddingPercentEncodingWithAllowedCharacters(
                NSCharacterSet.URLQueryAllowedCharacterSet()),
            url = NSURL(string: encodeString) {

            let request = NSMutableURLRequest(URL:url)
            request.HTTPMethod = "POST"
            let params = dictionaryToQueryString(["One":"1 and 1",
"Two":"2 and 2"])
            request.HTTPBody = params.dataUsingEncoding(
                NSUTF8StringEncoding, allowLossyConversion: true)

            let urlSession = NSURLSession(
                configuration:sessionConfiguration, delegate: nil,
delegateQueue: nil)

            let sessionTask =
urlSession.dataTaskWithRequest(request) {
                (data, response, error) in

                handler(response, data)
            }
            sessionTask.resume()
        }
    }
```

Now, let's walk though this code. Notice that we are using the same type alias, named `DataFromURLCompletionClosure`, that we used with the `sendGetRequest()` function. If you are not familiar with using a `typealias` object to define a closure type, please refer to *Chapter 12, Working with Closures*, for more information.

The `sendPostRequest()` function accepts one argument named `handler`, which is a closure that conforms to the `DataFromURLCompletionClosure` type. The handler closure will be used to process the data from the `http://httpbin.org` service once the service responds to our request.

Within our `sendPostRequest()` method, we start off by creating an instance of the `NSURLSessionConfiguration` class using the `defaultSessionConfiguration()` method, which creates a default session configuration instance. We are able to modify the session configuration properties after we create it, but, in this example, the default configuration is what we want.

After we created our session configuration, we create our URL string. This is the URL of the service we are connecting to. In this example, the URL is `http://httpbin.org/post`. Next, we run the URL string that we just created through the `stringByAddingPercentEncodingWithAllowedCharacters()` method to make sure our URL string is encoded properly. We use the `URLQueryAllowedCharacterSet` character set with this method to ensure we have a valid URL string.

Next, we use the URL string that we just built to create an instance of the `NSURL` class named `url`. Since this is a POST request, this `NSURL` instance will represent the location of the web service that we are connecting to.

We now create an instance of the `NSMutableURLRequest` class using the `NSURL` instance that we just created. We use the `NSMutableURLRequest` class, instead of the `NSURLRequest` class so that we can set the properties needed for our request. In this example, we set the `HTTPMethod` property; however, we can also set other properties such as the timeout interval or add items to our HTTP header.

Now, we use our `dictionaryToQueryString()` function, which we showed you at the beginning of this section, to build the data that we are going to post to the server. We use the `dataUsingEncoding()` function to make sure that our data is properly encoded prior to sending it to the server, and finally, the data is added to the `HTTPBody` property of the `NSMutableURLRequest` instance.

We use the `sessionConfiguration` variable (instance of the `NSURLSessionConfiguration class`) that we created at the beginning of the function to create an instance of the `NSURLSession` class. The `NSURLSession` class provides the API that we will use to connect to the post on `http://httpbin.org` post service. In this example, we use the `dataTaskWithRequest()` method of the `NSURLSession` instance to return an instance of the `NSURLSessionDataTask` class named `sessionTask`.

The `sessionTask` instance is what makes the request to the `http://httpbin.org` POST service. When we receive the response from the service, we use the handler callback to return both the `NSURLResponse` object and the `NSData` object. The `NSURLResponse` contains information about the response, and the `NSData` instance contains the body of the response.

Finally, we call the `resume()` method of the `NSURLSessionDataTask` instance to make the request to the web service. Remember, as we mentioned earlier, an `NSURLSessionTask` class will not send the request to the service until we call the `resume()` method.

We can then call the `sendPostRequest()` method in exactly the same way that we called the `sendGetRequest()` method.

When developing applications that communicate to other devices and services over the Internet, it is good practice to verify that we have a network connection. When developing mobile applications, it is also good practice to verify that we are not using a mobile connection (3G, 4G, and so on) to transfer large amounts of data.

Let's look at how to verify that we have a network connection and what type of connection we have.

Checking network connection

As we create applications that communicate with other devices and services over the Internet, eventually, we will want to verify that we have a network connection prior to making the network calls. Another thing to consider when we are writing mobile applications is the type of network connection that the user has. As mobile application developers, we need to keep in mind that our users probably have a mobile data plan that limits the amount of data they can send/receive in a month. If they exceed that limit, they may have to pay an extra fee. If our application sends large amounts of data, it might be appropriate to warn our user prior to sending this data if they are on a cellular network.

This next example will show us how we can verify that we have a network connection and it also tells us what type of connection we have. We will begin by importing the system configuration API and also defining an enum that contains the different connection types. We will import the system configuration API like this:

```
import SystemConfiguration
```

We create a `ConnectionType` enum. This enum will be used as the return type for `networkConnectionType()`:

```
public enum ConnectionType {
    case NONETWORK
    case MOBILE3GNETWORK
    case WIFINETWORK
}
```

Now, let's look at the code to check the network connection type:

```
public func networkConnectionType(hostname: NSString) ->
ConnectionType {

    let reachabilityRef =
SCNetworkReachabilityCreateWithName(nil,hostname.UTF8String)

    var flags: SCNetworkReachabilityFlags =
SCNetworkReachabilityFlags()
        SCNetworkReachabilityGetFlags(reachabilityRef!, &flags)

    let reachable: Bool = (flags.rawValue &
SCNetworkReachabilityFlags.Reachable.rawValue) != 0
    let needsConnection: Bool = (flags.rawValue &
SCNetworkReachabilityFlags.ConnectionRequired.rawValue) != 0
    if reachable && !needsConnection {
        // what type of connection is available
        let isCellularConnection = (flags.rawValue &
SCNetworkReachabilityFlags.IsWWAN.rawValue) != 0
        if isCellularConnection {
            // cellular connection available
            return ConnectionType.MOBILE3GNETWORK
        } else {
            // wifi connection available
            return ConnectionType.WIFINETWORK
        }
    }
    return ConnectionType.NONETWORK // no connection at all
}
```

The `networkConnectionType()` function begins by creating a `SCNetworkReachability` reference. To create the `SCNetworkRechabilityRef` reference, we use the `SCNetworkReachabilityCreateWithName()` function, which creates a reachability reference to the host provided.

After we get our `SCNetworkReachabilityRef` reference, we need to retrieve the `SCNetworkReachabilityFlags` enum from the reference. This is done with the `SCNetworkReachabilityGetFlags()` function.

Once we have the network reachability flags, we can begin testing our connection. We use the bitwise AND (`&`) operator to see whether the host is reachable and if we need to establish a connection before we can connect to the host (`needsConnection`). If the reachable flag is false (we cannot currently connect to the host), or if `needsConnection` is true (we need to establish a connection before we can connect), we return `NONETWORK`, which means the host is currently not reachable.

If we are able to connect to the host, we then check to see whether we have a cellular connection by checking the network reachability flags again. If we have a cellular connection, we return `MOBILE3GNETWORK`, otherwise, we assume we have a Wi-Fi connection and return `WIFINETWORK`.

If you are writing applications that connect to other devices or services over the Internet, I would recommend putting this function in a standard library to use because you will want to check for networking connectivity, and also the type of connection that you have pretty regularly.

Now that we have seen how to use Apple's networking APIs to connect to remote services, I would like to demonstrate a network library that you can use in your own applications. This network library makes it very easy and simple to connect to various types of services on the Internet. This is a library that I created and maintained, but I would definitely welcome anyone that would like to contribute to the code base. This library is called **RSNetworking**.

RSNetworking2 for Swift 2

You can find `RSNetworking2` on GitHub with `https://github.com/hoffmanjon/RSNetworking2`

The `RSNetworking2` library is a network library written entirely in the Swift programming language. `RSNetworking2` is built using Apple's powerful URL loading system (`https://developer.apple.com/library/mac/documentation/Cocoa/Conceptual/URLLoadingSystem/URLLoadingSystem.html`), which features the `NSURLSession` class that we used earlier in this chapter. The main design goal of `RSNetworking2` is to make it easy and quick for developers to add powerful asynchronous networking requests to their applications that are written in Swift.

There are the three ways in which we can use `RSNetworking2`:

- `RSURLRequest`: This API provides a very simple and easy interface to make single GET requests to a service.
- `RSTransaction` and `RSTransactionRequest`: These APIs provide a very powerful and flexible way to make both GET and POST requests to a service. This API also makes it very easy to make multiple requests to a service.
- `Extensions`: `RSNetworking2` provides extensions to both the `UIImageView` and `UIButton` classes to dynamically load images from a URL and insert them into the `UIImageView` or `UIButton` classes after they are loaded.

Let's look at each of these APIs in greater detail and then provide some examples of how to use them.

RSURLRequest

With the `RSURLRequest` API, we can make a GET request to a service and the only thing we need to provide is the URL and the parameters we wish to send to the service. The `RSURLRequest` API exposes four functions. These functions are as follows:

- `dataFromURL(url: NSURL, completionHandler handler: RSNetworking.dataFromURLCompletionClosure)`: This retrieves an `NSData` object from a URL. This is the main function and is used by the other three functions to retrieve an `NSData` object prior to converting it to the requested format.
- `stringFromURL(url: NSURL, completionHandler handler: RSNetworking.stringFromURLCompletionClosure)`: This retrieves an `NSString` object from a URL. This function uses the `dataFromURL()` function to retrieve an `NSData` object and then converts it to an `NSString` object.
- `dictionaryFromJsonURL(url: NSURL, completionHandler handler: RSNetworking.dictionaryFromURLCompletionClosure)`: This retrieves an `NSDictionary` object from a URL. This function uses the `dataFromURL()` function to retrieve an `NSData` object and then converts it to an `NSDictionary` object. The data returned from the URL should be in the JSON format for this function to work properly.
- `imageFromURL(url: NSURL, completionHandler handler: RSNetworking.imageFromURLCompletionClosure)`: This retrieves a `UIImage` object from a URL. This function uses the `dataFromURL()` function to retrieve an `NSData` object and then converts it to a `UIImage` object.

Now, let's look at an example on how to use the `RSURLRequest` API. In this example, we will make a request to Apple's iTunes search API, as we did in the *Making an HTTP GET request* section of this chapter:

```
func rsURLRequestExample() {
  var client = RSURLRequest()

  if let testURL =
NSURL(string:"https://itunes.apple.com/search?term=jimmy+buffett&m
edia=music") {

      client.dictionaryFromJsonURL(testURL, completionHandler:
        resultsHandler)
  }
}
```

Let's walk through this code. We begin by creating an instance of the `RSURLRequest` class and an instance of the `NSURL` class. The `NSURL` instance represents the URL of the service that we wish to connect to and since we are making a GET request, it also contains the parameters that we are sending to the service. If we recall from the previous *Making an HTTP GET Request* section, when we make a HTTP GET request, the parameters that we are sending to the service are contained within the URL itself.

Apple's iTunes search API returns the results of the search in the JSON format. We can see that in the API documentation and also by printing out the results of the search to the console; therefore, we will use the `dictionaryFromJsonURL()` method of the `RSURLRequest` class to make our request to the service. We could also use the `dataFromURL()` or `stringFromURL()` methods to retrieve the data if we wanted to, but this method is specifically written to handle JSON data that is returned form a REST-based web service.

The `dictionaryFromJsonURL()` method will take the data that is returned from the `NSURLSession` request and convert it to an `NSDictionary` object. We use the `NSDictionary` object here rather than Swift's `Dictionary` object because the web service could return multiple types (Strings, Arrays, Numbers, and so on), and if we recall, a Swift `Dictionary` object can have only a single type for the key and a single type for the value.

When we call the `dictionaryFromJsonURL()` method, we pass the URL that we want to connect to and also a completion handler that will be called once the information from the service is returned and converted to an `NSDicationary` object.

Now, let's look at our completion handler:

```
var resultsHandler:RSURLRequestRSURLRequestRSURLRequestRSURLRequest.
dictionaryFromURLCompletionClosure = {
  var response = $0
  var responseDictionary = $1
  var error = $2
  if error == nil {
    let res = "results"
    if let results = responseDictionary[res] as? NSArray {
      print(results[0])

    }
    else {
      print("Problem with data")
    }
  }
  else {
    //If there was an error, log it
    print("Error : \(error)")
  }
}
```

Our completion handler is of the `RSURLRequest.dictionaryFromURLCompletionClosure` type. This type is defined in the same way as the `RSTransactionRequest.dictionaryFromRSTransactionCompletionClosure` type, which allows us to use this same closure for the `RSURLRequests` and `RSTransactionRequest` requests.

We begin the completion handler by retrieving the three parameters that were passed and assign them to the `response`, `responseDictionary`, and `error` variables. We then check the `error` variable to see whether it is `nil`. If it is `nil`, we received a valid response and can retrieve values for the `NSDictionary` object.

In this example, we retrieve the `NSArray` value that is associated with the `results` key in the `NSDictionary` object that was returned from the service. This `NSArray` value will contain a list of items in the iTunes store that are associated with our search term. Once we have the `NSArray` value, we print out the first element of the array to the console.

The `RSURLRequest` API is very good for making single GET requests to a service. Now, let's look at the `RSTransaction` and `RSTransactionRequest` APIs, which can be used for both POST and GET requests and should be used when we need to make multiple requests to the same service.

RSTransaction and RSTransactionRequest

The `RSTransaction` and `RSTransactionRequest` classes allow us to configure a transaction (`RSTransaction`) and then use that transaction to make a request (`RSTransactionRequest`) to the service. One of the things that make, this API so powerful is how easy it is for us to make subsequent request by simply updating the transaction and resubmitting it. Let's look at the API that is exposed by these two classes.

RSTransaction

The `RSTransaction` class defines the transaction we wish to make. It exposes four properties and one initiator.

The properties are as follows:

- `TransactionType`: This defines the HTTP request method. Currently, there are three types defined—GET, POST, and UNKNOWN. Only the GET and POST actually send a request.
- `baseURL`: This is the base URL to use for the request. This will normally look something like `https://itunes.apple.com`. If we are using a nonstandard port, we would follow the server URL by a colon and the port number such as `http://mytestserver:8080`.
- `path`: This is the path that will be added to the base URL. This will be something like `search`. It can also include a longer path string such as `path/to/my/service`.
- `parameters`: This is a `Dictionary` object containing the parameters to send to the service.

The initiator is as follows:

- `init(transactionType: RSTransactionType, baseURL: String, path: String, parameters: [String: String])`: This will initialize the `RSTransaction` class with all the required properties

RSTransactionRequest

The `RSTransactionRequest` class builds and sends out the request that is defined by the four functions, which are as follows:

- `dataFromRSTransaction(transaction: RSTransaction, completionHandler handler: RSNetworking.dataFromRSTransactionCompletionCompletionClosure)`: This function retrieves an `NSData` object from the service defined by the `RSTransaction` class. This is the main function and is used by the other three functions to retrieve the `NSData` object prior to converting it to the requested format.
- `stringFromRSTransaction(transaction: RSTransaction, completionHandler handler: RSNetworking.stringFromRSTransactionCompletionCompletionClosure)`: This functionfn-= retrieves an `NSString` object from the service defined by the `RSTransaction` class. This function uses the `dataFromRSTransaction()` function to retrieve the `NSData` object and then converts it to an `NSString` object.
- `dictionaryFromRSTransaction(transaction: RSTransaction, completionHandler handler: RSNetworking.dictionaryFromRSTransactionCompletionCompletionClosure)`: This function retrieves an `NSDictionary` object from the service defined by the `RSTransaction` class. This function uses the `dataFromRSTransaction()` function to retrieve the `NSData` object and then converts it to an `NSDictionary` object. The data returned from the URL should be in the JSON format for this function to work properly.
- `imageFromRSTransaction(transaction: RSTransaction, completionHandler handler: RSNetworking.imageFromRSTransactionCompletionCompletionClosure)`: This function retrieves a `UIImage` object from the service defined by the `RSTransaction` class. This function uses the `dataFromRSTransaction()` function to retrieve the `NSData` object and then converts it to a `UIImage` object.

Now, let's look at an example of how we would use the `RSTransaction` and `RSTransactionRequest` classes to make a GET request to Apple's iTunes search API. In this example, we will use the same `resultsHandler` closure that we defined in the *RSURLRequest* section of this chapter. Let's take a look at the following code:

```
func rsTransactionExample() {

  let rsRequest = RSTransactionRequest()

   //First request
```

```
    let rsTransGet = RSTransaction(transactionType:
      RSTransactionType.GET, baseURL: "https://itunes.apple.com",
        path: "search", parameters: ["term":"jimmy+buffett",
          "media":"music"])
    rsRequest.dictionaryFromRSTransaction(rsTransGet,
      completionHandler: resultsHandler)

    //Second request
    rsTransGet.parameters = ["term":"jim", "media":"music"]
    rsRequest.dictionaryFromRSTransaction(rsTransGet,
      completionHandler: resultsHandler)
}
```

In this example, we begin by creating an instance of the `RSTransactionRequest` class named `rsRequest`. This `RSTransactionRequest` instance will be used to send our request to the service defined in our `RSTransaction` instance.

After we create the `RSTransactionRequest` instance, we use the `RSTransaction` initiator to create an instance of the `RSTransction` class named `rsTransGet`. In this initiator, we define the following properties as follows:

- `transactionType`: The `transactionType` is set to `RSTransactionType.` GET (this can also be `RSTransactionType`.POST or `RSTransactionType.` UNKNOWN)
- `baseURL`: The `baseURL` is set to `https://itunes.apple.com`
- `path`: The `path` is set to search
- `parameters`: The parameter is set to `["term":"jimmy+buffett", "media":"music"]`

Finally, we use the `dictionaryFromRSTransaction()` method of the `RSTransactionRequest` instance. This method accepts two parameters; the first being the `RSTransaction` instance that defines the transaction to send and the second being the completion handler that will be called once the data is returned from the service.

As we mentioned earlier, one of the things that makes the `RSTransaction` and `RSTransactionRequest` classes so nice to use is how easy it is to make subsequent requests to the same service. In our example, after we make the initial request, we then change the parameters and make a second request to the same service. One thing to watch out for is that since these are asynchronous requests, if we make two back-to-back requests like this, we cannot guarantee which request will be returned first.

Now, let's look at the last part of the `RSNetworking2` library—the extensions.

Extensions

In Swift, extensions add new functionality to the existing classes. `RSNetworking2` has extensions for the `UIImageView` and `UIbutton` classes. These extensions allow us to load images from a URL and then add them to `UIImageView` or `UIButton`, once the image has finished downloading. We can also put a placeholder image that will be displayed in `UIImageView` or `UIButton` until the final image is downloaded. Once the image finishes downloading, the placeholder image will be replaced by the downloaded image.

Both the `UIImageView` and `UIButton` extensions expose four new methods:

- `setImageForURL(url: NSString, placeHolder: UIImage)`: This method sets the image of the `UIImageView` or `UIButton` extensions to the placeholder image and then asynchronously downloads the image from the provided URL. Once the image downloads, it will replace the placeholder image with the downloaded image.
- `setImageForURL(url: NSString)`: This asynchronously downloads the image from the URL. Once the image is downloaded, it sets the image of the `UIImageView` or `UIButton` extensions to the downloaded image.
- `setImageForRSTransaction(transaction:RSTransaction, placeHolder: UIImage)`: This method sets the image in `UIImageView` or `UIButton` to the placeholder image and then asynchronously downloads the image from the provided `RSTransaction` object. Once the image downloads, it will replace the placeholder image with the downloaded image.
- `setImageForRSTransaction(transaction:RSTransaction)`: This asynchronously downloads the image from the provided `RSTransaction` object. Once the image downloads, it sets the image of the `UIImageView` or `UIButton` extensions to the downloaded image.

The `UIButton` and `UIImageView` extensions are used in exactly the same way. To see how to use these extensions, let's take a look at how we would use the `UIImageView` extension to view an image that we download from the Internet:

```
let url =
  "http://is4.mzstatic.com/image/pf/us/r30/Features/2a/b7/da/dj.kkir
mfzh.100x100-75.jpg"
 if let iView: UIImageView = imageView, image = UIImage(named:
"loading") {
   iView.setImageForURL(url, placeHolder: image)
}
```

In this example, we start off by defining the URL of our image. We then verify that the `imageView` variable contains an instance of a `UIImageView` class. Note that we normally would not define the constant type (the `UIImageView` type) in an `if-let` statement, but I defined the type in this example to show that the `imageView` constant should be an instance of the `UIImageView` class. Next, we create an instance of the `UIImage` class with the image named `loading`. This image will be used as the placeholder image and will be displayed while we are downloading the final image from the URL.

Now that we have the URL of the image and the placeholder image, we use the `setImageForURL()` extension method. This method accepts two parameters—the URL to download the image from and the placeholder image. Once we call this method, `RSNetworking2` will set the image of the `UIImageView` class to the placeholder image that is provided and then download the image from the URL provided. Once the image finishes downloading, `RSNetworking2` will replace the placeholder image with the downloaded image.

We looked at a few brief examples of `RSNetworking2` in this chapter. There are additional examples on the `RSNetworking2` GitHub site at `https://github.com/hoffmanjon/RSNetworking2`.

Summary

In today's world, it is essential that a developer have a good working knowledge of network development. In this chapter, we saw how to use Apple's `NSURLSession` API, with other classes, to connect to HTTP REST-based web services. The `NSURLSession` API was written as a replacement for the older `NSURLConnection` API and is now the recommended API to use when making network requests.

We also saw how to use Apple's system configuration API to figure out what type of network connection we have. If we are developing applications for a mobile device (iPhone, iPod, or iPad), it is essential to know whether we have a network connection and what type of connection it is.

We ended the chapter discussing `RSNetworking2`, which is an open source network library, written entirely in Swift, that I maintain. `RSNetworking2` allows us to very quickly and easily add network functionality to our applications. It also adds an extension to both the `UIImageView` and `UIButton` classes to dynamically load images from the Internet and display them after the download is complete. I would encourage anyone who wishes to participate in the development of RSNetworking.

17
Adopting Design Patterns in Swift

Although the Gang of Four's *Design Patterns: Elements of Reusable Object-Oriented Software* was first published in October 1994, it has only been in the last 6 or 7 years that I started paying attention to design patterns. Like most experienced developers, when I first started reading about design patterns, I recognized a lot of the patterns because I had already been using them without realizing what they were. I would have to say that in the past 6 or 7 years since I first read about design patterns, I did not write a serious application without using at least one of the Gang of Four's design patterns. I will tell you that I am definitely not a design pattern zealot, and actually, if I get into a conversation about design patterns, there is usually only a couple that I can name without having to look them up, but one thing that I do remember is the concepts of the major patterns and the problems they are written to solve. This way, when I encounter one of these problems, I can look up the appropriate pattern and apply it.

In this chapter, you will learn about the following topics:

- The difference between reference and value types
- What design patterns are
- What types of patterns make up the creational, structural, and behavioral categories of design patterns
- How to implement the builder, factory method, and singleton creational patterns in Swift
- How to implement the bridge, façade, and proxy structural patterns in Swift
- How to implement the strategy and command behavioral patterns in Swift

Value versus reference types

In *Chapter 5, Classes and Structures*, we discussed the difference between value and reference types. It is important that we understand the basic differences between the two types, especially when we are architecting our code. Certain design patterns work best with reference types, while other work best with value types; therefore, knowing when to use each type is important in design patterns. With that in mind, let's review the difference between reference and value types.

A class is a reference type. What this means is that when we pass an instance of a class around our code, we are passing a reference to the original instance. Since we are passing a reference to the original instance, any changes that are made to this instance are reflected back to the original instance.

Structures, enums, and tuples are all value types. When we pass an instance of a value type, we are passing a copy of the type. This means that any changes made to this copy is not reflected back to the original. Let's take a look at the difference between a value and reference types by looking at some code. We will begin by creating a class named `MyClass` and a structure named `MyStruct`. Both of these types contain a single property named `number` that will be of the Int type:

```
class MyClass {
    var number = 0
}

struct MyStruct {
    var number = 0
}
```

Now let's create an instance of the `MyClass` class. We will also create a second constant of the `MyClass` type that is created from the first instance. We will then change the `number` property in one of the instances, and see what the value is in both:

```
let myClass1 = MyClass()
let myClass2 = myClass1

myClass2.number = 5

print("myClass1 = \(myClass1.number)")
print("myClass2 = \(myClass2.number)")
```

If we ran this code, we would see the following output:

```
myClass1 = 5
myClass2 = 5
```

As we can see, when we changed the `number` property in one instance, it changed the value in both. This also means that there is only one instance of the `MyClass` class in memory.

Now let's look at this same example, but this time, we will use the `MyStruct` structure (value type) rather than the `MyClass` class (reference type):

```
var myStruct1 = MyStruct()
var myStruct2 = myStruct1

myStruct2.number = 5

print("myStruct1 = \(myStruct1.number)")
print("myStruct2 = \(myStruct2.number)")
```

If we ran this code, we would see the following output:

```
myStruct1 = 0
myStruct2 = 5
```

Notice that in this example, when we change the `number` property of one instance, it did not change the property in the other. Since the `myStruct2` structure was created with a copy of the `myStruct` structure, we now have two instances of the `MyStruct` structure in memory.

Also notice that we defined the instances of the `MyClass` class as constants with the `let` keyword; however, we defined the instances of the `MyStruct` structure as variables with the `var` keyword.

When a constant refers to an instance of a reference type, we are unable to change the instance that the constant is referring to; however, we are able to change the values of the properties of that instances, as shown in the previous example. When a constant refers to an instance of a value type, we will not only be unable to change the instance that the constant is referring to, but we will also be unable to change any of the property values. Swift arrays and dictionaries are value types which is why when they are declared constants, they are immutable. This means, in our previous example, in order to change the values of the `number` properties, we needed to create the instances of the `MyStruct` structures as variables and not constants.

For some of the design patterns in this chapter, we used structures and for some other, we used classes. The choice to use either a structure or class for these examples is based on the experience of the author. For most of the patterns, the choice of using either a structure or a class should be based on the needs of the individual application. In each section, we will explain why we chose either a structure or a class to help you understand why it was chosen.

What are design patterns

Every experienced developer has a set of informal strategies that shape how he/she designs and writes applications. These strategies are shaped by their past experiences and the obstacles that they have had to overcome in previous projects. Though these developers might swear by their strategies, it does not mean that their strategies have been fully vetted and proven. The use of these strategies also introduces inconsistent implementations between different developers.

A design pattern identifies a common software development problem and provides a strategy for dealing with it. Over the years, the strategies behind these design patterns have been proven to effectively solve the problem they are intended to solve.

While there is a lot to like about design patterns, and they are extremely beneficial to developers and architects, they are not the solution for world hunger that some developers make them out to be. Sometimes in your development career, you will probably meet a developer or architect who thinks that design patterns are immutable laws. These developers usually try to force the use of design patterns even when they are not necessary. A good rule of thumb is to make sure that you have a problem to fix before you try to fix it.

Keep in mind that design patterns are starting points for avoiding and solving common programming problems. We can think of each design pattern as a recipe for a food dish, and just like a good recipe, we can tinker and adjust it to meet our particular taste, but we usually do not want to stray too far from the original recipe because we may mess it up.

There are also times that we do not have a recipe for a certain dish, just like there are times when there isn't a design pattern to solve the problem we face. In these cases, we can use our knowledge of design patterns and their underlying philosophy to come up with an effective solution to the problem.

Design patterns can be broken into three categories:

- **Creational patterns**: These support the creation of objects

- **Structural patterns**: These are concerned with class and object compositions
- **Behavioral patterns**: These are concerned with communication between classes

While the Gang of Four defined over 20 design patterns, we are only going to give examples of some of the most popular patterns in this chapter. Let's start off by looking at the creational patterns.

Creational patterns

Creational patterns are design patterns that deal with how an object is created. These patterns create objects in a manner that is suitable for the particular situation. There are two basic ideas behind creational patterns. The first is encapsulating the knowledge of which concrete classes should be created and the second is hiding how the instances of these classes are created. There are five well-known patterns that are part of the creational pattern category:

- **Abstract factory pattern**: This provides an interface for creating related objects without specifying the concrete class
- **Builder pattern**: This separates the construction of a complex object from its representation so the same process can be used to create similar types
- **Factory method pattern**: This creates objects without exposing the underlying logic of how the object or which type is created
- **Prototype pattern**: This creates an object by cloning an existing one
- **Singleton pattern**: This allows one and only one instance of a class for the lifetime of an application

In this chapter, we are going to show you examples of how to use the builder, factory method, and singleton patterns in Swift. Let's start off by looking at one of the most controversial and possibly overused design patterns—the singleton pattern.

The singleton design pattern

The use of the singleton pattern is a fairly controversial subject among certain corners of the development community. One of the main reasons for this is the singleton pattern is probably the most overused and misused pattern. Another reason why this pattern is controversial is that the singleton pattern introduces a global state into an application, which allows the ability to change the object at any point within the application, thereby ignoring the scope. My personal opinion is, if the singleton pattern is used correctly, there is nothing wrong with using it; however, we do need to be careful not to misuse it.

The singleton pattern restricts the instantiation of a class to one instance for the lifetime of an application. This pattern is very effective when we need exactly one object to coordinate actions within our application. An example of a good use of a singleton is if our application communicates with a remote device over Bluetooth and we also want to maintain that connection throughout our application. While some would say that we can pass the instance of the connection class from one page to the next, that is essentially what a singleton is.

In my opinion, the singleton pattern, in this instance, is much cleaner because with the singleton pattern, any page that needs the connection can get it without forcing every page to maintain the instance. This also allows us to maintain the connection without having to reconnect each time we go to another page.

There are several ways to implement the singleton pattern in Swift. The way that is presented here uses class constants, which were introduced in version 1.2 of Swift.

Let's look at how we would implement the singleton pattern with Swift. The following code example shows how to create a singleton class:

```
class MySingleton {
  static let sharedInstance = MySingleton()
  var number = 0

  private init() {}

}
```

We can see that within the `MySingleton` class, we create a static constant named `sharedInstance`, which contains an instance of the `MySingleton` class. A static constant can be called without having to instantiate the class. Since we declared the `sharedInstance` constant static, only one instance will exist throughout the life cycle of the application, thereby creating the singleton pattern.

We also create a private initiator that will restrict other code from creating another instance of the `MySingleton` class.

Now, let's see how this pattern works. The `MySingleton` pattern has another property named `number`, which is of the Int type. We will monitor how this property changes as we use the `sharedInstance` property to create multiple variables of the `MySingleton` type, as shown in the following code:

```
var singleA = MySingleton.sharedInstance
var singleB = MySingleton.sharedInstance
```

```
var singleC = MySingleton.sharedInstance

singleB.number = 2

print(singleA.number)
print(singleB.number)
print(singleC.number)

singleC.number = 3

print(singleA.number)
print(singleB.number)
print(singleC.number)
```

In this example, we use the `sharedInstance` property to create three variables of the `MySingleton` type. We initially set the `number` property of the second `MySingleton` variable (`singleB`) to the number `2`. When we print out the value of the `number` property for `singleA`, `singleB`, and `singleC`, we see that the `number` property for all the three equals to `2`. We then change the value of the `number` property of the third `MySingleton` variable (`singleC`) to the number `3`. When we print out the value of the `number` property again, we see that this time, all the three now have the value of `3`. Therefore, when we change the value of the `number` property in any of the instances, it changes the values for all the three because each variable is pointed to the same instance.

The singleton pattern can be very useful when we need to maintain the state of an object throughout our application, but be careful not to overuse it. The singleton pattern should not be used unless there is a specific requirement (requirement is the keyword here) for having one, and only one, instance of our class throughout the life cycle of our application. If we are using the singleton pattern simply for convenience, then we are misusing it.

For the singleton pattern, we created the `MySingleton` type as a class (reference type) because we wanted to ensure that only one instance of the type existed throughout our application. If we created the `MySingleton` type as a structure (value type), we would run the risk of the existence of multiple instances because structures are value type.

Now, let's look at the builder design pattern.

The builder design pattern

The builder pattern helps us in the creation of complex objects and enforces the process of how these objects are created. With this pattern, we generally separate the creation logic from the complex class and put it in another class. This allows us to use the same construction process to create different representations of the class.

In this section, we will see how to use the builder pattern by creating a `Burger` class and then use various different burger builders to create different types of burgers. Before we see how to use the builder pattern, let's look at how to create a `Burger` class without the builder pattern and the problems we'll run into.

The following code creates a class named `BurgerOld` and does not use the builder pattern:

```
class BurgerOld {
    var name: String
    var patties: Int
    var bacon: Bool
    var cheese: Bool
    var pickles: Bool
    var ketchup: Bool
    var mustard: Bool
    var lettuce: Bool
    var tomato: Bool

    init(name: String, patties: Int, bacon: Bool, cheese: Bool,
pickles: Bool,ketchup: Bool,mustard: Bool,lettuce: Bool,tomato: Bool)
{
        self.name = name
        self.patties = patties
        self.bacon = bacon
        self.cheese = cheese
        self.pickles = pickles
        self.ketchup = ketchup
        self.mustard = mustard
        self.lettuce = lettuce
        self.tomato = tomato
    }
}
```

In the BurgerOld class, we have several properties that define what is on the burger and also the name of the burger. Since we need to know which items are on the burgers and which aren't, when we create an instance of the BurgerOld class, the initializer requires us to define each item. This can lead to some complex initializations throughout our application, not to mention that if we had more than one standard burger (bacon cheeseburger, cheeseburger, hamburger, and so on), we would need to make sure that we define each correctly. Let's see how to create the instances of the BurgerOld class:

```
// Create Hamburger
var burgerOld = BurgerOld(name: "Hamburger", patties: 1, bacon:
  false, cheese: false, pickles: false, ketchup: false, mustard:
    false, lettuce: false, tomato: false)

// Create Cheeseburger
var burgerOld = BurgerOld(name: "Cheeseburger", patties: 1, bacon:
  false, cheese: false, pickles: false, ketchup: false, mustard:
    false, lettuce: false, tomato: false)
```

Now, let's look at a better way to do this. We will begin by creating a BurgerBuilder protocol that will have the following code in it:

```
protocol BurgerBuilder {
    var name: String {get}
    var patties: Int {get}
    var bacon: Bool {get}
    var cheese: Bool {get}
    var pickles: Bool {get}
    var ketchup: Bool {get}
    var mustard: Bool {get}
    var lettuce: Bool {get}
    var tomato: Bool {get}
}
```

This protocol simply defines the nine properties that will be required for any class that implements this protocol. Now, let's create two classes that implement this protocol—the HamburgerBuilder and CheeseBurgerBuilder classes:

```
class HamBurgerBuilder: BurgerBuilder {
    let name = "Burger"
    let patties = 1
    let bacon = false
    let cheese = false
    let pickles = true
```

```
        let ketchup = true
        let mustard = true
        let lettuce = false
        let tomato = false
    }

    class CheeseBurgerBuilder: BurgerBuilder {
        let name = "CheeseBurger"
        let patties = 1
        let bacon = false
        let cheese = true
        let pickles = true
        let ketchup = true
        let mustard = true
        let lettuce = false
        let tomato = false
    }
```

In both the `HamburgerBuilder` and `CheeseBurgerBuilder` classes, all we are doing is defining the values for each of the required properties. In more complex classes, we might need to initialize other objects that are required by this instance.

Now, let's look at our `Burger` class that will use implementations of the `BugerBuilder` protocol to create instances of itself. Let's take a look at the following code:

```
class Burger {
    var name: String
    var patties: Int
    var bacon: Bool
    var cheese: Bool
    var pickles: Bool
    var ketchup: Bool
    var mustard: Bool
    var lettuce: Bool
    var tomato: Bool

    init(builder: BurgerBuilder) {
        self.name = builder.name
        self.patties = builder.patties
        self.bacon = builder.bacon
        self.cheese = builder.cheese
        self.pickles = builder.pickles
```

```
        self.ketchup = builder.ketchup
        self.mustard = builder.mustard
        self.lettuce = builder.lettuce
        self.tomato = builder.tomato
    }

func showBurger() {
    print("Name:     \(name)")
    print("Patties: \(patties)")
    print("Bacon:    \(bacon)")
    print("Cheese:   \(cheese)")
    print("Pickles: \(pickles)")
    print("Ketchup: \(ketchup)")
    print("Mustard: \(mustard)")
    print("Lettuce: \(lettuce)")
    print("Tomato:   \(tomato)")
}
}
```

The difference between this `Burger` class and the `BurgerOld` class, shown earlier in this section, is the initializer. In the previous `BurgerOld` class, the initializer took nine arguments—one for each constant defined in the class. In the new `Burger` class, the initializer takes one argument, which is an instance of a class that conforms to the `BurgerBuilder` protocol. This new initializer allows us to create instances of the `Burger` class like this:

```
// Create Hamburger
var myBurger = Burger(builder: HamBurgerBuilder())
myBurger.showBurger()

// Create Cheeseburger with tomatoes
var myCheeseBurgerBuilder = CheeseBurgerBuilder()
var myCheeseBurger = Burger(builder: myCheeseBurgerBuilder)
myCheeseBurger.tomato = false
myCheeseBurger.showBurger()
```

If we compare how we created instances of the new `Burger` class to the earlier `BurgerOld` class, we can see that it is much easier to create instances of the `Burger` class. We also know that we are setting the values for each type of burger correctly because the values are set directly in the builder classes.

As we can see, the builder pattern helps us to simplify the creation of complex objects. It also ensures that our objects are fully created.

In this example, for our builder types, we chose to use classes (reference types). There really is not a huge advantage to using either a reference or value type; therefore, the reference type was chosen because it did not make sense to make multiple copies of our builder types.

For our last example of a creational pattern, we will look at the factory method pattern.

The factory method pattern

The factory method pattern uses factory methods to create instance of objects without specifying the exact class that will be created. This allows us to pick the exact class to create at runtime.

Let's look at how to use the factory method pattern by creating a computer store class that allows us to pick a computer from multiple models. We will begin by creating a protocol named `Computer`. Each class that represents a different computer model will implement the `Computer` protocol. Here is the code for the `Computer` protocol:

```
protocol Computer {
  func getType() -> String
}
```

The only method in the `Computer` protocol is a method that returns a string type that represents the model of the computer. Now, let's create three concrete classes that implement the `Computer` protocol:

```
class MacbookPro: Computer {
  func getType() -> String {
    return "Macbook Pro"
  }
}
class IMac: Computer {
  func getType() -> String {
    return "iMac"
  }
}

class MacMini: Computer {
  func getType() -> String {
    return "MacMini"
  }
}
```

Each of the three classes that implement the `Computer` protocol return a unique string type in the `getType()` method. This will identify which class was created. Now, let's look at our `ComputerStore` class that will create an instance of one of these three classes depending on the type of computer we are looking for. Let's take a look at the following code:

```
class ComputerStore {
  enum ComputerType {
    case Laptop
    case Desktop
    case Headless
  }

  func getModel(type: ComputerType) -> Computer {
    switch(type) {
    case ComputerType.Laptop:
      return MacbookPro()
    case ComputerType.Desktop:
      return IMac()
    case ComputerType.Headless:
      return MacMini()
    }
  }
}
```

In the `ComputerStore` class, we begin by creating an enum named `ComputerType`, which defines the types of computers that we sell. These types are `Laptop`, `Desktop`, and `Headless`.

The `ComputerStore` class has one method and that is the `getModel()` method. This method accepts one argument, which is of the `ComputerType` types and returns an instance of a type that conforms to the `Computer` protocol, depending on the `ComputerType` enum that was passed in. Within this method, we create a `switch` statement that will create and return an instance of a class that confirms to the `Computer` protocol.

Now, let's look at how to use the `ComputerStore` class:

```
var laptop = store.getModel(.Laptop)
print(laptop.getType())
```

In this example, we begin by creating an instance of the `ComputerStore` class. We then call the `getModel()` method to retrieve an instance of a class that conforms the `Computer` protocol by passing in a `ComputerType` value. The code that is calling the `getModel()` method does not need to know how the backend code selects which type of class to create; all it knows is that it should get a valid instance of a type that conforms to the `Computer` protocol or `nil`.

I find myself using this pattern a lot. Anytime we have multiple types that conform to the same protocol, we may want to consider using the factory method pattern to centralize the creation of these objects; otherwise, we may find that we are repeating the object creation code in multiple parts of our application.

Like the builder pattern, we chose to use classes to represent the different computer types mainly because it does not make sense to create multiple copies of the computer types.

One of the key ideas about design patterns, especially the creational patterns, is that we take the logic about how and what to create out of our general code and put it into specific classes or functions. Then, when we need to make changes to our code in the future, the logic is embedded in a single spot and can be easily changed, rather than having the logic in multiple spots throughout our code.

Now, let's look at the structural design patterns.

Structural design patterns

Structural design patterns describe how classes can be combined to form larger structures. These larger structures can generally be easier to work with and hide a lot of the complexity of the individual classes. Most of the patterns in the structural pattern category involve connections between objects.

There are seven well-known patterns that are part of the structural design pattern type:

- **Adapter**: This allows classes with incompatible interfaces to work together
- **Bridge**: This is used to separate the abstract elements of a class from the implementation so that the two can vary
- **Composite**: This allows us to treat a group of objects as a single object
- **Decorator**: This lets us add or override behavior in an existing method of an object

- **Façade**: This provides a simplified interface for a larger and more complex body of code
- **Flyweight**: This allows us to reduce the resources needed to create and use a large number of similar objects
- **Proxy**: This is a class acting as an interface for another class or classes

In this chapter, we are going to give examples of how to use bridge, façade, and proxy patterns in Swift. Let's start off by looking at the bridge pattern.

The bridge pattern

The bridge pattern decouples the abstraction from the implementation so that they can both vary independently. The bridge pattern can also be thought of as a two-layer abstraction.

In this section, we will show you how to use the bridge pattern by creating a simple universal remote class that can control multiple TV objects. We will begin by creating protocols for both the remote control and the TVs, as shown in the following code:

```
protocol TV {
  var currentChannel: Int {get set}

  func turnOn()
  func turnOff()
}

protocol RemoteControl {
  var tv: TV {get set}
  init(tv: TV)
}
```

The `TV` protocol defines one property and two functions. The `currentChannel` property is used to keep track of the current channel that the TV is on. The functions are `turnOn()` and `turnOff()`,which are used to turn the TV on or off.

The `RemoteControl` protocol defines one property and one initializer. The `tv` property holds the instance of the TV that we want to control. The initializer will initiate the remote with a type that conforms to the `TV` protocol.

Now we will extend both the `TV` and `RemoteControl` protocols to add common functionalities for types that conform to the protocols. Keep in mind that the functionality added here could be overridden in the types that conform to the protocol:

```
extension TV {
    mutating func changeChannel(channel: Int) {
        self.currentChannel = channel
    }
}

extension RemoteControl {
    func turnOn() {
        tv.turnOn()
    }
    func turnOff() {
        tv.turnOff()
    }
    mutating func setChannel(channel: Int) {
        tv.changeChannel(channel)
    }
    mutating func nextChannel() {
        tv.changeChannel(tv.currentChannel + 1)
    }
    mutating func prevChannel() {
        tv.changeChannel(tv.currentChannel - 1)
    }
}
```

In the `TV` extension, we are adding a method to change the channel on the TV. In the `RemoteControl` extension, we are adding five methods that turn the TV on/off or change the channel on the TV.

Now, let's look at how to create structures that conform to the `TV` protocol. For this, we will define two concrete implementations of the protocol, which are as follows:

```
struct VizioTV: TV {

    var currentChannel = 1

    func turnOn() {
        print("Vizio On")
    }
    func turnOff() {
```

```
        print("Vizio Off")
    }
}

struct SonyTV: TV {

    var currentChannel = 1

    func turnOn() {
        print("Sony On")
    }
    func turnOff() {
        print("Sony Off")
    }
}
```

With this code, we define both the `SonyTV` and `VizioTV` implementations of the `TV` protocol. Within these structures, we implement all of the requirements for the `TV` protocol. We will be using these implementations to tell the universal remote which TV to control. Now, let's see how to implement the `RemoteControl` protocol, which is as follows:

```
class MyUniversalRemote: RemoteControl {
    var tv: TV

    required init(tv: TV) {
        self.tv = tv
    }
}
```

Within the `MyUniversalRemote` class, we implement the required initializer for the `Remote` protocol.

To use this pattern, we would begin by creating an instance of the `TV` type that we wish to control. We would then use that instance to initiate our remote control type, as shown in the following code:

```
var myTv = VizioTV()
var remote = MyUniversalRemote(tv: myTv)
remote.turnOn()
remote.nextChannel()
print("Channel on: \(myTv.currentChannel)")
remote.nextChannel()
print("Channel on: \(myTv.currentChannel)")
remote.turnOff()
```

The bridge pattern can be thought of as two layers of abstraction where the abstraction and implementations should not be bound at compile time. This allows us to define which objects to use at runtime. This also allows us to add more TVs to our `myUniversalRemote` class simply by creating new classes that implement the `TV` protocol.

> For this pattern, we implemented the types that conform to the `TV` protocol using structures. Structures were chosen because it is very easy to create one instance of a TV type and then use it to create multiple instances of the remote control types, as shown in the following example:
>
> ```
> var myTv = VizioTV()
> var remoteForTV1 = MyUniversalRemote(tv: myTv)
> var remoteForTV2 = MyUniversalRemote (tv: myTv)
> ```
>
> In this example, if the `VizioTV` type were implemented with a class, then the both `MyUniversalRemote` instances would refer to the same TV rather than different TVs. Therefore, even though we had two TVs, each with separate remotes, both of the remotes would actually on work on one of the TVs.
>
> There are times when we want this behavior and for those times, we should use classes; however, in my experience, this is usually not the desired behavior.

Now, let's look at the next pattern in the structural category—the façade pattern.

The façade pattern

The façade pattern provides a simplified interface to a larger and more complex body of code. This allows us to make our libraries easier to use and understand by hiding some of the complexities. It also allows us to combine multiple API's into a single, easier to use API, which is what we will see in our example.

In this example, we will make a simplified travel API that combines the hotel, flight, and rental car APIs into a single, easy-to-use interface. We will start off by defining the hotel, flight, and rental car classes, which are as follows:

```
struct HotelBooking {
    static func getHotelNameForDates(to: NSDate, from: NSDate) ->
[String]? {
        let hotels = [String]()
        //logic to get hotels
        return hotels
    }
```

```
}

struct FlightBooking {
    static func getFlightNameForDates(to: NSDate, from: NSDate) ->
[String]? {
        let flights = [String]()
        //logic to get flights
        return flights
    }
}

struct RentalCarBooking {
    static func getRentalCarNameForDates(to: NSDate, from: NSDate) ->
[String]? {
        let cars = [String]()
        //logic to get flights
        return cars
    }
}
```

In each of these APIs, we define a single static method that will return a list of items (hotels, flights, or rental cars) that are available for the requested date. We actually do not implement any logic here because we would need to define a data source, and I would prefer to keep the example simple to concentrate on how the pattern works.

Now, let's look at our `TravelFacade` class that will combine these three APIs into a single, easier to use API, as shown in the following code:

```
class TravelFacade {
var hotels: [String]?
var flights: [String]?
var cars: [String]?

    init(to: NSDate, from: NSDate) {
        hotels = HotelBooking.getHotelNameForDates(to, from: from)
        flights = FlightBooking.getFlightNameForDates(to, from: from)
        cars = RentalCarBooking.getRentalCarNameForDates(to, from:
from)
    }
}
```

Inside the `TravelFacade` class, we create a single initializer that accepts two `NSDate` objects as the parameters. We then use those two `NSDate` objects to retrieve the hotels, flights, and rental cars that are available for the time period defined by the dates.

The façade pattern is very useful when we have a complex API structure that we want to simplify. It is also very useful when we have a series of multiple related APIs, as we saw in our example, to consolidate them in a single API.

For this pattern, we chose to use structures when we implemented the three booking types; however, which type is used (classes or structures) is really dependent on the individual design of the application. In the *The bridge pattern* section of this chapter, we were able to say that the majority of the time structures would be preferred; however, in this pattern, we really cannot say that either type is preferred the majority of the time.

Now, let's look at our last structural pattern, which is the proxy design pattern.

The proxy design pattern

In the proxy design pattern, there is one object acting as an interface for other objects. This wrapper class, which is the proxy, can then add functionality to the object, make the object available over a network, or restrict access to the object.

In this section, we will demonstrate the proxy pattern by creating a house class that we can add multiple floor plans to, where each floor plan represents a different story of the house. Let's begin by creating a `FloorPlanProtocol` protocol:

```
protocol FloorPlanProtocol {
  var bedRooms: Int {get set}
  var utilityRooms: Int {get set}
  var bathRooms: Int {get set}
  var kitchen: Int {get set}
  var livingRooms: Int {get set}
}
```

In `FloorPlanProtocol`, we define five properties that will represent the number of rooms contained in each floor plan. Now, let's create an implementation of the `FloorPlanProtocol` protocol named `FloorPlan`, which is as follows:

```
struct FloorPlan: FloorPlanProtocol {
  var bedRooms = 0
  var utilityRooms = 0
  var bathRooms = 0
  var kitchen = 0
  var livingRooms = 0
}
```

The `FloorPlan` class implements all the five properties required from `FloorPlanProtocol` and assigns default values to them. Next, we will create the `House` class, which will represent a house:

```
class House {
  private var stories = [FloorPlanProtocol]()

  func addStory(floorPlan: FloorPlanProtocol) {
    stories.append(floorPlan)
  }
}
```

Within our `House` class, we have an array of the `FloorPlanProtocols` objects where each floor plan will represent one story of the house. We also have one function named `addStory()`, which accepts an instance of an object that conforms to the `FloorPlanProtocol` protocol. This function will add the floor plan to the array of the `FloorPlanProtocols` protocols.

If we think about the logic of this class, there is one problem that we might encounter. The problem is that we are allowed to add as many floor plans as we want, which may lead to houses that are 60 or 70 stories high. This would be great if we were building skyscrapers, but we just want to build basic single-family houses. If we want to limit the number of floor plans without changing the `House` class (either we cannot change it or we simply do not want to), we can implement the proxy pattern. The following example shows how to implement the `HouseProxy` class, where we limit the number of floor plans we can add to the house, which is as follows;

```
class HouseProxy {
 var house = House()

  func addStory(floorPlan: FloorPlanProtocol) -> Bool {
    if house.stories.count < 3 {
      house.addStory(floorPlan)
      return true
    }
    else {
      return false
    }
  }
}
```

We begin the `HouseProxy` class by creating an instance of the `House` class. We then create a method named `addStory()` that lets us add a new floor plan to the house. In the `addStory()` method, we check whether the number of stories in the house is less than three, and if so, we add the floor plan to the house and return `true`. If the number of stories is equal to or greater than three, then we do not add the floor plan to the house and return `false`. Let's see how we use this proxy:

```
var ourHouse = HouseProxy()

var basement = FloorPlan(bedRooms: 0, utilityRooms: 1, bathRooms:
  1, kitchen: 0, livingRooms: 1)
var firstStory = FloorPlan(bedRooms: 1, utilityRooms: 0,
  bathRooms: 2, kitchen: 1, livingRooms: 1)
var secondStory = FloorPlan(bedRooms: 2, utilityRooms: 0,
  bathRooms: 1, kitchen: 0, livingRooms: 1)
var additionalStory = FloorPlan(bedRooms: 1, utilityRooms: 0,
  bathRooms: 1, kitchen: 1, livingRooms: 1)

print(ourHouse.addStory(basement))
print(ourHouse.addStory(firstStory))
print(ourHouse.addStory(secondStory))
print(ourHouse.addStory(additionalStory))
```

In our example code, we start off by creating an instance of the `HouseProxy` class named `ourHouse`. We then create four instances of the `FloorPlan` class, each with a different number of rooms. Finally, we attempt to add each of the floor plans to the `ourHouse` instance. If we then run the code, we see that the first three instances of the `FloorPlan` class were added to the house successfully, but the last one wasn't because we are only allowed to add three floors.

The proxy pattern is very useful when we want to add some additional functionality or error-checking to a class, but we do not want to change the actual class itself.

For the proxy pattern, we chose to use a class to implement the pattern because normally, we would not want to make copies of the type we are proxying. Instead, we would normally want to maintain the changes made to the instance. This is kind of the reverse of the bridge pattern where, in my experience, the structure would be preferred the majority of the time.

Now, let's look at the behavioral design patterns.

Behavioral design patterns

Behavioral design patterns explain how objects interact with each other. These patterns describe how different objects send messages to each other to make things happen.

There are nine well-known patterns that are part of the structural design pattern type:

- **Chain of responsibility**: This is used to process a variety of requests, each of which may be delegated to a different handler.
- **Command**: This creates objects that can encapsulate actions or parameters so that they can be invoked later or by a different component.
- **Iterator**: This allows us to access the elements of an object sequentially without exposing the underlying structure.
- **Mediator**: This is used to reduce coupling between classes that communicate with each other.
- **Memento**: This is used to capture the current state of an object and store it in a manner that can be restored later.
- **Observer**: This allows an object to publish changes to its state. Other objects can then subscribe so that they can be notified of any changes.
- **State**: This is used to alter the behavior of an object when its internal state changes.
- **Strategy**: This allows one out of a family of algorithms to be chosen at runtime.
- **Visitor**: This is a way of separating an algorithm from an object structure.

In this section, we are going to give examples of how to use strategy and command patterns in Swift. Let's start off by looking at the command pattern.

The command design pattern

The command design pattern lets us define actions that we can execute later. This pattern generally encapsulates all the information needed to call or trigger the actions at a later time.

In this section, we will demonstrate how to use the command pattern by creating a `Light` class. In this example, we will define two commands—`lightOnCommand` and `lightOffCommand`. We will then use the `turnOnLight()` and `turnOffLight()` methods to call the commands.

We will begin by creating a protocol named `Command` that all of our commands will need to conform to. Here is the `Command` protocol:

```
protocol Command {
  func execute()
}
```

This protocol contains one method named `execute`, which will be used to execute the command. Now, let's look at our `LightOneCommand` and `LightOffCommand` classes that the `Light` class will use to turn the light on and off. They are as follows:

```
struct RockerSwitchLightOnCommand: Command {
  func execute() {
    print("Rocker Switch:  Turning Light On")
  }
}

struct RockerSwitchLightOffCommand: Command {
  func execute() {
    print("Rocker Switch:  Turning Light Off")
  }
}
struct PullSwitchLightOnCommand: Command {
  func execute() {
    print("Pull Switch:  Turning Light On")
  }
}

struct PullSwitchLightOffCommand: Command {
  func execute() {
    print("Pull Switch:  Turning Light Off")
  }
}
```

The `RockerSwitchLightOffCommand`, `RockerSwitchLightOnCommand`, `PullSwitchLightOnCommand`, and `PullSwitchLightOffCommand` commands conform to the `Command` protocol by implementing the `execute()` method, so we will be able to use them in our `Light` class. Now, let's look at how to implement the `Light` class:

```
class Light {
  var lightOnCommand: Command
  var lightOffCommand: Command

  init(lightOnCommand: Command, lightOffCommand: Command) {
```

```
        self.lightOnCommand = lightOnCommand
        self.lightOffCommand = lightOffCommand
    }

    func turnOnLight() {
        self.lightOnCommand.execute()
    }

    func turnOffLight() {
        self.lightOffCommand.execute()
    }
}
```

In the `Light` class, we start off by creating two variables named `lightOnCommand` and `lightOffCommand`, which hold instances of classes that conform to the `Command` protocol. We then create an initiator that lets us set both of the commands when we initiate the class. Finally, we create the `turnOnLight()` and `turnOffLight()` methods that we will use to turn the light on and off. In these methods, we call the appropriate command to turn the light on or off.

We would then use the `Light` class like this:

```
var on = PullSwitchLightOnCommand()
var off = PullSwitchLightOffCommand()
var light = Light(lightOnCommand: on, lightOffCommand: off)

light.turnOnLight()
light.turnOffLight()

light.lightOnCommand = RockerSwitchLightOnCommand()
light.turnOnLight()
```

In this example, we begin by creating an instance of the `PullSwitchLightOnCommand` class named `on` and an instance of the `PullSwitchLightOffCommand` class named `off`. We then create an instance of the `Light` class using the two commands that we just created and call the `turnOnLight()` and `turnOffLight()` methods of the `Light` instance to turn our light on and off. In the last two lines, we changed the `lightOnCommand` method, which was originally set to an instance of the `PullSwitchLightOnCommand` class to an instance of the `RockerSwitchLightOnCommand` class. The `light` instance will now use the `RockerSwitchLightOnCommand` class whenever we turn the light on. This allows us to change the functionality of the `Light` class during runtime.

There are a number of benefits of using the command pattern. One of the main benefits is that we are able to set the implementation of the commands at runtime, which also lets us swap the commands out with different implementations that conform to the `Command` protocol, as needed throughout the life of the application. Another advantage of the command pattern is that we encapsulate the details of the command implementations within the command classes themselves rather than in the container class.

For the command pattern, we used structures to implement our command types because it is very easy to create one instance of a command type and then use it to create multiple instances of the `Light` class. In that case, if one `Light` class changed anything in the command instance, it would then be reflexed in all the instances of the `Light` class that used that command instance. Generally, this is not the behavior we want; however, if that is the behavior your application needs, then you should use a class rather than a structure.

Now, let's look at our last design pattern, which is the strategy pattern.

The strategy pattern

The strategy pattern is pretty similar to the command pattern in the fact that they both allow us to decouple implementation details from our calling class and also allow us to switch the implementation out at runtime. The big difference is, the strategy pattern is intended to encapsulate algorithms. By swapping out an algorithm, we are expecting the object to perform the same functionality but in a different way. In the command pattern, when we swap out the commands, we are expecting the object to function differently.

In this section, we will demonstrate the strategy pattern by showing you how we could swap out compression strategies at runtime. Let's begin this example by creating a `CompressionStrategy` protocol that each one of our compression classes will conform to. Let's take a look at the following code:

```
protocol CompressionStrategy {
  func compressFiles(filePaths: [String])
}
```

This protocol defines one method named `compressFiles()` that accepts a single parameter, which is an array of strings that contain the paths of the files to compress. We will now create two structures that conform to the `CompressionStrategy` protocol. These classes are the `ZipCompressionStrategy` and `RarCompressionStrategy` classes, which are as follows:

```
struct ZipCompressionStrategy: CompressionStrategy {
  func compressFiles(filePaths: [String]) {
    print("Using Zip Compression")
  }
}

struct RarCompressionStrategy: CompressionStrategy {
  func compressFiles(filePaths: [String]) {
    print("Using RAR Compression")
  }
}
```

Both of these structures implement the `CompressionStrategy` protocol by having a method named `compressFiles()`, which accepts an array of strings. Within these methods, we simply print out the name of the compression that we are using. Normally, we would implement the compression logic in these methods.

Now, let's look at our `CompressContent` class that will be called to compress the files:

```
class CompressContent {
  var strategy: CompressionStrategy

  init(strategy: CompressionStrategy) {
    self.strategy = strategy
  }

  func compressFiles(filePaths: [String]) {
    self.strategy.compressFiles(filePaths)
  }
}
```

In this class, we start off by defining a variable named `strategy` that will contain an instance of a class that conforms to the `CompressStrategy` protocol. We then create an initiator that will be used to set the compression type when the class is initiated. Finally, we create a method named `compressFiles()` that accepts an array of strings that contain the paths to the list of files that we wish to compress. In this method, we compress the files using the compression strategy that is set in the strategy variable.

We will use the `CompressContent` class like this:

```
var filePaths = ["file1.txt", "file2.txt"]
var zip = ZipCompressionStrategy()
var rar = RarCompressionStrategy()

var compress = CompressContent(strategy: zip)
compress.compressFiles(filePaths)

compress.strategy = rar
compress.compressFiles(filePaths)
```

We begin by creating an array of strings that contain the files we wish to compress. We also create an instance of both the `ZipCompressionStrategy` and `RarCompressionStrategy` classes. We then create an instance of the `CompressContent` class, setting the compression strategy to the `ZipCompressionStrategy` instance and call the `compressFiles()` method, which will print the `Using zip compression` message to the console. We then set the compression strategy to the `RarCompressionStrategy` instance and call the `compressFiles()` method again, which will print the `Using rar compression` message to the console.

The strategy pattern is really good for setting the algorithms to use at runtime, which also lets us swap the algorithms out with different implementations as needed by the application. Another advantage of the strategy pattern is, we encapsulate the details of the algorithm within the strategy classes themselves and not in the main implementation class.

Just like the command pattern, we used structures to implement the strategy pattern because it is very easy to create one instance of a strategy type and then use it to create multiple instances of the `CompressContent` class. In this case, if anything is changed in the strategy instance, it would be reflexed in all of the `CompressContent` types. Generally, this is not the behavior we want; however, if that is the behavior your application needs, then you should use a class rather than a structure.

This concludes our tour of design patterns in Swift.

Summary

Design patterns are solutions to software design problems that we tend to see over and over again in real-world application designs. These patterns are designed to help us create reusable and flexible code. Design patterns can also make our code easier to read and understand for other developers and also for ourselves when we look back at out code months/years later.

If we looked at the examples in the chapter carefully, we would notice that one of the backbones of design patterns is protocols. Almost all the design patterns (the singleton design pattern is an exception) use protocols to help us create very flexible and reusable code.

If this was the first time that you really looked at design patterns, you probably noticed some similarities to strategies that you may have used in the past in your own code. This is expected when experienced developers are first introduced to design patterns. I would also encourage you to read about design patterns more because they will definitely help you to create more flexible and reusable code.

Index

D

E

F

G

H

I

J

L

M

N

O

P

Q

R

S

T

U

V

W

X

About Packt Publishing

Packt, pronounced 'packed', published its first book, *Mastering phpMyAdmin for Effective MySQL Management*, in April 2004, and subsequently continued to specialize in publishing highly focused books on specific technologies and solutions.

Our books and publications share the experiences of your fellow IT professionals in adapting and customizing today's systems, applications, and frameworks. Our solution-based books give you the knowledge and power to customize the software and technologies you're using to get the job done. Packt books are more specific and less general than the IT books you have seen in the past. Our unique business model allows us to bring you more focused information, giving you more of what you need to know, and less of what you don't.

Packt is a modern yet unique publishing company that focuses on producing quality, cutting-edge books for communities of developers, administrators, and newbies alike. For more information, please visit our website at `www.packtpub.com`.

Writing for Packt

We welcome all inquiries from people who are interested in authoring. Book proposals should be sent to `author@packtpub.com`. If your book idea is still at an early stage and you would like to discuss it first before writing a formal book proposal, then please contact us; one of our commissioning editors will get in touch with you.

We're not just looking for published authors; if you have strong technical skills but no writing experience, our experienced editors can help you develop a writing career, or simply get some additional reward for your expertise.

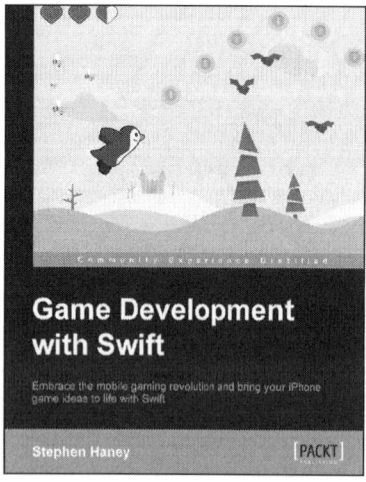

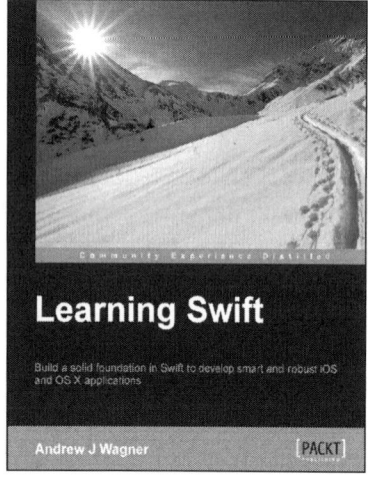

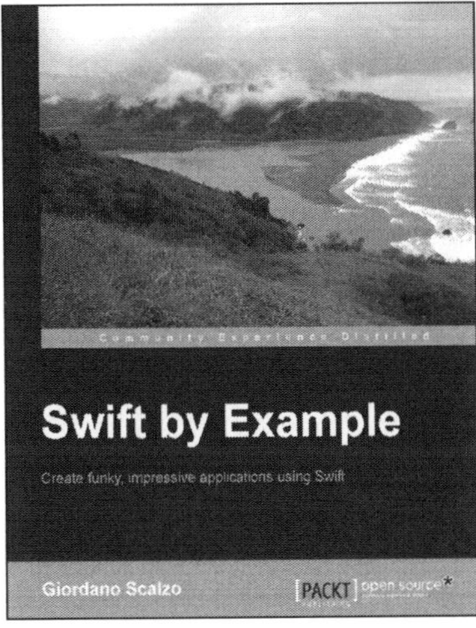

Swift by Example

ISBN: 978-1-78528-470-0 Paperback: 284 pages

Create funky, impressive applications using Swift

1. Learn Swift language features quickly with playgrounds and in-depth examples.
2. Implement real iOS apps using Swift and Cocoapods.
3. Create professional video games with SpriteKit, SceneKit, and Swift.

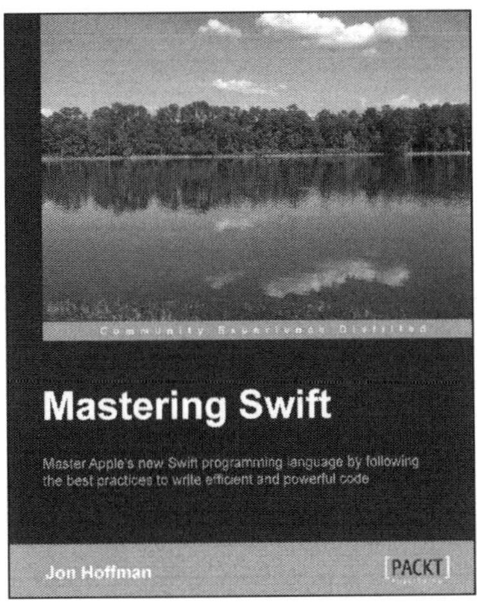

Mastering Swift

ISBN: 978-1-78439-215-4 Paperback: 358 pages

Master Apple's new Swift programming language by following the best practices to write efficient and powerful code

1. Start with basic language features and progressively move to more advanced features.
2. Learn to use Xcode's new Playground feature as you work through the immense number of examples in the book.
3. Learn what makes development with Swift so exiting and also get pointers on pitfalls to avoid.

16131822R00226

Printed in Great Britain
by Amazon